FREEDOM OF RELIGION,
MINORITIES, AND THE LAW

FREEDOM OF RELIGION, MINORITIES, AND THE LAW

Samantha Knights

OXFORD

UNIVERSITY PRESS

This book has been printed digitally and produced in a standard specification in order to ensure its continuing availability

OXFORD
UNIVERSITY PRESS

Great Clarendon Street, Oxford OX2 6DP

Oxford University Press is a department of the University of Oxford.
It furthers the University's objective of excellence in research, scholarship,
and education by publishing worldwide in

Oxford New York

Auckland   Cape Town Dar es Salaam   Hong Kong   Karachi
Kuala Lumpur Madrid Melbourne Mexico City   Nairobi
New Delhi Shanghai Taipei Toronto
With offices in
Argentina Austria Brazil Chile Czech Republic France Greece
Guatemala Hungary Italy Japan South Korea Poland Portugal
Singapore Switzerland Thailand Turkey Ukraine Vietnam

Oxford is a registered trade mark of Oxford University Press
in the UK and in certain other countries

Published in the United States
by Oxford University Press Inc., New York

ISBN 978-0-19-929062-8

Printed and bound by CPI Group (UK) Ltd, Croydon, CR0 4YY

To M, J & J

PREFACE

The boundary between freedom of religion and freedom from religion has always been controversial. History is littered with examples of religious conflict—Jews and Romans, Persian Sasanians and Christians, and Islam and Christianity. From the murder of the pagan philosopher Hypatia of Alexandria by a Christian mob in the fifth century AD, to the recent riots following the publication of satirical cartoons of the prophet Muhammad in newspapers across Europe, actions of a few in the name of religion have often unleashed widespread unrest.

There are two popular narratives relating to religion, one stressing the clash of civilizations and the conflict between forces of good and evil, and the other more quietly pointing to long term co-operation and co-existence. The reality is of course more complex and cannot easily be reduced to diametrically opposed sides. The challenge for society as a whole is to overcome the fiction of polarized battle lines and to carve a way forward that respects both civil liberties and promotes the common good. This task is far from easy, not least because concepts of the common good are themselves subjective and highly contestable.

England has from the earliest times been a religiously diverse country. Today it is home to the largest Sikh gurdwara in Europe, Druid celebrations of the summer and winter solstices at Stonehenge and Avebury, and the sound of the call to prayer from the minarets of mosques. The results of the 2001 United Kingdom Census included a voluntary question about religious affiliation for the first time. Notably in the light of the long lamented decline of Anglicanism by the established Church of England, a majority of the population identified their religion as Christian. However, other surveys have shown that the levels of active worship for the Church of England are proportionately low compared to other religions.

Although there has been considerable tolerance of religious diversity in England for some time, freedom of thought, conscience and religion was not protected under the common law or any domestic statute until the enactment of the Human Rights Act 1998. This contrasted with the express provisions relating to freedom of religion in the written constitutions of many other countries. Nor was there any express protection under English law against discrimination on the grounds of religion until the enactment of this Act. This legislation, therefore, marks a fundamental change in English law and its protection of civil liberties. But the rights are framed as highly general principles that leave considerable scope for debate as to their particular application. The protection against discrimination on the grounds of religion or belief has been further extended by the adoption of the Employment Equality (Religion or Belief) Regulations 2003 and the enactment of the Equality Act 2006.

In considering the ambit of legal protection it is, therefore, important to have regard to the historical, sociological, religious and political contexts. This includes consideration of national identity, the role and function of religion in society, how far religion is valued and protected, the position of the established Church of England, and the relative position of other religions in society. These factors raise questions about how a liberal democracy should balance the interests of the individual or group against the interests of the modern state, the extent to which the state will intervene in the affairs of religious organizations, and about the politics of assimilation and multiculturalism. In the legal context they prompt debates as to whether there should be separate laws for different religious groups, whether exemptions from generally applicable laws should be granted on religious grounds, and whether separate religious courts should deal with disputes in certain areas of law.

In these debates the treatment of minorities is fundamental. Typically, the legal system accommodates the needs, traditions and culture of the majority and packages them in the language of apparently neutral rules that conceal their religious, sociological and cultural underpinnings. The legal system needs to be sensitive to this and should not simply accede to the views of a majority in a modern democratic society without consideration of the minority. Moreover, views about religious minorities are affected by their portrayal in historical sources, fiction and the media. In the popular media certain religious communities are invariably associated with positive values such as artistic expression, promotion of peaceful values and community welfare, while others are linked directly to violence, extremism and terrorism, leaving the positive aspects of the communities largely unreported. In recent times, for example, the image of Islam has been predominantly associated with acts of terrorism perpetrated by a minority group of extremists acting in the name of religion.

In *Singh v Entry Clearance Officer New Delhi*,[1] Munby LJ noted:

> We live, or strive to live, in a tolerant society increasingly alive to the need to guard against the tyranny which majority opinion may impose on those who, for whatever reason, comprise a weak or voiceless minority. Equality under the law, human rights and the protection of minorities have to be more than what Brennan J in the High Court of Australia once memorably described as 'the incantations of legal rhetoric'.

---

[1] [2004] EWCA Civ 1075 [67]. See also *Matadeen v Pointu* [1999] 1 AC 98, 109–10 where Lord Hoffmann noted that certain fundamental rights needed protection against being overridden by the majority.

This book aims to provide a bridge between some of the underlying issues that feature in academic writing, and the practice of law. It is intended as a user-friendly guide for practitioners, while at the same time placing these issues in context. More broadly the book may be of interest to anyone engaged and interested in the legal aspects of this topic.

Chapter 1 sets the issues in context first by looking briefly at the historical and political background by reference to the formation of national identity and migration trends that have led to a highly religiously diverse population. It then examines the relationship between religion and the state, and the position of the established Church of England. Finally, the chapter looks at the development of philosophical, political and legal thinking in the modern period on the issues of diversity, individual freedom and tolerance.

Chapter 2 sets out the current applicable legal framework on freedom of thought, conscience and religion applicable in England at common law and in statute, and most notably in the Human Rights Act 1998. Chapter 3 examines the issue of balancing conflicting rights and respective interests in a case involving freedom of religion. In particular it considers three areas where difficulties may arise, namely between religious freedom of the individual and that of the religious group, between rights of a child and rights of a parent, and between rights of the majority and those of the minority.

The remaining chapters deal in turn with different specialist civil law areas of practice. They set out in each case the legal framework, the key case law, and current legal issues. Chapter 4 looks at education, Chapter 5 deals with employment, Chapter 6 looks at immigration and asylum, while Chapter 7 deals with miscellaneous public law areas such as health and safety regulations, animal rights, planning and prison law. Detailed treatment of two other areas—criminal law and family law—is beyond the scope of this book, although some reference is made to the law in these areas in Chapter 2.

Finally, a word on citations, ever the subject of interest to practitioners and judges. A decision has been taken in this book to use wherever possible a neutral citation alone in order to overcome the difficulty of progressive 'best citation' in the recent cases cited.

ACKNOWLEDGEMENTS

This book is the culmination of a project that began in 2002 at the School of Oriental and African Studies, London, shifted to the Law Faculty at Harvard University, Massachusetts, and back to Matrix Chambers, London.

En route I am deeply indebted to the inspiration provided by Professor Werner Menski and Dr Prakash Shah at SOAS who teach what ought to be a compulsory subject for all law students, *Ethnic Minorities and the Law*. At Harvard University I am very grateful to Professor David Little and Professor Jacqueline Bhahba for their insightful thoughts, and to Professor Frank Vogel and Dr Peri Bearman at the Islamic Legal Studies Program that so generously funded and supported a year of research providing the backbone of the book. Thank you also to Professor Noah Feldman at NYU for his ever incisive discussions on the topic. Lastly, a mention of three wonderful companions during my stint at Harvard who provided an endless source of debate and kept me sane after long hours in a library, Masha Hedberg, Brenna Marea Powell and Natalie Ruotsinoja.

Back on home turf I am enormously appreciative of a number of colleagues at Matrix for their support, reading chapters and providing invaluable comments— Helen Mountfield, Dan Squires, Raza Husain, Karon Monaghan, Alison Macdonald and Hugh Tomlinson QC in particular. Thanks also to Nick Lane, Katie Young, Sophie Bessemer, Ravinder Thukral, Ros Dixon, Andrew Shorten and Joy de Menil for reading and commenting on parts of the work in progress. The editorial team at OUP and Sarah McGrath, Annabel Moss, Kate Bailey and Roxanne Selby deserve special mention for their assistance, and patience throughout with the fluidity of deadlines. Finally, none of this would have been possible without the unwavering support of my parents and sister Julia. And lastly to Bijan for his engaging discussion, ideas and passion for the subject, not to mention his astute editorial eye.

CONTENTS—SUMMARY

CONTENTS

TABLE OF CASES

GERMANY

TABLE OF LEGISLATION

LIST OF ABBREVIATIONS

AINA	Asylum, Immigration and Nationality Act
CRC	UN Convention on the Rights of the Child
DfES	Department for Education and Skills
EA	Equality Act
EAT	Employment Appeal Tribunal
EdA	Education Act
ECHR	European Convention on Human Rights and Fundamental Freedoms
ECJ	European Court of Justice
ECtHR	European Court of Human Rights
HEA	Higher Education Act
HRA	Human Rights Act
IA	Immigration Act
ICCPR	International Covenant on Civil and Political Rights
ICERD	Convention on the Elimination of all Forms of Racial Discrimination
IDI	Immigration Directorate Instructions
JCHR	Joint Committee on Human Rights
LEA	Local education authority
LSA	Learning and Skills Act
RRA	Race Relations Act
SDA	Sex Discrimination Act
SSFA	School Standards and Framework Act
THEA	Teaching and Higher Education Act
UDHR	Universal Declaration of Human Rights

1

CONTEXT AND BACKGROUND

Introduction

From the earliest times, religion has been both a divisive and cohesive force in **1.01** society. Spiritual belief has been the inspiration for immense good, but also the driving force and justification for mass persecution, intolerance of difference, and abuse of the rights of others. As Lord Walker commented in the House of Lords judgment in *R (Williamson) v Secretary of State for Education and Employment*:[1]

> Countless thousands have suffered cruel deaths because at different periods during the last two thousand years parts of the Christian Church thought that the Bible not merely permitted but enjoined them to torture and kill apostates, heretics and witches.

The protection afforded by freedom of religion is important for society as a whole **1.02** and minorities in particular. Minorities are especially vulnerable to biased perceptions and negative stereotyping and may not easily be able to secure their rights through the normal democratic process. At the same time there is a need to place

---

[1] [2005] UKHL 15 [56]. See also Rix LJ in CA who noted: '. . .it is impossible to shut one's eyes to the great dangers which exist and have always existed in the very potency of religious belief and in its potential for conflict. *Tantum religio potuit suadere malorum* was the comment of a classical poet (Lucretius, De Rerum Natura, I. 101).' Reported at [2004] EWCA Civ 1926 [95].

limits on the freedom so that it does not become a means of infringing the freedom and rights of others. Throughout history, religious orthodoxies that began as the views of a persecuted minority, once associated with power have become the basis for persecution of others. The fine balance between the competing rights of individuals and groups in the context of freedom of religion is a constant theme in the case law. In order to assess the balance fairly it is necessary to view a case in its particular religious, cultural and sociological setting.[2]

Development of Freedom of Religion

Migration, immigration and religion

1.03 Various groups of people with diverse belief systems have been migrating to the areas now occupied by the United Kingdom from different locations from the earliest times.[3] Recent scholarship has challenged the concept of a homogenous national identity, but the Anglo-Saxon Protestant myth is ever present. The account of the British and English nations is still rarely told as a story of immigration, but more often as a story of a narrowly defined 'indigenous' group with waves of immigration thereafter.[4]

1.04 Religious activity in Britain is traceable to circa 4,000 BC when ceremonial monuments such as Stonehenge were constructed and elaborate tombs suggest a tendency towards ritual and some community of beliefs. The Roman invasion from circa 43 BC brought Roman cults and gods to Britain, which were mixed with local beliefs. The conquest had a major impact on the spread of Christianity in Britain following Emperor Constantine's conversion in the fourth century AD, although it had to be later reintroduced by Christian missionaries at the end of the sixth century following the fifth century invasion of pagan Germanic tribes. But the Reformation in England in the 1530s and establishment of the monarch as head of the Church of England, an event sparked by the desire of Henry VIII for an heir to the throne and his failure to secure a royal divorce from the papacy, remains the single largest influence on the current religious identity of the population.

1.05 Tolerance and fairness are two characteristics that are today frequently cited as British values, and Britain has a long history of granting asylum to certain groups persecuted around the world. However, overall religious freedom has a precarious

---

2 See *Singh v Entry Clearance Officer New Delhi* [2004] EWCA Civ 1075 [57].

3 VG Kiernan, 'Britons Old and New' in C Holmes (ed), *Immigrants and Minorities in British Society* (Allen and Unwin, 1978).

4 K Paul, *Whitewashing Britain: Race and Citizenship in the Postwar Era* (Cornell University Press, 1997) 64.

history in England.[5] Druids were persecuted in Roman Britain, Jews were expelled from the realm under Edward II and were not officially readmitted until 1656, and early Protestant groups such as the Lollards were stamped out. But it was the link between religion and the state in England under Henry VIII that unleashed a particularly long and bloody period of religious and political persecution. The period following the Reformation was dangerous for any religious dissenters involved in public life, a number of whom were executed or burnt at the stake, depending upon the official orthodoxy of the day. Protestants fled England during the reign of Catholic Mary I, Catholics escaped from Protestant Elizabeth I, and Puritans left under James I. Anabaptists who refused to bear arms, pay taxes or use law courts were oppressed by all three.

Discrimination against Catholics was both legally entrenched and prevalent in practice, particularly after the gunpowder plot of 1605. Legal restrictions were also placed on dissenting Protestants or Nonconformists. Under the Test Acts 1673 and 1678, Catholics were excluded from office and Parliament, and Nonconformists from office. Freedom of worship in licensed premises in England and Wales was granted generally to trinitarian dissenters but not to Catholics or Jews under the Toleration Act 1689. And anyone who would not take an oath of allegiance to the monarch as head of the Church of England was barred from office. It was not until the nineteenth century that Catholics were granted a period of greater toleration and most of the discriminatory laws reversed. There was a limited extension of civil rights to those outside the established Church by the repeal of the Test and Corporation Acts in 1828 and the Act for Catholic Emancipation in 1829. A little later, limited toleration was extended to the Jewish population.[6] **1.06**

In the twentieth century, despite the lack of formal barriers to office or institutions, discrimination against certain religious groups continued in a variety of ways. Some of this was indirect. For example, immigration regulations were used to prevent the migration of certain individuals and groups. Prior to the twentieth century, British subjects were free to come and go, as generally were foreigners, subject to a few known exceptions, notably Jews and Gypsies. But by the late nineteenth century, Britain's industrial lead was being undermined and from the 1870s a severe economic depression led to a series of boom and bust cycles. Against this backdrop came increasing hostility to immigration and in particular to the Jewish refugees fleeing from pogroms and persecution in Russia and other parts of Eastern Europe. This was coupled with the rise of now discredited crude **1.07**

---

[5] See R Ahdar & I Leigh, *Religious Freedom in the Liberal State* (OUP, 2005) 15.

[6] The Jewish Disabilities Removal Act 1845 and the Jewish Relief Act 1858 removed some of the religious obstacles to office and employment that had existed due to requirements to take Christian oaths. Formal freedom of worship was not guaranteed until the Religious Disabilities Act 1846.

scientific, philosophical and historical theories about the categorization of the human race.[7]

1.08 Fears about a stream of poor Jewish refugees arriving in Britain led to the Aliens Act 1905 that sought to exclude steerage passengers on 'immigrant ships' carrying more than 20 aliens. There were also various attempts made in the nineteenth century to remove the non-white population of Lascars, the Indian seamen who had worked in the British merchant navy.[8] These controls marked the beginnings of a series of nationality and immigration statutes and regulations that continue to this day.

1.09 In post World War II Britain, during a period of considerable labour shortage, a fall in the birth rate and wide-scale emigration to the Dominions created an immediate need for immigration. In response the British government adopted policies and passed legislation, principally contained in the Commonwealth Immigrants Acts 1962 and 1968, that facilitated the immigration of European aliens and Irish citizens to the United Kingdom, but at the same time made it increasingly difficult for non-white British subjects living in the Colonies and Dominions to immigrate. This was achieved through the segregation of British nationality into different categories of 'Britishness', some with the right of abode in the United Kingdom and some without.[9] Despite the restrictions on non-white immigration to the United Kingdom, the period from the 1950s still saw a significant increase in people migrating from the Caribbean and South Asia. The distinction between British citizens with the right of abode, and various other types of British nationality, unique among nationality laws in the world, continues to this day. It has had dramatic consequential effects on the religious diversity of the population.

1.10 Historically, there has been a strong correlation at the state level between national identity and the Church of England. However, current debates about nationality in political circles are at least expressed differently. In 2004 the Home Office stated that 'integration is not about assimilation into a single homogenous culture and there is space within the concept of "British" for people to express their religious and cultural beliefs'.[10] But the policy on what it means to be British, English, Welsh, Scottish or Irish and the relative role that religion plays as an aspect of

---

[7] See generally A Dummett & A Nicol, *Subjects, Citizens, Aliens and Others: Nationality and Immigration Law* (Northwestern University Press, 1990); P Shar, *Refugees, Race and the Legal Concept of Asylum in Britain* (Cavendish, 2000).

[8] The Merchant Shipping Act of 1906 introduced a language test that was intended to discriminate against non-white sailors.

[9] This is a now well documented but until relatively recently a largely ignored aspect of British history. See L Fransman, *British Nationality Law* (Butterworths, 1998) and I Spencer, *British Immigration Policy: The Making of Multi-Racial Britain* (Routledge, 1997).

[10] Home Office Communications Directorate, *Strength in Diversity: Towards a Community Cohesion and Race Equality Strategy* (2004) 5.

identity is far from clear.[11] There is little consensus about whether nationality should embody certain prescribed values and what those values should be. While the sentiment of inclusive identity is an important first step, research done about identity and minorities points to the considerable social exclusion that is felt by certain ethnic and religious groups.[12] And within the wider community there is considerable tension as to the concept of nationality and possibly as many different views as there are people. Moreover, feelings of exclusion are heightened by the increasing restrictions on civil liberties, in particular for the Muslim population, under the guise of anti-terrorism measures.

Religious diversity in the United Kingdom

There were no official statistics collected on religion in the United Kingdom until   **1.11** a voluntary question about religious affiliation was included for the first time in the 2001 Census. The summary results are as follows:

Population of Great Britain: by religion, April 2001[13]

Religion	Numbers	Percentages
Christian	41,014,811	71.8
Muslim	1,588,890	2.8
Hindu	558,342	1.0
Sikh	336,179	0.6
Jewish	267,373	0.5
Buddhist	149,157	0.3
Any other religion[14]	159,167	0.3
All non-Christian religion	3,059,108	5.4
No religion[15]	8,596,488	15.1
Religion not stated	4,433,520	7.8
All population	57,103,927	100.0

As the results show, a majority of the population identified itself as Christian,   **1.12** although the results conflict with other surveys showing Christianity on the wane replaced by a rise in spirituality rather than affiliation to any one religion, and

---

[11] J Jacobson, 'Perceptions of Britishness' [1997] 3(2) Nations and Nationalism 181–99; S Spencer (ed), *Strangers and Citizens: A Positive Approach to Migrants and Refugees* (IPPR and Rivers Oram Press, 1994).

[12] See *The Parekh Report: The Future of Multi-Ethnic Britain* (Profile Books, 2002); see also on Muslims: OSI/EU Monitoring and Advocacy Program, *Muslims in the UK: Policies for Engaged Citizens* (Open Society Institute, 2005).

[13] See <http://www.statistics.gov.uk/census2001/census2001.asp>.

[14] In England and Wales 151,000 people belonged to religious groups that did not fall into any of the main religions. The largest of these were Spiritualists (32,000) and Pagans (31,000), followed by Jain (15,000), Wicca (7,000), Rastafarian (5,000), Baha'i (5,000) and Zoroastrian (4,000).

[15] The category of no religion includes people who ticked None and those who wrote in Jedi Knight, Agnostic, Atheist and Heathen and those who ticked Other but did not write in a religion.

a substantial proportion of atheists among the population.[16] But, the survey did not require a breakdown of different branches of Christianity despite the fact that the Church of England represents only one branch of that religion and is itself highly diverse.[17] The method of questioning has been criticized for not separating issues of identification and actual belief. But the results do show that religion is an important aspect of identity for minorities.[18] And they reveal the high concentration of particular religious groups in certain areas. For example, as regards the Muslim population, about two fifths of all British Muslims live in London.[19]

1.13 There are various explanations as to why large numbers of people identify with Christianity in the Census, contradicting other evidence of a decline in faith. One sociologist explains the dichotomy on the basis of 'vicarious religion' whereby people constituting an active minority perform the function of exercising religion on behalf of the majority that implicitly endorses this form of exercise.[20] Another explanation is that some people officially prefer to identify with the majority religion as a descriptive label rather than claiming to have no religious identity, or that some people identify Christianity with Britishness.

1.14 Whatever the explanation behind the results of the Census, it appears that England is becoming increasingly secular and increasingly religiously diverse at the same time. As Munby LJ noted in *Singh v Entry Clearance Officer New Delhi*:[21]

> [T]here have been enormous changes in the social and religious life of our country. The fact is that we live in a secular and pluralistic society. But we also live in a multi-cultural community of many faiths. One of the paradoxes of our lives is that we live in a society which is at one and the same time becoming both increasingly secular but also increasingly diverse in religious affiliation. Our society includes men and women from every corner of the globe and of every creed and colour under the sun.

---

[16] A YouGov Poll commissioned by the *Daily Telegraph* in 2004 revealed highly contradictory results. Eg in answer to the question: Do you believe in God? 44% said yes, 35% said no and 21% said don't know. Of the sample 46% described themselves as agnostic, 35% as atheist, 16% as neither and 2% didn't know.

[17] The YouGov Poll found that 49% were Church of England, 14% Other Protestant Christian, 16% Roman Catholic Christian, and 8% Other Christian suggesting a great degree of diversity within Christianity.

[18] M O'Beirne, *Religion in England and Wales: Findings from the Home Office Citizenship Study 2001*, Home Office Research Study 274 (Home Office, 2004) 20.

[19] The boroughs with the highest numbers were Newham, Tower Hamlets, Brent, Waltham Forest, Redbridge, Hackney, Haringey, Camden and Westminster where the proportions range from 36% (Tower Hamlets) to 11% (Haringey).

[20] G Davie, *Religion in Modern Europe: A Memory Mutates* (OUP, 2000).

[21] [2004] EWCA Civ 1075 [62].

International law

England was not alone in its intolerance of difference and dissent in the early **1.15** modern period.[22] But from the sixteenth century a number of treaties were signed between European states granting recognition between them to the different branches of Christianity.[23] The turning point in the struggle for religious liberty of the state in Europe was the Treaty of Westphalia (1648), which guaranteed equal rights for both Roman Catholic and Protestant states in central Europe. But it was the religious freedom of the state that was guaranteed rather than that of the individual. Other treaties did grant more protection for individual freedom of religion but the principal motivation in these treaties was the avoidance of conflict.[24] During the nineteenth century several international treaties relating to territorial settlement contained clauses dealing with the respect of religious freedom.[25] Again, these treaties were negotiated according to political expediency and there was no consensus in Europe about the importance of religious tolerance.

The concept of an international framework on human rights and rights of minori- **1.16** ties began to be developed in the aftermath of World War I. As regards religious tolerance and freedom, religious factors had little impact in the post-war peace concluded by the Treaty of Versailles (1919).[26] A proposal that a provision dealing with religious equality should be included in the Covenant of the League of Nations was dropped, and instead religious intolerance was dealt with by the Minority Treaties of 1919–20. The Minority Treaties contained provision for protection of religious groups against discrimination, but enforcement of this protection was the sole responsibility of member states. The focus was also on injustices experienced by groups and not by the individual.[27]

After the dissolution of the League of Nations in 1946 and in the aftermath **1.17** of World War II, a more prevalent attitude in favour of human rights emerged. This focused on general and universal protection of all human beings as individuals as expressed in the Universal Declaration of Human Rights 1948 ('UDHR'). Article 18 UDHR relating to freedom of religion proved to be one of the most

---

[22] See generally M Evans, *Religious Liberty and International Law in Europe* (CUP, 1997) Chs 1 and 2.

[23] See eg Religious Peace of Augsburg (1555) that recognized that the Lutheran princes should enjoy equal status to Catholic Princes in the Holy Roman Empire.

[24] See eg the Treaties of Konigsberg, Marienburg and Labiau (1656) in which Brandenburg promised to respect the freedom of worship for Lutherans in the areas which were to pass to it.

[25] See eg the Treaty of Berlin (1878) that obliged the newly established Romanian state to respect the religious liberties of its citizens and in particular of the Jews.

[26] The sole exception to this was in the Saar basin where Germany ceded governance to the League of Nations and the right to exploit the region's coal mines to France for a 15 year period during which time the inhabitants were to be entitled to retain their local assemblies, religious liberties, their schools and language.

[27] See further N Lerner, *Group Rights and Discrimination in International Law* (Kluwer Law, 1991).

controversial articles. It influenced subsequent texts including Article 18 of the International Covenant on Civil and Political Rights 1966 ('ICCPR') and Article 1 of the Declaration on the Elimination of All Forms of Intolerance and of Discrimination Based on Religion or Belief 1981. It also provided the basis of Article 9 of the European Convention on Human Rights and Fundamental Freedoms 1950 ('ECHR'). The wording of the respective articles relating to freedom of religion in these instruments differs, but all contain the principle that freedom of religion or belief may be manifested in 'teaching, practice, worship and observance' and that the exercise of such freedom may be limited on a number of specified grounds.[28]

1.18   As regards minorities' protection the proposals for inclusion of an article in the UDHR were rejected. The Commission on Human Rights established in 1946 created a Sub-Commission on Prevention of Discrimination and Protection of Minorities. This Sub-Commission helped in developing Article 27 ICCPR that grants the right to ethnic, religious and linguistic minorities to enjoy their own culture, profess and practise their own religion, and use their own language. The Council of Europe has adopted the 1995 Framework Convention for the Protection of National Minorities.[29] This is the first legally binding multilateral instrument devoted to the protection of national minorities in general.

Philosophical, Political, and Legal Theory

Function of religion

1.19   In considering the importance of freedom of religion, a necessary anterior issue is the function of religion in society. In examining this it is hard to avoid becoming entangled in the very problem that courts have sought to avoid—namely from whose perspective should religion be judged. But a view on the importance of religion or of a particular religion and its manifestation will be implicit in the balancing exercise between the interests of religion, the state and individuals in a given case.

1.20   A religion may provide a coherent world-view, an explanation of origins of peoples, of this and the after-life, a common morality, guiding principles of ethics, and both emotional and physical support to the individual. From outside the religion, others may indirectly benefit from the religious beliefs of diverse groups within a society to the extent that different religions share many common values that allow and encourage tolerant behaviour towards all those

---

[28] See B Tahzib, *Freedom of Religion or Belief: Ensuring Effective International Legal Protection* (Kluwer Law, 1996).

[29] (1995) ETS 157.

around them.[30] The state may value religion or religions as encouraging core values among its citizenship, providing essential support that the state does not itself wish to or cannot provide, and enhancing social harmony and cohesiveness.[31] The presence of different religions allows for a fertile interaction of different cultural concepts and ideas. Nafziger has identified five specific functions of religion—creative, aspirational, didactic, custodial and mediative.[32]

In short, religion is far more than a set of private beliefs and the manifestation of those beliefs through rituals and practices. It provides a link between thought and action and thereby has a direct impact on the social sphere. In addition many religious groups perform important social functions such as education, welfare and medical care.   **1.21**

Philosophical and political theory

For a thousand years between the fall of the Roman Empire and the Renaissance in the fifteenth century, literature and philosophical writing in Europe emanated mostly from the Christian church. Much of this early writing in Europe on tolerance and religious freedom would be regarded as far from tolerant by today's standards in its implicit or express justification of forced conversions to Christianity, persecution of heretics and mass murder in the name of religion. John Locke's *Letter on Toleration* (1688), for example, was written against a backdrop of persecution against Protestants following the revocation of the Edict of Nantes, and his own exile under James II. Tolerance for Locke, however, was confined to Anglicans and dissenting Protestants but did not extend to Catholics, Muslims, Jews or atheists.[33]   **1.22**

Following the enactment of international norms in the twentieth century, the emphasis for philosophers shifted. Many writers have sought to identify the roots of religious freedom and tolerance from within the world's religions as a means of promoting co-existence and suggesting the compatibility of international human rights standards and religion.[34] Another concern is with the concept of individual   **1.23**

---

[30] See L Bloss, *European Law of Religion—organisational and institutional analysis of national systems and their implications for the future European Integration Process*, Jean Monnet Working Paper 13/03 (NYU School of Law).

[31] See H Berman, *The Interaction of Law and Religion* (Abingdon Press, 1974) 25.

[32] J Nafziger, 'The Functions of Religion in the International Legal System' in M Janis & C Evans (eds), *Religion and International Law* (Kluwer Law, 1999) 155–76.

[33] At this time there were however a number of writers who were inspired by the rediscovery of ancient mystical texts and Plato to seek a transcendence of religious differences: see further F Yates, *Giordano Bruno and the Hermetic Tradition* (University of Chicago Press, 1991).

[34] See A An-Naim (ed), *Human Rights in Cross-Cultural Perspectives: A Quest for Consensus* (University of Pennsylvania Press, 1992); J Runzo, N Martin & A Sharma, *Human Rights and Responsibilities in the World Religions* (Oneworld, 2003); J Witte & J van der Vyver, *Religious Human Rights in Global Perspective: Religious Perspectives* (M Nijhoff Publishers, 1996).

freedom, autonomy and human dignity within a democracy.[35] Joseph Raz, Ronald Dworkin and John Rawls in their respective works have all formulated ideas on personal autonomy and pluralism that apply to religious freedom.[36]

1.24   Theory may assist in taking a principled approach but does not always provide solutions to the myriad problems that arise in practice. Many people would have little difficulty with the idea that the state should intervene in the internal affairs of a religious group in order to protect children against physical harm by members of that group. But what about invention where adults fully and freely consent to forms of physical harm? And should the state intervene if a religious group discriminates against women or against certain ethnic groups by refusing to permit them to hold positions within the organization?

Cultural diversity and multiculturalism

1.25   One important contemporary debate in this field focuses on cultural diversity and multicultural accommodation within liberal democracies in general. The basic concern is how to divide authority in the multicultural state so as to strike a balance between the rights of individuals, the accommodation of minority group traditions, and the interests of the state as a whole. Many political and legal theorists have argued in favour of accommodating distinctive identity groups by granting them special rights and exemptions.[37] But the concept of good and therefore the relevant needs of each of the individual, the group and the state is contestable, and a group may not respect individual rights within that group.

1.26   The assimilation approach has been the standard approach in many places. This 'when in Rome do as the Romans do' approach involves minorities and new members assimilating to the majority and in its extreme form leads to the eventual diminution of cultural, religious and ethnic differences. The French state has favoured an assimilation approach and has officially not recognized diversity in race or ethnicity, although in practice it turns out that its ethnic minority population is far from assimilated. The United Kingdom, on the other hand, has attempted to adopt a more pluralistic approach in its treatment of ethnic and religious groups.

1.27   Reacting to the assimilation standard, Will Kymlicka, Charles Taylor and Iris Young writing in the 1990s marked the beginnings of the current multiculturalism debate. This writing in various different ways emphasized the importance of

---

[35] See the discussion in Ahdar & Leigh (n 5 above) Ch 2 on liberal perspectives on freedom of religion.

[36] See J Raz, *The Morality of Freedom* (OUP, 1986); J Raz, *Ethics in the Public Domain* (OUP, 1994); R Dworkin, *Taking Rights Seriously* (Harvard University Press, 1978); J Rawls, *A Theory of Justice* (Harvard University Press, 1999).

[37] See A Shachar, *Multicultural Jurisdictions: Cultural Differences and Women's Rights* (CUP, 2001) 1–16.

autonomy and cultural identity for groups, and the need to transform power structures in society. Kymlicka's particular concern is with national minorities rather than religious groups per se.[38] Young and Taylor both accord significance to group membership as an important social relationship.[39]

A second wave of writing on multiculturalism in the late 1990s discussed the **1.28** complexities of the multicultural approach. This acknowledged the tripartite conflict between the interests of the individual, the group and the state. For example, Brian Barry aims to provide a theory of group rights that respects both internal diversity and universal rights. The key in his view is the right to freedom of association and the ability freely to join or leave any group. The freedom to exit the group must be genuine so that if there are economic, educational or social barriers to leaving the group this is problematic.[40] A stronger form of multiculturalism is advocated by Chandran Kukathas. He takes an extreme liberal position and proposes a minimal constitutional structure that would solve the problem of group rights by allowing extensive autonomy for all groups and minorities in a society and takes as its principal objective the protection of one group from another.[41]

More recent scholarship tends to stress the reality that people have multiple overlap- **1.29** ping identities that are highly fluid and may be constantly shifting in an infinite variety of patterns. An approach that either gives emphasis to the individual's rights or to the group or state may not be sufficiently responsive to these mutating identities. Linked to this is an increasing understanding of the complexities of discrimination and the fact that many people are simultaneously subjected to more than one form of discrimination so that a woman may be treated less favourably because she is both Muslim and female, or a man may be discriminated against because he is homosexual, Jewish, and Israeli. Some of this has emanated from post-colonial theory that focuses on the simplification, essentializing and stereo-typing that have taken place under the forces of colonial powers that have purported to speak on behalf of large sections of the world's population.[42]

Overall, there is a need to develop ideas that allow for flexibility, renegotiation **1.30** and continued bargaining. But at the same time there is also a need to develop

---

[38] W Kymlicka, *Multicultural Citizenship: A Liberal Theory of Minority Rights* (Clarendon Press, 1995).

[39] I Young, *Justice and the Politics of Difference* (Princeton University Press, 1990); C Taylor, *Multiculturalism: Examining the Politics of Recognition* (ed A Gutmann) (Princeton University Press, 1994).

[40] B Barry, *Culture and Equality: An Egalitarian Critique of Multiculturalism* (Polity Press, 2001).

[41] C Kukathas, *Liberalism and Multiculturalism: the Politics of Indifference* (1998) 26 Political Theory 686–99.

[42] See G C Spivak, *A Critique of Post-Colonial Reason: Toward a History of the Vanishing Present* (Harvard University Press, 1999).

a minimum core set of values by which everyone within the state can live. While sensitivity to religious and cultural difference is important, it should not be used as a means of undermining the rights of the vulnerable and weak in society. Further, the law needs to be responsive to multiple and overlapping forms of discrimination that take place.

Legal models

1.31 Just as the political system may adopt different models, so the legal system in a pluralist and multicultural society may develop different approaches both in terms of jurisdiction and substantive rules. A wide variety of models have been tried and tested throughout the world, such as the millet system under the Ottoman empire, the separate personal law systems in operation in India that differentiate between Muslims, Hindus, Parsis and Christians, and the system in Israel that creates separate personal laws for Jews, Muslims and Druzes.[43]

1.32 The assimilationist approach assumes one legal system for all citizens with neutral, generally applicable laws and a common court system. This may appear attractive particularly from the perspective of the state and the majority who are likely to find their needs adequately met by such a system. It also finds support among strong universalists who want state recognition for generally applicable individual rights. But it may not be sufficiently responsive to the needs of minorities and ignores the basic problem that so-called neutral laws are in fact premised on the dominant culture and may not be neutral in their application.

1.33 Within a liberal framework there are a number of possible responses as to how a system might accord respect to individuals or groups. One solution is to allow groups the right to govern themselves through their own set of rules and courts. But there are many variables on this option as regards the areas of law that are parcelled out to the group and the extent to which separate jurisdiction is granted. Some systems have made a division between substantive areas of the law so that, for example, family and criminal laws may be governed by religious law while other areas such as commercial law, tax and torts are governed by general secular laws. Some systems allow groups jurisdiction over their own personal laws at the lowest level and then may incorporate a right of appeal to a state court from the decision of the group. This was advocated by the province of Ontario in Canada by a proposal to set up a Shar'ia court that would adjudicate on matters relating to Muslims but with a possibility of appeal to the federal court system, but now appears to have been rejected.

---

[43] For a discussion of legal pluralism see P Shah, *Legal Pluralism in Conflict: Coping with Cultural Diversity in Law* (Glasshouse Press, 2005).

Another approach and one used to some degree in many legal systems is the rule **1.34** and exemption model. On this basis generally applicable laws are passed according to the needs of the majority but it is recognized that certain categories of people will have considerable difficulty in conforming to the general rule and a special exemption is enacted for them. The English legal system has used this approach in a number of areas and has granted exemptions to turbaned Sikhs from wearing motorcycle helmets, and Jews and Muslims from being subject to rules requiring the stunning of animals before slaughter for food. But it raises a number of issues including who in the community decides what rules they need exemption from, and which groups get exemptions, and it ultimately reifies religious practice, belief and group identity.

In the United Kingdom, there are a number of separate religious courts which **1.35** have jurisdiction over a variety of matters relating to religious law. In the Church of England a series of ecclesiastical courts have jurisdiction over matters dealing with the rights and obligations of church members, church doctrine, and ceremony or ritual. The ecclesiastical courts are part of the English court system. A number of other religions also have their own courts systems or forums for dispute resolution. Some of their decisions, such as arbitration awards, may be enforceable through the English court system. For example, the London Beth Din, in its capacity as Court of the Chief Rabbi, is historically the supreme Halakhic Authority for several commonwealth countries and additionally is consulted by Batei Din throughout Europe. The range of questions with which the Beth Din deals is vast and covers all areas of Jewish law. The Islamic Shar'ia Council guides Muslims in the United Kingdom in matters related to religious issues as well as solving their matrimonial problems which are referred to it.

Religion and the State

Significance of relationship

Consideration of the divide between church and state is important in a number of **1.36** respects to understanding the approach to cases involving religion. The European Union has expressly recognized the competence of its Member States to have an established church.[44] The European Court of Human Rights ('ECtHR') and the European Commission for Human Rights (the 'Commission') have similarly held that the establishment of a state church is not in itself a breach of the ECHR but the system must include specific safeguards for the individual's freedom

---

[44] See Declaration (No 11) on the Status of Churches and Non-Confessional Organisations to the Final Act of the Treaty of Amsterdam, signed 2 October 1997.

of religion.[45] As a result, many of the decisions from Strasbourg relating to freedom of religion reveal a wide margin of appreciation granted to the decision of the domestic authorities. A key factor in this is the differing relationships between church and state across Europe.

1.37 An understanding of the divide assists in understanding the level of state interference in religious affairs. It may explain the importance ascribed to religion within a country and the way in which the state seeks to regulate the internal affairs of that religion. It is also important in understanding the relative positions of differing religions within a state and the extent to which some religions have been disadvantaged over a dominant and privileged religion.

1.38 In any given case, the particular label ascribed to the relationship may not be determinative. The fact that a state describes itself as secular or *laïc* does not necessarily mean that in practice particular religions are not given state support, or it may disguise a situation where religious beliefs are widespread and profoundly held and therefore influence the state in many ways. A secular state may also intervene in the affairs of religious groups and may be hostile or discriminatory towards certain religions. Similarly the fact that a state is described as religious or has an established church does not necessarily mean that other faiths are disadvantaged in practical terms although there may well be a presumption that this is the case.[46]

Different models

1.39 There are broadly three different categories of church and state divide. The first involves countries where there is a very close link between church and state. Many Muslim countries fall into this category such as Saudi Arabia and Iran. A European example of this is Greece.[47] Other models have a weaker form of establishment such as the arrangement between the Church of England and the state in the United Kingdom.[48] The second category includes countries where there is a separation between church and state. In such states religion, in theory at least, is relegated to the private sphere and opposes any legal, administrative and political institutionalization. The precise nature of the relationship may take many forms. In the United States this is referred to as the 'wall of separation' and enshrined in the so-called free exercise and non-establishment clauses contained in the First

---

[45] See eg *Darby v Sweden* (1991) 13 EHRR 774. It follows from this that the ECtHR does not consider that in democratic societies the state needs to take steps to ensure that religious communities have unified leadership: see *Mehmet Agga v Greece (Nos 3 & 4)* Applications 32186/02 & 33331/02 (13 July 2006).

[46] See V Bader, 'Religious Diversity and Democratic Institutional Pluralism' (2003) 31(2) Political Theory 265–94, 268.

[47] Constitution of Greece, 7 June 1975 (as amended), Art 3.

[48] Note too the model of plural establishment that exists in Finland where there are two state churches: the Lutheran Church of Finland and the Orthodox Church of Finland.

Amendment to the Constitution.[49] In practice, as the number of cases concerning religion show, the boundaries of this wall are far from clear. In France, for example, the separation is based on the principle of *laïcité*, which is linked to the anti-clerical reaction to absolute monarchy and its link to the Catholic Church that was a driving force of the French Revolution.[50] Although the French state claims not to support religion, there are exceptions to this in the Moselle-Alsace region.

The third category includes a range of other models that combine non-establishment **1.40** with restricted legal, administrative and political pluralism. Some countries have adopted a so-called position of neutrality towards religion. An example of this is the Constitution of India that requires equal treatment of all religions within the state. In this regard the state is free to support religion so long as it is not done in a way that favours one religion over another. Similarly, the German constitution does not establish any one religion. The German Basic Law provides that there 'shall be no state church', although the preamble refers to the 'responsibility before God and humankind' of the German people.[51]

In practice a number of arrangements between church and state have evolved **1.41** while at the same time providing for freedom of religion and non-discrimination. But regardless of the form, in practice the state is unable to ensure a total disassociation from religious affairs or to free itself entirely from providing support to religious groups whether directly or indirectly. In this respect arguably the precise relationship matters less than the practical effects for individuals and various religious groups. But in a religiously diverse society, the fact that one particular church is established and thereby is accorded status over and above other religions, itself creates a presumption of bias even without taking into account the tangible privileges that such establishment will confer, and requires scrutiny.

The Church of England

The position of the Church of England appears in many respects to be an anomaly **1.42** in the present day. It establishes on the one hand a denomination of Protestantism and grants special privileges to that church. Its bishops are entitled as of right to sit in the House of Lords, the monarch is head of the Church of England and may not marry a Catholic, and it conducts certain public ceremonies such as the Coronation. While it has been the subject of much discussion, there has been

---

[49] The First Amendment reads 'Congress shall make no law respecting an establishment of religion, nor prohibiting the free exercise thereof'. See generally J Noonan & E McGlynn Gaffney, *Religious Freedom* (Foundation Press, 2001).

[50] The Constitution of the Republic of France describes France as 'a Republic, indivisible, laic, democratic and social'.

[51] Basic Law of Germany, 23 May 1949, preamble and Art 137(1) of the Weimar Constitution of 1919 which is an integral part of the Basic Law pursuant to Art 140 of the Basic Law.

little political pressure to reform to date, although increasingly questions are being asked about the role of religion in the public sphere.[52] The role of the Church of England, its privileges and obligations and the relationship between other religious groups and the state in any given set of circumstances must be examined closely in the light of the norms protecting freedom of religion and non-discrimination.[53]

1.43   As regards political influence, the 26 most senior bishops of the Church of England have by right a seat and a vote in the House of Lords as Lords Spiritual.[54] No other religious organization has such a right to seats in either House.[55] Although the Church of England does not receive any direct funding from the government, it has vast assets of around £4.8 billion managed by the Church Commissioners and an annual income of £138 million.[56] The Church of England alone is protected from expressions of contempt for its beliefs. The common law offences of blasphemy and blasphemous libel limit free speech only where the Church of England is the subject, although the legal protection is very rarely invoked. An unsuccessful challenge to this situation was brought by a member of the Muslim Action Front following the publication of Salman Rushdie's *The Satanic Verses*.[57]

1.44   There are a number of organized religions with representative bodies in England including the Muslim Council of Britain, the Board of Deputies of British Jews, the Buddhist Society, Hindu Council (UK) and Network of Sikh Organisations (UK). The relative political bargaining position of these groups will vary according to individual members, history and current politics, but none possess guaranteed political representation in the House of Lords in the way in which the Church of England does. In England, the position of the Church of England has been under attack from a number of sides at various points in history. The enactment of the Human Rights Act 1998 was not intended to affect the established position of the

---

[52] Note that Prince Charles has previously suggested that he might be 'defender of faith' rather than 'Defender of The Faith'.

[53] A February 2001 Home Office study suggested that the establishment status of the Church of England causes 'religious disadvantage' to other religious communities. See P Weller, A Feldman & K Pudman, 'Religious discrimination in England and Wales' Home Office Research Study 220, February 2001.

[54] Note that the Church of England has a special status on the Isle of Man, where the Bishop of Sodor and Man is a member of parliament, and in Guernsey and Jersey although none of these three territories forms part of the UK.

[55] Note that the Removal of Clergy Disqualification Act 2001 removed restrictions that prohibited all clergy ordained by an Anglican bishop, as well as ministers of the Church of Scotland, from seeking or holding membership in the House of Commons.

[56] See <http://www.cofe.anglican.org/info/funding>. Of the 33 Church Commissioners, six hold state office and include the Prime Minister, the Lord Chancellor, the Lord President of the Council, the Home Secretary, the Secretary of State for Culture, Media and Sport, and the Speaker of the House of Commons. The fund has its historical roots in money accrued by Henry VIII that was given to the Anglican Church in 1704.

[57] See *Choudhury v United Kingdom* [1991] 12(4) HRLJ 172.

Church of England. However, in the same period the Wakeham Report circulated in 2000 reviewed the position of the bishops in the House of Lords. It proposed that their numbers should be reduced to allow for more non-Christian representatives and other Christian denominations so that the House of Lords would represent all major religions.[58]

Advocates of disestablishment of the Church of England come from a variety of   **1.45**
arenas. George Carey, former Archbishop of Canterbury, expressed the opinion that he expects the Church of England to be disestablished one day. Disestablishment is also supported by many religious leaders in the United Kingdom outside the Church of England including the Libertarian Alliance and the Christian Socialist Movement. Many academics and other writers have similarly advocated reform. Most recently the Fabian Society has called for the end of the Church of England's preferential status and the removal of bishops from the House of Lords.[59] However, there are also vociferous supporters of maintaining an established church.[60]

Concluding Remarks

This chapter has briefly mapped some of the theoretical aspects of this topic as   **1.46**
a prelude to consideration of the practical issues. No overarching theory about the relationship between religion, church, individuals and the state is likely to provide a solution in a specific case although it is important to understand the links. As regards religious minorities as groups, it should not be assumed that leaders of the group represent the views of the majority within that group. Religious groups, like all other groups, may be subject to the dictates of small and often male elites. Their views may be imposed on the wider group to the detriment of contrasting views and in particular the views of women. Rather the emphasis should be on looking at the competing interests in any given case, taking into account the need to protect the vulnerable, and to strike a fair balance in the context of the particular case. The words of Rosa Luxembourg, socialist philosopher and revolutionary, writing from prison in 1916 are ever resonant and as relevant to the issue of freedom of religion as they are to freedom and rights generally: 'Freedom only for supporters of the government, for members of the party—though they are quite numerous— is no freedom at all. Freedom always means freedom for the dissenters.'[61]

---

[58] See Wakeham Report (Royal Commission on the House of Lords, Cm 4524, January 2000).
[59] See Report of the Fabian Commission, *Future of the Monarchy* (Fabian Society, 2003).
[60] See the defence articulated in Ahdar & Leigh (n 5 above) Ch 5.
[61] See MA Waters (ed), *Rosa Luxemburg Speaks* (Pathfinder Press, 1970).

2

LEGAL FRAMEWORK

Introduction

Freedom of religion has always been one of the most controversial of rights at the **2.01** international level. It is no less so in the domestic setting. While the freedom privately to hold particular religious or philosophical views is unlikely to give rise to practical difficulties, the extent to which manifestations of religious belief are considered acceptable in society is a vexed issue. The diversity of views on substantive beliefs, on the position of religion in the public sphere, and the balance between the right to express and manifest religious views on the one hand, and the legitimate restrictions that may be imposed by the state on the other, all create considerable challenges for society today.

The right to freedom of thought, conscience and religion contained in Article 9 of **2.02** the European Convention on Human Rights ('ECHR') was derived from Article 18 of the Universal Declaration of Human Rights 1948 ('UDHR').[1] The signing of

---

[1] Adopted by General Assembly Resolution 217 A (III) of 10 December 1948. Art 18 UDHR provides: 'Everyone has the right to freedom of thought, conscience and religion; this right includes freedom to change his religion or belief, and freedom, either alone or in community with others and in public or private, to manifest his religion or belief in teaching, practice, worship and observance.'

the UDHR marked a significant step forward in recognizing a common framework for the protection of individual rights. During the drafting process, Article 18 proved to be one of the most controversial articles, with Muslim states in particular being concerned about missionaries and the freedom to change religion or belief.[2] There was, and remains to this day, little consensus between states as to the meaning of freedom of religion in practice. The approach taken by Saudi Arabia and the United Kingdom on the issue of freedom to change religion, for example, could not be more different, despite the common standard reflected in the UDHR.[3]

2.03 The drafting of the provision for freedom of religion was less controversial in the European context, but its application varies widely even among members of the European Union and even more so among members of the Council of Europe (the 'Council'). A comparison of the positions taken by France, Germany and the United Kingdom on religious clothing in state schools, for example, shows the considerable gulf in interpretation of the ECHR rights relating to religion.[4] Individual states have interpreted their obligations under the ECHR according to a variety of factors including the political regime, the nature and history of the relationship between church and state, the degree of religious plurality within the state, the nature of the dominant religion and its commitment to religious liberty, and the interaction between religious groups.[5]

2.04 It is fundamental to the understanding of the approach taken by the European organs to recognize that the European Union, the European Commission on Human Rights ('the Commission') and the European Court of Human Rights ('ECtHR') all accept in principle that individual states have the right to determine the nature of the relationship between church and state within their respective borders.[6] As a consequence the Strasbourg decisions can often be hard to reconcile with each other because of the local circumstances and the relatively wide margin of appreciation granted to domestic courts by the European organs.

---

[2] See B Tahzib, *Freedom of Religion or Belief: Ensuring Effective International Legal Protection* (Kluwer Law International, 1996) 70–81; N Lerner, 'Religious Human Rights under the United Nations' in J van der Vyver & J Witte (eds), *Religious Human Rights in Global Perspective: Legal Perspectives* (Kluwer Law, 1996) 86–8; M Evans, *Religious Liberty and International Law in Europe* (CUP, 1997) 172–93.

[3] Conversion from the Muslim faith is regarded as apostasy in Saudi Arabia and punishable under Shar'ia law as applied there by death. Note that Saudi Arabia abstained from voting on the final text of the UDHR: see Tahzib (n 2 above) 76.

[4] See A Riley, 'Headscarves, Skull Caps and Crosses' CEPS Policy Brief No 49/April 2004; S Knights, 'Religious Symbols in the School: Freedom of Religion, Minorities and Education' [2005] EHRLR 499–516.

[5] See W Cole Durham, 'Perspectives on Religious Liberty: A Comparative Framework' in van der Vyver & Witte (n 2 above) 2.

[6] See Declaration (No 11) on the Status of Churches and Non-Confessional Organisations to the Final Act of the Treaty of Amsterdam, signed 2 October 1997; *Darby v Sweden* (1991) 13 EHRR 774.

Despite the differing interpretations, there are core principles that underpin the pro- **2.05**
tection contained in Article 9. In particular in a liberal democracy the constitution
aims to protect the minority and should provide a check against the unwarranted
imposition of the views of the majority. The ECtHR in *Young, James and Webster v
United Kingdom*[7] stated in the context of an employee who had conscientious
objections to a 'closed-shop' policy:

> [P]luralism, tolerance and broadmindedness are the hallmarks of a 'democratic society'
> . . . Although individual interests must on occasion be subordinated to those of a
> group, democracy does not simply mean that the views of a majority must always
> prevail: a balance must be achieved which ensures the fair and proper treatment of
> minorities and avoids any abuse of a dominant position. Accordingly, the mere fact
> that the applicants' standpoint was adopted by very few of their colleagues is again
> not conclusive of the issue now before the Court.[8]

As regards protection for religious minorities, there are now a number of provi- **2.06**
sions relating to equality and non-discrimination applicable domestically.
Non-discrimination on the basis of religion is protected by Article 14 ECHR in
conjunction with Article 9 or another substantive ECHR right. Some, but not all
religious groups, have also been afforded protection against discrimination under
the provisions of the Race Relations Act 1976 ('RRA 1976') as amended by the
Race Relations Act (Amendment) Regulations 2003 implementing the Race
Equality Directive.[9] More specifically, protection against discrimination on religious grounds in certain circumstances (employment and vocational education)
is expressly granted by the Employment Equality (Religion or Belief) Regulations
2003 giving effect to the Framework Employment Directive.[10] The Equality Act
2006 ('EA 2006') extends the scope of protection and makes discrimination on
the grounds of religion or belief unlawful in the provision of goods, facilities and
services, education, the use and disposal of premises, and the exercise of public
functions.[11]

At the domestic level it is important that the case law is developed consistently **2.07**
with the best practice and interpretation of Strasbourg decisions. This requires
a critical approach to the ECHR rights and the case law in order to identify the
underlying principles. However, it does not imply a blind following of cases in

---

[7] (1982) 4 EHRR 38 [63].

[8] See also *Sorensen and Rasmussen v Denmark*, Applications 52562/99 and 52620/99 (11 January 2006) [58].

[9] SI 2003/1626 implementing Council Directive (EC) 2000/43 implementing the principle of equal treatment between persons irrespective of racial or ethnic origin [2000] OJ L180/22.

[10] SI 2003/1660 implementing Council Directive (EC) 2000/78 establishing a general framework for equal treatment in employment and occupation [2000] OJ L303/16.

[11] Received Royal Assent on 16 February 2006. The relevant provisions of the EA 2006 are expected to enter into force in 2007.

which the circumstances may be very different to those under consideration. Domestically the fact that there is an established religion in the Church of England means that the state is not hostile per se to religion in the public sphere and there are numerous examples of how religion is promoted and supported by the state. This is important for religious minorities, because many of the arguments raised in secular states such as Turkey to justify the restriction on manifestations of religion will not necessarily be applicable to the situation in England. Decisions of the European Court of Justice ('ECJ') are of course binding authority on the United Kingdom.

2.08 This chapter examines the interpretation of the relevant legal provisions at the European and domestic levels. In Europe the case law is principally derived from the former Commission and the ECtHR. There is as yet very little relevant case law in this area from the ECJ although this is an area that is likely to develop with the Race Equality and Framework Employment Directives recently implemented by EU Member States.

Overview of Legal Provisions

Common law

2.09 By the beginning of the twentieth century, the repeal of various restrictive pieces of legislation meant that there were as such no legal prohibitions in England on freedom of religious belief and worship. Nor did legal bars prevent people from entering public office or employment on the grounds of religion. But there was no positive right to freedom of religion or belief, no protection against discrimination on the grounds of religion, and no guarantee of equal treatment.[12] Given the historical context of religious freedom, the dominance of Christian values as expressed in the legal system, and the position of the Church of England, other religions and their adherents were at risk of less favourable treatment than that afforded to the established church, its followers and the majority of the population. The legislative framework in England prior to the enactment of the Human Rights Act 1998 ('HRA 1998') contrasted directly with the positive right to freedom of religion contained in many of the bills of rights and constitutions around the world.[13]

---

[12] See St JA Robilliard, *Religion and the Law: Religious Liberty in Modern English Law* (Manchester University Press, 1984) ix–xii; C Hamilton, *Family, Law and Religion* (Sweet & Maxwell, 1995) 1–11 for a brief history of the development of religious freedom in English law.

[13] See eg US Constitution (1791) 1st Amendment; India Constitution (1950) Arts 15, 16, 25, 26; Canada Constitution (1982) Art 2; France Constitution (1953) Arts 2, 77; German Basic Law (1949) Arts 4, 7, 140, 141.

In England, despite the lack of formal protection, there was some judicial recog- **2.10** nition of aspects of freedom of religion prior to the enactment of the HRA 1998. In a case in the mid 1990s, Sedley J referred to the position as follows:

> The common law, like the European Convention on Human Rights, recognizes the freedom of individuals to adopt, practise and (relevantly) to change their religion. Any administrative decision impinging upon this liberty must be justified by a suffi- ciently weighty competing public interest . . . [14]

However, the fact that freedom of religion was not expressly protected and the ECHR not part of domestic law would allow considerable room for divergent approaches among decision makers.

As regards discrimination, the position at common law prior to the HRA 1998 **2.11** was also unclear as there was traditionally no express protection against it. In a case in the 1990s, Lord Hoffmann giving the opinion of the Privy Council in *Matadeen v Pointu*[15] recognized that '[e]quality before the law requires that persons should be uniformly treated, unless there is some valid reason to treat them differently'. This was one of the 'building blocks of democracy and necessarily permeates any democratic constitution'. But the Privy Council also noted that 'it by no means follows, however, that the rights which are constitutionally protected and subject to judicial review include a general justiciable principle of equality'.[16] As regards freedom of religion and discrimination, in the absence of prescribed legal norms, there was no guarantee that these basic rights would be justiciable through the courts. The lack of adequate protection is highlighted by another case in which the Court of Appeal doubted that the Privy Council in *Matadeen v Pointu* was propounding a free-standing principle of equality in English domestic law.[17]

Although there was de facto recognition to a large extent of both religious expression **2.12** and religious practice in English law, both have been circumscribed by criminal sanctions in common law and statute. The restrictions fall into two categories: first, criminal law applies in relation to certain actions by individuals regardless of their religious beliefs and may criminalize actions closely connected to religion or to culture. Secondly, criminal law provides for particular sanctions aimed to protect religion against criticism through free expression.[18]

---

[14] *R v Secretary of State for the Home Department, ex p Moon* (1995) 8 Admin LR 477, 480. See also *Ahmad v Inner London Education Authority* [1978] QB 36, 41 where Denning MR said that although the ECHR was not part of English law, the courts would 'pay regard' to it. Scarman LJ at 48 in a dissenting judgment stated that it could always be employed as an aid to the interpretation of statutes.

[15] [1999] 1 AC 98, 109 citing *Police v Rose* [1976] MR 79.

[16] Ibid, 110.

[17] *R (Association of British Civilian Internees: Far East Region) v Secretary of State for Defence* [2003] EWCA Civ 473 [85] (per Dyson LJ).

[18] For a more detailed treatment of this subject see R Ahdar & I Leigh, *Religious Freedom in the Liberal State* (OUP, 2005) Ch 12.

2.13   As regards manifestations of belief and religious practice, various criminal sanctions are imposed specifically to restrict and protect against religious or cultural actions that are considered harmful. For example, the Female Genital Mutilation Act 2003 makes it an offence to perform circumcision on a female.[19] Further, acting in accordance with religious beliefs in taking drugs, in general is not considered to be a defence to a criminal charge relating to the possession of drugs.[20] However, in a variety of areas of criminal law the lack of 'reasonable excuse' is an element of the offence or having a 'reasonable excuse' may be a defence to a charge. It may therefore be appropriate to consider the manifestation of religious beliefs in considering whether a defendant has an excuse. There may also be room for argument about the proportionality of a prosecution depending on the circumstances.

2.14   There has been some legislation passed to provide exemptions from criminal and regulatory sanctions for certain religious groups to enable them to practise their religion. For example, turbaned Sikhs have been granted an exemption from the general requirement to wear motor cycle helmets,[21] and Muslims and Jews have been able to obtain exemptions from meat slaughter regulations to allow them to prepare and sell kosher and halal meat.[22] There is also an exemption with regard to Sikhs wearing a kirpan (ceremonial sword) from the prohibition on carrying offensive weapons.[23] The exemptions to date have been ad hoc rather than systematic and largely confined to major world religions with greater bargaining power vis-à-vis the state.[24]

2.15   The expression of religious and other views is subject to the common law sanctions of breach of the peace, sedition and blasphemy laws.[25] These are relatively rarely applied in practice. Until the furore sparked by the publication of Salman Rushdie's *The Satanic Verses*, and the ensuing claim alleging seditious and blasphemous libel, blasphemy had been rarely invoked.[26] In *R v Chief Metropolitan*

---

[19] In force from 3 March 2004, repealing and re-enacting the Prohibition of Female Circumcision Act 1985.

[20] *R v Andrews* [2004] EWCA Crim 947; *R v Taylor* [2001] EWCA Crim 2263.

[21] Road Traffic Act 1988, s 17 (formerly Motor-Cycle Crash Helmets (Religious Exemption) Act 1976). See 7.06–7.08 below.

[22] Slaughterhouses Act 1976, s 36. See 7.19–7.24 below.

[23] Criminal Justice Act 1988, s 139 (as amended by Offensive Weapons Act 1996, s 4). See also Canadian Supreme Court decision in *Multani v Commission Scolaire Marguerite-Bourgeoys* (2006) SCC 6 (order of a Quebec school board that prohibited a Sikh child from wearing a kirpan to school was struck down as a violation of freedom of religion under the Charter of Rights and Freedoms). See 7.09–7.12 below.

[24] See eg reference in debates of the historical record of service by Sikhs to the British military and to their contributions in WWI and WWII in which they had not been forced to wear protective headgear: Report of HC Standing Committee 'F', 23 June 1976, cols 5–12; *Hansard*, HL Vol 374, cols 1060–2 (23 June 1976).

[25] See further Robilliard (n 12 above) 1–45.

[26] The last successful prosecution was by Mrs Mary Whitehouse in the Gay News case: see *Whitehouse v Gay News Ltd and Lemon* [1979] AC 617.

Stipendiary Magistrate, ex p Choudhury,[27] the case concerning *The Satanic Verses*, the court ruled that the law of blasphemy only protected the established Church of England. Despite consideration in the light of non-discrimination provisions in the HRA 1998 and widespread criticism, the offence has not been repealed or extended to cover other religions.[28]

Religious expression is subject to provisions contained in the Public Order Act **2.16** 1986 against displaying writing or signs or representations that are threatening, abusive or insulting.[29] It is also subject to the provisions of the Anti-social Behaviour Act 2003. In *R (Parminder Singh) v Chief Constable of West Midlands*[30] the applicant challenged the the validity of the decision of the respondent police force to issue a dispersal order in the context of a demonstration. The applicant was one of a number of Sikhs who had demonstrated inside and outside a theatre for several nights during the run of a play to which they took great exception, believing it to be grossly offensive to their religion and their religious beliefs. The Court of Appeal dismissed the case, holding that the use of the police powers had a legitimate aim, namely the prevention of crime and disorder, the protection of public safety, and the protection of the rights and freedoms of others, including the right to freedom of expression of those producing the play and the right of others present in the area to go about their business without being subjected to scenes that were unnecessarily frightening, intimidating and distressing. The court further held that the use of the power had been necessary in a demo- cratic society and constituted the right balance between the rights of protesters to express their opinions and the rights of others to be protected from distressing conduct. Religious expression is also subject to statutory provisions against incitement to racial hatred contained in s 18 of the Public Order Act 1986, but only protects those groups such as Sikhs and Jews who were considered to be a racial or ethnic group, but not Muslims. The Racial and Religious Hatred Act 2006 creates offences of stirring up hatred against a person on the grounds of

---

27 [1991] QB 429.

28 See also *Choudhury v United Kingdom* (1991) 12 HRLJ 172 (upholding domestic court find- ing that blasphemy only applies to Church of England). Note the Law Commission Working Paper No 79, *Offences against Religion and Public Worship* at 82 in which they refer to the anomalous posi- tion of the law of blasphemy. See further discussion of the arguments for and against abolition of the offence in Ahdar & Leigh (n 18 above) 371–4.

29 Public Order Act 1986, s 5. See *Harry John Hammond v DPP* [2004] EWHC 69 (Admin) where the case was put principally on the grounds of Art 10, and it was submitted that Art 9 consid- erations were broadly similar to those under Art 10. See further Crime and Disorder Act 1998, ss 28, 31 (as amended by Anti-terrorism, Crime and Security Act 2001, s 39) and *Norwood v DPP* [2003] EWHC 1564 (Admin).

30 [2006] EWCA Civ 1118.

their religion.[31] There are also restrictions on the broadcasting opportunities for religious groups although the Communications Act 2003 lifted some of the limitations.[32]

2.17   Recently, the government has indirectly made further incursions into the right to free expression and association through anti-terrorism measures contained in the Prevention of Terrorism Act 2005 which allows the Secretary of State to place control orders on certain individuals.[33] The obligations that may be imposed by a control order include a 'restriction on his association or communications with specified persons or with other persons generally'.[34] The Terrorism Act 2000 (Proscribed Organisations) (Amendment) Order 2005 added a list of 15 Muslim organizations to those already proscribed under the Terrorism Act 2000.[35] The Terrorism Act 2006 creates additional offences under the guise of encouragement of terrorism including the nebulous concept of 'glorification of terrorism'. It also extends the scheme of proscribing groups to those that glorify terrorism.[36]

Race Relations Act 1976

2.18   Although the express prohibitions on non-Church of England adherents taking office were removed by the mid-nineteenth century, there was no express protection against religious discrimination under the common law or statute until the enactment of the HRA 1998.[37] During the passage of the bill leading to the RRA 1976, consideration was given as to whether to protect against religious

---

[31] The Act received Royal Assent on 17 February 2006 but at the date of publication had not yet entered into force. It was the Labour government's third attempt to bring in this offence. The provisions were originally included as part of the Anti-Terrorism, Crime and Security Bill in 2001, but were dropped after objections from the House of Lords. The measure was again brought forward as part of the Serious Organised Crime and Police Bill in 2004–5, but was again dropped in order to get the body of that Bill passed before the 2005 general election. See I Hare, 'Crosses, Crescents and Sacred Cows: Criminalising Incitement to Religious Hatred' [2006] PL 521.

[32] Communications Act 2003, Sch 14 Pt 4; Broadcasting Act 1990, Sch 2 Pt 2. The new provisions permit religious bodies to hold local and national digital radio and digital terrestrial licences, although they are still prohibited from holding analogue licences and radio and television multiplex licences.

[33] Note that in *Secretary of State for the Home Department v JJ, KK, GG, HH, NN, LL* [2006] EWCA 1141 the Court of Appeal held purported non-derogating control orders made by the Secretary of State were in fact derogating control orders that he had no power to make, as the obligations imposed were so severe that they amounted to a deprivation of liberty contrary to Art 5, ECHR.

[34] Prevention of Terrorism Act 2005, s 1(4)(d).

[35] SI 2892/2005, came into force on 14 October 2005. Note that the Terrorism Act 2000 (Proscribed Organisations) (Amendment) Order 2006, SI 2016/2006 entered into force on 26 July 2006 and added a further four organizations.

[36] Received Royal Assent on 30 March 2006; entered into force on 13 April 2006.

[37] Note that the Northern Ireland Act 1998 prohibits discrimination by the government and public bodies on the grounds of religious belief or political opinion. Discrimination on these grounds in employment is prohibited by the Fair Employment and Treatment (Northern Ireland) Order 1998, SI 1998/3162 (NI 21).

discrimination, but it was decided not to provide expressly for this.[38] Under the provisions of the RRA 1976, discrimination against an individual on the grounds of 'colour, race, nationality or ethnic or national origins' but not religion is prohibited.

The RRA 1976 must now be construed to give effect to the Race Equality **2.19** Directive as a result of the Race Relations Act (Amendment) Regulations 2003, and other relevant provisions of EC law.[39] The EC Directives represent the most wide-ranging EC response to discrimination to date but their impact is as yet largely untested.[40] As amended the RRA 1976 now generally applies to the fields of employment, planning, housing, the exercise of public functions, the provision of goods, facilities and services, and education.[41]

The Race Equality Directive, like the RRA 1976, does not provide any definition **2.20** of the words 'racial' or 'ethnic origins' and it has been left to the national courts to decide.[42] The Race Equality Directive expressly acknowledges that the European Union rejects theories that attempt to determine the existence of separate human races, and that the use of the term 'racial origin' does not imply any acceptance of such theories. However, it is precisely the difficulty in defining 'racial' and 'ethnic origins' that is likely to reduce its impact at the domestic level.[43]

The concept of a 'racial' or 'ethnic' group as referred to in the RRA 1976 has led to a **2.21** wholly unsatisfactory state in case law whereby Sikhs, Jews and Gypsies are currently considered covered by the legislation but Muslims, Hindus and Rastafarians are not.[44] This anomalous state of affairs has resulted from the application of the decision of the House of Lords in *Mandla v Dowell Lee*,[45] a case involving a Sikh pupil at a private school in England whose father wished him to wear his turban

---

[38] HC, Standing Committee A, 29 April and 4 May 1976, cols 84–118. Note that subsequent attempts were made to introduce religious discrimination legislation by a private members' bill. See *Hansard*, HC col 859 (3 March 1998). See also *Hansard*, HL cols 454–78 (28 October 1999) and HL cols 1189–1209 (7 June 2000).

[39] See eg *Bossa v Nordstress* [1998] ICR 694.

[40] See D Chalmers, 'The Application of EC Law in the United Kingdom 1994–1999' (2000) 37 CML REV 7 for a discussion of the history of EC race discrimination provisions.

[41] See generally H Hill, *Blackstone's Guide to the Race Relations (Amendment) Act 2000* (Blackstone, 2002).

[42] One possibility would have been to have a reference to the definition contained in Art 1 of the 1966 Convention on the Elimination of all Forms of Racial Discrimination (ICERD) which includes race, colour, descent and national or ethnic origin. Article 1 is relied upon in the case law of the ECtHR for the purpose of defining race, see *Jersild v Denmark* (1995) 19 EHRR 1.

[43] See L Waddington & M Bell, *More Equal Than Others: Distinguishing European Union Equality Directives* (2001) 38 CML REV 587–611. Note too that doctrines of racial superiority based upon 19th century biological theories which have since been scientifically discredited are condemned in ICERD preambular para 6 and Art 14.

[44] See A McColgan, *Discrimination Law: Text, Cases and Materials* (Hart Publishing, 2005); R Jones & W Gnanapala, *Ethnic Minorities in English Law* (Trentham Books, 2000) 27–58.

[45] [1983] 2 AC 548.

in school. The main issue was whether Sikhs were a 'racial group' defined by reference to their 'ethnic origins' within the meaning of s 3(1) RRA 1976. The House of Lords in that case accepted the argument that Sikhs were an ethnic group and established a set of criteria for determining the status of other groups in this regard.

2.22 The House of Lords held that the two essential characteristics of a racial group under s 3(1) RRA 1976 were: (1) a long shared history, which the group is conscious of as distinguishing it from other groups; and (2) a cultural tradition of its own, including family and social customs and manners, often but not necessarily associated with religious observance. Five other characteristics were identified as relevant but not essential: (1) either a common geographical origin, or descent from a small number of common ancestors; (2) a common language, not necessarily peculiar to the group; (3) a common literature peculiar to that group; (4) a common religion different from that of neighbouring groups or from the general community around it; (5) being a minority or being an oppressed or dominant group within a larger community. Under this test, Gypsies[46] and Jews[47] have been found to constitute a racial group. On the other hand, Muslims,[48] Rastafarians[49] and Jehovah's Witnesses[50] have been held not to constitute a racial or ethnic group.[51]

2.23 The approach taken by the English courts has been the subject of intense criticism. Much of the criticism understandably has come from the Muslim community, which remains excluded from protections against discrimination afforded to other religious groups under the RRA 1976, despite the fact that it is a numerically more significant group and has historically suffered and continues to suffer discrimination in the United Kingdom.[52]

2.24 The European Community itself has very little case law on racial or religious discrimination and therefore the ECJ is likely to draw upon the case law of the member states to assist in the interpretation of the Race Equality Directive.

---

[46] Ibid, 562 (per Lord Fraser); see also *Commission for Racial Equality v Dutton* [1989] IRLR 8.

[47] *Seide v Gillette Industries Ltd* [1980] IRLR 427.

[48] *Tariq v Young*, Case 247738/88, EOR Discrimination Case Law Digest No 2. Cf K Dobe & S Chhokar, 'Muslims, Ethnicity and the Law' (2000) 4 International Journal of Discrimination and the Law 369–86 in which they argue that the criteria in *Mandla v Dowell Lee* are sufficiently broad to recognize British Muslims as an ethnic group.

[49] *Crown Suppliers (Property Services Agency) v Dawkins* [1993] ICR 517.

[50] *Lovell-Badge v Norwich City College of Further and Higher Education*, Case 1502237/97 (1999) 39 EOR Discrimination Case Law Digest 4.

[51] Note that Scots, English and Welsh are not recognized by English law as ethnic or racial groups, see *Northern Joint Police Board v Power* [1997] IRLR 610.

[52] See *Muslims in the UK: Policies for Engaged Citizens* (Open Society Institute, 2005); H Ansari, *Muslims in Britain* (Minority Rights Group International, 2002); K Dobe, *Muslims, Ethnicity and the Law*, (Consilio, 9 November 2000) at <http://www.spr-consilio.com/muslims.pdf>; Jones & Gananapala (n 44 above) 244.

There is little consensus on the meaning of race and ethnicity. This is hardly surprising considering that the first is largely based upon a discredited biological theory, while the second term, now used more frequently as a replacement for race, is only capable of a loose definition in which a number of characteristics of an individual may be taken into account.[53]

Of the EU Member States, the United Kingdom has some of the most developed **2.25** case law in this area, which is, therefore, likely to be referred to at the ECJ level.[54] Some states such as France have taken a very different approach to anti-discrimination policy. France does not collect official statistics on race and rejects the very notion of a distinction between different races. Consequentially the case law is much less developed on the definition of race.[55] The ECJ will determine an autonomous European definition of race but is likely to be guided by the highest domestic courts in member states. However, if a restrictive interpretation of the criteria set out in *Mandla v Dowell Lee*[56] is followed, the Race Equality Directive will have no application for many religious minority groups. A far more flexible working definition of 'racial' or 'ethnic' group should be adopted to avoid the anomalous situation at present and in order to provide protection for the groups that require it.

The RRA 1976 prohibits both direct and indirect discrimination. A person is subject **2.26** to direct race discrimination if, on the ground of race, he is treated less favourably than someone of another race is treated or would be treated.[57] In order to show discrimination, a claimant must be able to point to a hypothetical comparator. He must show that he has been treated less favourably than an actual or hypothetical person of a different race whose relevant circumstances were not materially different to his.

Indirect discrimination is designed to prevent particular groups being disadvan- **2.27** taged by apparently neutral practices that in practice disproportionately impact on them. The RRA 1976 has two different definitions of indirect discrimination.

---

[53] Note the wide definition contained in ICERD.

[54] See A Riley, *Headscarves, Skull Caps and Crosses*, CEPS Policy Brief No 49/April 2004.

[55] France maintains a 'colour-blind' model of public policy. This means that it targets virtually no policies directly at racial or ethnic groups. Instead, it uses geographic or class criteria to address issues of social inequalities: see E Bleich, *Race Policy in France* at <http://www.brookings.edu/fp/cuse/analysis/race.htm>.

[56] By contrast, at the international level there has been recognition of contemporary forms of racism that effectively includes racism on religious grounds. The Special Rapporteur on Contemporary Forms of Racism, Racial Discrimination, Xenophobia and Related Intolerance first appointed in 1993 had its mandate extended by the Human Rights Commission in 1994 and now embraces 'incidents of contemporary forms of racism, racial discrimination, any form of discrimination against Blacks, Arabs, Muslims, xenophobia, negrophobia, anti-Semitism and related intolerance'.

[57] RRA 1976, s 1(1)(a).

The first and original one applies broadly only to discrimination on the grounds of nationality or colour. This requires that the claimant show that he has had applied to him a requirement or condition that is applied to all racial groups but that a considerably smaller proportion of the claimant's racial group than of others is able to comply, and which is to his detriment because he is unable to comply with it.[58] The second definition introduced by the Race Equality Directive refers to employment related indirect race discrimination. This applies where a 'provision, criterion or practice' is applied to him that applies or would apply equally to persons not of the same race or ethnic or national origins as that other but (a) which puts or would put persons of the same race or ethnic or national origins as that other at a particular disadvantage when compared with other persons, (b) which puts that other at that disadvantage, and (c) which he cannot show to be a proportionate means of achieving a legitimate aim.[59]

2.28   Religious groups that are not protected per se under the prohibition on direct discrimination under the RRA 1976 may still be protected by the prohibition on indirect discrimination. In *JH Walker v Hussain*,[60] a group of Asian Muslims claimed discrimination when they were not permitted to take a day of leave to observe a religious holiday. The only group that was affected by the blanket rule preventing taking leave at that time was the group of Asian Muslims. It was held that as the group originated from the subcontinent they could claim indirect discrimination but that they could not claim direct discrimination as Muslims in general did not fall within the RRA 1976.

2.29   The RRA 1976 as amended does not prevent difference of treatment based on ethnic or racial characteristics if the latter constitutes a genuine and determining occupational requirement provided that the objective is legitimate and the requirement is proportionate. This exception is to be given a restrictive interpretation. This exception may affect employers such as schools with the need to have teachers with particular qualifications or characteristics, and thereby may indirectly affect pupils.[61]

2.30   The RRA 1976 also expressly prohibits victimization and harassment. Victimization is considered as less favourable treatment in circumstances including where a person has complained of discrimination under the RRA 1976 or has taken steps in connection with legal action thereunder.[62] Previously, racial harassment was not mentioned in the RRA 1976, although courts and tribunals have considered harassment to be a form of unlawful direct discrimination. Now the RRA 1976 as

---

[58] Ibid, s 1(1)(b).
[59] Ibid, s 1(1A).
[60] [1996] ICR 291.
[61] See Chapters 4 and 5 below.
[62] RRA 1976, s 2.

amended states that harassment on the relevant grounds is unlawful. It occurs when someone's actions or words are unwelcome and violate another person's dignity or create an environment that is intimidating, hostile, degrading, humiliating or offensive.

Human Rights Act 1998

Section 2 HRA 1998

When determining a question that has arisen in connection with a right contained in the ECHR, courts and tribunals must take into account relevant decisions from Strasbourg pursuant to s 2(1) HRA 1998. The domestic courts are obliged to take the case law into account but importantly are not bound to follow it. The extent of the obligation was referred to by Lord Bingham in *R (Ullah) v Special Adjudicator*[63] where he stated that in the absence of special circumstances the courts should follow 'clear and constant' jurisprudence of the European courts. It is important to stress, however, that while Strasbourg case law is persuasive and must be taken into account by the domestic courts, the task of the domestic court is not to search in the European case law for similar fact scenarios and seek to analogize from fact-specific cases.[64] Rather, the domestic courts should aim to identify guiding principles from the Strasbourg cases and apply these to the facts of the case. This is of particular relevance in the context of cases concerning religion where superficially the facts may be similar but the contexts from which the cases arise are very different.

2.31

Section 3 HRA 1998

A further guiding principle of construction is set out in s 3 HRA 1998, which requires all legislation—primary and subordinate, past and future—to be read and given effect, so far as possible, in a way which is compatible with ECHR rights. This reading requirement does not depend upon statutory ambiguity as the House of Lords previously held in *R v Secretary of State for the Home Department, ex p Brind*.[65] It effectively establishes a new canon of interpretation as referred to in the decision of the House of Lords in *Ghaidan v Godin-Mendoza*,[66] which stated that s 3 allowed a reading in of words into an otherwise unambiguous legislative provision to grant equal protection for homosexual partnerships

2.32

---

[63] [2004] UKHL 26 [20] citing *Alconbury Developments Ltd v Secretary of State for the Environment, Transport and the Regions* [2001] UKHL 23 [26].

[64] See Court of Appeal in *Aston Cantlow and Wilmcote with Billesley Parochial Church Council v Wallbank* [2001] EWCA Civ 713 [44] (per Sir Andrew Morritt V-C): 'Our job is not to cast around in the European Human Rights Reports like blackletter lawyers seeking clues. In the light of s 2(1) of the Human Rights Act 1998 it is to draw out the broad principles which animate the Convention.' This comment was undisturbed by the decision of the House of Lords [2003] UKHL 37.

[65] [1991] 1 AC 696.

[66] [2004] UKHL 30.

as that accorded to heterosexuals.[67] If incompatibility of legislation cannot be remedied by construction, the only remedy is a declaration of incompatibility.[68]

Section 6 HRA 1998

2.33 Under s 6 HRA 1998 it is unlawful for a public authority to act in a way which is incompatible with an ECHR right. It is generally understood that there is a distinction between on the one hand a 'core' or 'standard' public authority, and on the other a 'hybrid' body which will come within the extended definition of public authority in s 6(3)(b) because some of the functions which it exercises are of a public nature. A primary consideration in any case, therefore, will be whether a particular body has public functions such that it is considered a public authority within the meaning of s 6.[69] This has implications too on whether a body may also be a victim for the purposes of protection from violation of ECHR rights. The position as regards the types of body that are likely to be relevant to particular areas of law, for example educational institutions or employers, are considered in the relevant chapters. The position of religious organizations is considered below.

2.34 In *Aston Cantlow and Wilmcote with Billesley Parochial Church Council v Wallbank*[70] the House of Lords considered whether a parochial church council was a public authority under s 6 and concluded that it was neither a standard nor a hybrid public body. As regards the meaning of a core public authority, Lord Nicholls considered that it was 'essentially a reference to a body whose nature is governmental in a broad sense of that expression'.[71] He gave as obvious examples: government departments, local authorities, the police and the armed forces, stating that behind the instinctive classification of these organizations as bodies whose nature is governmental were 'factors such as the possession of special powers, democratic accountability, public funding in whole or in part, an obligation to act only in the public interest, and a statutory constitution'. As regards the meaning of s 6(3)(b), Lord Nicholls focused on the 'function' based nature of the test rather than examining the character of the institution or its relationship with a public authority. He noted that in the interests of efficiency and economy, and for other reasons, functions of a governmental nature

---

[67] At [30] (per Lord Nicholls). Reference was made to *Marleasing SA v La Comercial Internacional de Alimentación SA* [1990] ECR I-4135, 4159 where it was held that the obligation under the EEC Treaty on national courts was, as far as possible, to interpret national legislation in the light of the wording and purpose of directives.

[68] HRA 1998, s 4(2).

[69] See JCHR, Seventh Report of 2003–04, *The Meaning of Public Authority under the Human Rights Act* (HL 39, HC 382) paras 110–126.

[70] [2003] UKHL 37.

[71] Ibid [7].

are frequently discharged by non-governmental bodies, sometimes as a result of privatization.[72]

The ECtHR considered the position and characterization of religious organiza-   **2.35**
tions in the case of *Holy Monasteries v Greece*.[73] The Greek government argued that the applicant monasteries were public authorities as they were hierarchically integrated into the organic structure of the Greek Orthodox Church. In addition it argued that legal personality was attributed to the church and its constituent parts in public law and that the church and its institutions, which played a direct and active part in public administration, took administrative decisions whose lawfulness was subject to judicial review by the Supreme Administrative Court like those of any other public authority. Rejecting this argument, the ECtHR said:

> Like the Commission in its admissibility decision, the Court notes at the outset that the applicant monasteries do not exercise governmental powers. Section 39(1) of the Charter of the Greek Church describes the monasteries as ascetic religious institutions. Their objectives—essentially ecclesiastical and spiritual ones, but also cultural and social ones in some cases—are not such as to enable them to be classed with governmental organizations established for public administration purposes.[74]

Although Strasbourg case law is not directly relevant to the construction of   **2.36**
s 6 HRA 1998, the Strasbourg jurisprudence was referred to by the House of Lords in *Aston Cantlow*. In holding that a parochial church council was not a core public authority and was not carrying out public functions when repairing the chancel of the church, Lord Nicholls made the following observations about the position of the Church of England:

> Historically the Church of England has discharged an important and influential role in the life of this country. As the established church it still has special links with central government. But the Church of England remains essentially a religious organization. This is so even though some of the emanations of the church discharge functions which may qualify as governmental. Church schools and the conduct of marriage services are two instances. The legislative powers of the General Synod of the Church of England are another. This should not be regarded as infecting the Church of England as a whole, or its emanations in general, with the character of a governmental organization . . . . The contrary conclusion, that the church authorities in general and parochial church councils in particular are 'core' public authorities, would mean these bodies are not capable of being victims within the meaning of the Human Rights Act.[75]

---

[72] Ibid [10]–[12]. See also *R (A) v Partnerships in Care Ltd* [2002] EWHC 529 (Admin). Compare with the approach in *R (Heather) v Leonard Cheshire Foundation* [2002] EWCA Civ 366; *Donoghue v Poplar Housing and Regeneration Community Association Ltd* [2001] EWCA Civ 595; *Hampshire CC v Beer (t/a Hammer Trout Farm)* [2003] EWCA Civ 1056; and *Johnson v Havering London Borough Council* [2006] EWHC 1714 (Admin).

[73] (1995) 20 EHRR 1.

[74] Ibid [49]. See also *Hautaniemi v Sweden* (1996) 22 EHRR CD 156 (Church of Sweden and its member parishes were regarded as corporations of public law in the domestic legal order but it was held nevertheless that the applicant parish was a victim for ECHR purposes, on the ground that the church and its member parishes could not be considered to have been exercising governmental powers).

[75] At [13]–[15]; see also [61] (per Lord Hope); [86] (per Lord Hobhouse).

2.37   The House of Lords in *Aston Cantlow* left open the possibility that certain functions carried out by ministers or religious organizations such as burials and marriages might be considered functions of a public nature.[76] In addition, all courts and tribunals are public authorities by virtue of s 6(3)(a) HRA 1998. This means that they have a positive obligation to give effect to the HRA 1998 and to interpret legislation so as to give effect to ECHR rights where possible.

Section 13 HRA 1998

2.38   During the passage of the Human Rights Bill through Parliament there were extensive debates about how the other ECHR rights would affect the rights of religious individuals and organizations. Would religious bodies, for example, be prevented from discriminating against potential applicants for leadership positions or other posts on the grounds of sex or religion? Partly as a result of such concerns, s 13 HRA 1998 was enacted which provides as follows:

> If a court's determination of any question arising under this Act might affect the exercise by a religious organization (itself or its members collectively) of the Convention right to freedom of thought, conscience and religion, it must have particular regard to the importance of that right.

2.39   It appears that it was intended to minimize the possibility of the state intervening in the internal organization of religious groups and in particular in that of the Church of England. But there has been much judicial and academic doubt as to whether this section has any practical effect and adds anything to the way in which a court would approach a question involving the balance of rights and the existing restrictions in the law relating to discrimination.[77]

ECHR rights

2.40   The most important provision in the ECHR dealing with freedom of religion is Article 9. Additionally, in the context of the right to education, Article 2 Protocol 1 provides for respect for the philosophical and religious convictions of parents. Article 14 is important in the context of equality and religious freedom.

2.41   Other articles may also be engaged in considering protection of freedom of religion such as Article 8 (respect for private and family life), Article 10 (freedom

---

[76] At [170] (per Lord Rodger).

[77] See eg the Court of Appeal in *R (Williamson) v Secretary of State for Education and Employment* [2002] EWCA Civ 1820 [49] (per Buxton LJ), [181] (per Rix LJ) whose comments were undisturbed by the House of Lords [2005] UKHL 15; *R (Amicus) v Secretary of State for Trade and Industry* [2004] EWHC 860 (Admin) [41] (it was common ground in the case that s 13 did not provide greater weight for rights than a religious organization would otherwise enjoy under the ECHR); *Douglas v Hello!* [2001] 2 All ER 289 [135]; see also A Lester & D Pannick, *Human Rights Law and Practice* (Butterworths, 2004) 67 and P Cumper, 'The Protection of Religious Rights under Section 13 of the Human Rights Act 1998' [2000] PL 254.

of expression), Article 11 (freedom of association and peaceful assembly) and Article 1 Protocol 1 (right to peaceful enjoyment of possessions).[78] For example a religious group that wishes to organize a religious procession may also rely on Article 11, while a religious leader who wishes to make a religious speech may refer to Article 10 as well as to Article 9. An extreme case of religious persecution could give rise to claims on the basis of the prohibition on torture, inhuman and degrading punishment as protected by Article 3. The focus in this chapter is on Articles 9 and 14 ECHR.[79] But it should be noted that the Commission and ECtHR have often preferred to deal with a particular case which may involve an aspect of religion and thereby potentially engage Article 9, under one of the other ECHR articles where they are also engaged and appear to be closer to the nature of another article.[80]

Equality Act 2006

The EA 2006 contains important provisions in Part 2 relating to discrimination on the grounds of religion or belief.[81] It provides far wider scope for protection against discrimination in this area than was previously covered by the existing provisions. It contains a broad definition of what is meant by 'religion or belief' for the purposes of the EA 2006 and in this regard should be viewed as falling in line with the wide definition applied to Article 9.[82] As with the protection against discrimination contained in the RRA 1976 and the EC Directives, the EA 2006 protects against both direct discrimination and indirect discrimination, and victimization. The definitions of each of these forms of discrimination are similar to those contained in the EC Directives.[83]   **2.42**

The EA 2006 prohibits discrimination in a number of areas including the provision of goods, facilities and services (s 46), the disposal and management of premises (s 47), the terms and conditions on which pupils are admitted to or access benefits, facilities, and services, and excluded from certain educational establishments (s 49), the provision of schools and transport by local education authorities (s 51), and the exercise of the functions of all public authorities (s 52). In addition the   **2.43**

---

[78] See eg *Otto-Preminger-Institut v Austria* (1995) 19 EHRR 34; *Wingrove v United Kingdom* (1997) 24 EHRR 1.

[79] See generally on ECHR rights R Clayton & H Tomlinson (eds), *The Law of Human Rights* (OUP, 2007); J Simor (ed), *Human Rights Practice* (Sweet & Maxwell, 2000–); Lester & Pannick (n 77 above); J Wadham, H Mountfield, A Edmunson & C Gallagher, *Blackstone's Guide to the Human Rights Act 1998* (OUP, 2007).

[80] See eg *Riera Blume v Spain* (2000) 30 EHRR 632 in which the ECtHR held that permitting parents to imprison their children in order to 'deprogramme' them from their cult was a breach of Art 5(1) and decided that as a result they did not need to decide whether Art 9 was also breached. See also 2.62 below.

[81] The relevant provisions in Part 2 are expected to come into force in 2007.

[82] EA 2006.

[83] Ibid s 45.

Commission for Equality and Human Rights, which is established under the provisions of the EA 2006, will have the power to bring proceedings relating to practices which would be likely to result in unlawful discrimination on the grounds of religion or belief (s 53), discriminatory advertisements (s 54), and relating to instructing or causing discrimination (s 55).

2.44 There are a number of general exceptions that apply. In particular the provisions of the EA 2006 will not make it unlawful to do anything that is necessary for the purpose of complying with an Act of Parliament, legislation made or to be made by a Minister of the Crown, or by Order in Council, or by virtue of a Measure of the General Synod of the Church of England (s 56). There are also specific exemptions for religious organizations (s 57), religious charities (s 58), faith schools (s 59), for the membership requirements for charities in general (s 60), for education, training and welfare (s 61), for care within the family (s 62), and for the purpose of safeguarding national security (s 63). The provisions relating to educational establishments and to faith schools are considered further in Chapter 4.

EC Directives

2.45 The European Community in 2000 adopted two new directives as part of a package of anti-discrimination measures.[84] The Race Equality Directive addresses discrimination based on racial or ethnic origins, whilst the Framework Employment Directive covers discrimination on the grounds of religion or belief, disability, age, sex and sexual orientation.[85] The Race Equality Directive, implemented in English law by the Race Relations Act (Amendment) Regulations 2003, is referred to above in the section relating to the RRA 1976.[86]

2.46 The Framework Employment Directive, implemented in the United Kingdom by the Employment Equality (Religion or Belief) Regulations 2003, prohibits both direct and indirect discrimination. It is, however, much narrower than the Race Equality Directive in that it applies only in the fields of employment, occupation, vocational guidance and vocational training. In this regard it only has a narrow impact in the field of education confined to vocational courses in universities and other institutions such as law, medicine and engineering and courses aimed directly at the workplace. The Employment Equality (Religion or Belief) Regulations 2003 are considered further in Chapter 5.[87]

---

[84] Provided for by Treaty of Amsterdam (1997) Art 13.

[85] EU Member States were required to adopt provisions necessary to comply with the Race Equality Directive of 29 June 2000 by 19 July 2003 and with the Framework Employment Directive of 27 November 2000 by 2 December 2003.

[86] See 2.18–2.30 above.

[87] See generally N De Marco, *Blackstone's Guide to The Employment Equality Regulations 2003* (OUP, 2004).

It should also be noted that the ECJ has held in relation to an employment issue   **2.47**
within the civil service that the right to non-discrimination on religious grounds
is a fundamental right protected by Community law.[88]

Other European instruments

Although the following instruments are not directly enforceable through the   **2.48**
English courts, they are relevant to and worth mentioning in connection with freedom of religion and minority rights. The first is the 1995 Framework Convention
for the Protection of National Minorities.[89] Proposals for an additional Protocol to
the ECHR protecting national minorities were rejected in favour of the Framework
Convention. As its main enforcement mechanism is five-yearly reporting, it is not
likely to have any direct impact in determining controversies that arise in the
domestic courts of those states that have ratified it. However, it could be used as
an aid to interpretation where there are gaps in the ECHR.[90] The ECtHR has
referred to the emerging international consensus among Council members recognizing the special needs of minorities and the obligation to protect their security,
identity and lifestyle by reference to the Framework Convention.[91]

In addition, the EU Charter of Fundamental Rights guarantees freedom of religion,   **2.49**
religious diversity and protects religious equality.[92] It is not yet binding law, and
is dependent upon ratification of the European Constitution. It may be seen
by the ECJ as a source of inspiration that EU members must respect although the
UK government has rejected this approach.[93] The current position on ratification
of the Constitution is very unclear in the light of the negative results of state
referendums.[94]

---

[88] Case 130/75 *Prais v EC Council* (1976) ECR 1589.
[89] (1995) ETS 157. Article 7 obliges states to 'ensure respect for the right of every person belonging
to a national minority to . . . freedom of thought, conscience and religion'. Article 8 provides that: 'The
parties undertake to recognize that every person belonging to a national minority has the right to manifest his or her religion or belief and to establish religious institutions, organizations and associations.'
[90] See generally on this subject D Fottrell & B Bowring, *Minority and Group Rights in the New
Millennium* (Martinus Nijhoff, 1999).
[91] *Chapman v United Kingdom* (2001) 33 EHRR 18 [93]–[94].
[92] Proclaimed on 7 December 2000; [2000] OJ C364/01. Article 10 states: '1. Everyone has the
right to freedom of thought, conscience and religion. This right includes freedom to change religion
or belief, and freedom, either alone or in community with others, and in public or in private, to
manifest religion or belief, in worship, teaching, practice and observance. 2. The right to conscientious objection is recognized in accordance with the national laws governing the exercise of this
right.' Article 21 prohibits discrimination on any ground including religion or belief. Article 22
states: 'The Union shall respect cultural, religious and linguistic diversity.'
[93] This is the view of the European Commission COM (2000) 644 but the UK government has stated
'it should have no legal status, and we do not intend it to': *Hansard*, HC col 354 (11 December 2000).
[94] See official website of the EC at <http://www.europa.eu.int> for details of the current status of
the Charter.

Freedom of Religion: Article 9 ECHR

General comments

2.50 Article 9 ECHR provides:

1. Everyone has the right to freedom of thought, conscience and religion; this right includes freedom to change his religion or belief, and freedom, either alone or in community with others and in public or private, to manifest his religion or belief, in worship, teaching, practice and observance.
2. Freedom to manifest one's religion or beliefs shall be subject only to such limitations as are prescribed by law and are necessary in a democratic society in the interests of public safety, for the protection of public order, health or morals, or for the protection of the rights and freedoms of others.

2.51 There is a general consensus that the right is fundamentally important although a lack of agreement as to precisely what it entails. The importance of the right was referred to by the ECtHR in a much cited passage in *Kokkinakis v Greece*[95] as follows:

> As enshrined in Article 9, freedom of thought, conscience and religion is one of the foundations of a 'democratic society' within the meaning of the Convention. It is, in its religious dimension, one of the most vital elements which go to make up the identity of believers and their conception of life, but it is also a precious asset to atheists, agnostics, sceptics and the unconcerned. The pluralism indissociable from a democratic society, which has been dearly won over the centuries, depends on it.

2.52 The right can be seen as having two aspects. There is the right to hold a particular belief, which is absolute, and the right to manifest beliefs, which is subject to limitations. These aspects are sometimes referred to as the *forum internum* and the *forum externum*. The European courts have tended to distinguish between the two aspects and have generally assumed that the *forum internum* is incapable of being interfered with in democratic societies. In summarizing the protection under Article 9, the Commission in one case has commented:

> Article 9 primarily protects the sphere of personal beliefs and religious creeds, i.e. the area which is sometimes called the forum internum. In addition, it protects acts which are intimately linked to these attitudes, such as acts of worship or devotion which are aspects of the practice of a religion or belief in a generally recognized form.[96]

2.53 Any legal provision guaranteeing a qualified right to freedom of religion will be subject to controversial issues of authority, perspective and subjectivity, which makes precise definition of the right difficult. The wording of Article 9 itself

---

[95] (1994) 17 EHRR 397 [31].
[96] See *Van den Dungen v Netherlands*, Application 22838/93 (1995) 80-A DR 147, 150.

gives little guidance as to what the right entails and as a result there is potential for considerable discretion in formulating the relevant guiding principles of interpretation. The *travaux préparatoires* do not provide much enlightenment as regards the background to the drafting of Article 9. They reveal that freedom of religion was an important priority for those involved in the drafting but there appears to have been little discussion as to the meaning and scope of that right. There was more interest in the drafting of the limitation clause. Proposals by some countries relating to a saving provision for existing laws or to more specific limitations were rejected ultimately in favour of a permissive limitation clause.[97]

Approach to Article 9

The Commission and ECtHR have not always approached Article 9 cases in a systematic fashion by reference to the various aspects of the right. It is however often helpful when arguing a case to separate the constituent elements of the right and address them individually. As with other qualified rights set out in the ECHR, it is suggested that the court should approach a claim under Article 9 in five stages as follows: **2.54**

  (i) Has the claimant established a right that qualifies for protection under Article 9(1)?
 (ii) Has that right been interfered with?
(iii) Was the interference prescribed by law?
 (iv) Did the interference have one of the legitimate aims set out in Article 9(2)?
  (v) Was the interference proportionate to that legitimate aim?[98]

These questions are considered in turn below: (i) and (ii) are considered separately while (iii) to (v) are linked to the limitations on the freedom and are dealt with together. In each case, the issues particular to each limb of Article 9 are referred to and relevant European and domestic case law is then considered. At the outset it should be noted that the House of Lords in *R (Begum) v Headteacher and Governors of Denbigh High School*,[99] held that Article 9 was concerned with substance and not procedure and roundly rejected the approach taken by the Court of Appeal below. The focus at Strasbourg was on whether an ECHR right had been violated and not whether a decision or action was the product of a defective decision making process. The court was therefore **2.55**

---

[97] See C Evans, *Freedom of Religion under the European Convention on Human Rights* (OUP, 2001) Ch 2.

[98] See *R (Razgar) v Secretary of State for the Home Department* [2004] UKHL 27 [17] (per Lord Bingham); *R (Begum) v Headteacher and Governors of Denbigh High School* [2006] UKHL 15 [66] (per Lord Hoffmann).

[99] [2006] UKHL 15 [29] (per Lord Bingham), [68] (per Lord Hoffmann).

required to come to a conclusion substantively as to whether Article 9 had been violated or not.[100]

Scope of Article 9(1)

Individuals and groups as claimants

2.56 A preliminary point now resolved by the courts is whether religious organizations or groups as well as individuals can rely on Article 9. This arose from the fact that the ECHR rights were primarily intended to protect natural persons. A distinction has been drawn between the freedom of thought and conscience, which may only be exercised by an individual and the freedom of religion, which may be exercised by religious bodies.[101] It is accepted that in addition to individual claimants, a religious organization may bring a claim in its own name on behalf of its adherents.[102]

Definition of religion or belief

2.57 The controversial question of what constitutes a religion, who has authority to define it, and whether a particular person falls within the religion is to a considerable degree circumvented by the terms of Article 9(1) and the fact that protection is afforded to non-religious as well as religious beliefs.[103] On the whole the Commission and ECtHR have given a wide interpretation to the meaning of religion or belief in Article 9(1). It has been held to cover non-religious beliefs such as pacifism,[104] veganism[105] and atheism[106] as well as the more traditional religions and beliefs.[107] In some cases the ECtHR and Commission have simply assumed that the particular beliefs in question are covered, such as druidism,[108] the Divine

---

[100] See also T Poole, 'Of headscarves and heresies: The Denbigh High School case and public authority decision making under the Human Rights Act' [2005] PL 685; T Linden & T Hetherington, 'Schools and Human Rights' [2005] Educational Law Journal 229.

[101] See *X v Switzerland*, Application 7865/77 (1981) 16 DR 85 (but the right under Art 9 cannot be held by a profit-making organization); *Verein 'Kontakt-Information-Therapie' v Austria*, Application 11921/86 (1988) 57 DR 81; *X and Church of Scientology v Sweden*, Application 7805/77 (1979) 16 DR 68; *Chappell v United Kingdom* (1990) 12 EHRR 1.

[102] See *Supreme Holy Council of the Muslim Community v Bulgaria*, Application 39023/97 (16 December 2004).

[103] Note UNHRC General Comment No 22(48) on Art 18: 'Art 18 protects theistic, non-theistic and atheistic beliefs, as well as the right to profess any religion or belief. The terms belief and religion are to be broadly construed. Article 18 is not limited in its application to traditional religions or to religions and beliefs with institutional characteristics or practices analogous to those of traditional religions.' UN Doc CCPR/C/21/Rev.1/Add.4 para 2 (1993).

[104] *Arrowsmith v United Kingdom* (1978) 3 EHRR 218.

[105] *X v United Kingdom*, Application 18187/91 (10 February 1993).

[106] *Angeleni v Sweden*, Application 10491/83 (1983) 35 DR 199.

[107] See eg *Knudsen v Norway*, Application 11045/84 (1985) 42 DR 247 (Christian denomination); *Ahmed v United Kingdom*, Application 8160/78 (1981) 22 DR 27 (Islam); *ISKCON v United Kingdom*, Application 20490/92 (1994) 76-A DR 90 (Hinduism).

[108] *Chappell v United Kingdom*, (1988) 10 EHRR CD 510.

Light Zentrum,[109] and the Church of Scientology,[110] without making an express finding on the point. At the domestic level, the House of Lords in *R (Williamson) v Secretary of State for Education and Employment*[111] has stressed the importance of giving the benefit of the doubt to the claimant in this area to avoid the problem of subjective interpretation.[112]

There are, however, two potentially difficult areas in deciding what beliefs are **2.58** covered. The first relates to beliefs that might be considered as inherently unreasonable or highly individualistic and as to what evidence is required to prove the existence of such beliefs. In *Campbell and Cosans v United Kingdom*,[113] a case concerning corporal punishment in a school and Article 2 Protocol 1, it was stated that a belief should attain a certain level of cogency, seriousness, cohesion and importance for the individual in order to acquire protection. While some evidence of a genuinely held belief is necessary, the references to cogency and cohesion may give rise to difficulty for applicants. It is unclear why these are important characteristics and from whose perspective they should be judged.

In *R (Williamson) v Secretary of State for Education and Employment*, Lord Bingham **2.59** stated:

> The belief must be consistent with basic standards of human dignity or integrity. Manifestation of a religious belief, for instance, which involved subjecting others to torture or inhuman punishment would not qualify for protection. The belief must relate to matters more than merely trivial. It must possess an adequate degree of seriousness and importance. As has been said, it must be a belief on a fundamental problem. With religious belief this requisite is readily satisfied. The belief must also be coherent in the sense of being intelligible and capable of being understood. But, again, too much should not be demanded in this regard. Typically, religion involves belief in the supernatural. It is not always susceptible to lucid exposition or, still less, rational justification. The language used is often the language of allegory, symbol

---

[109] *Omkarananda and Divine Light Zentrum v Switzerland*, Application 8118/77 (1981) 25 DR 105.

[110] *X and Church of Scientology v Sweden*, Application 7805/77 (1979) 16 DR 68. But see 6.74 below for restrictions relating to Scientologists and the Unification Church (Moonies) under immigration law and refusal by Charity Commission to register the Church of Scientology as a charity.

[111] [2005] UKHL 15 [22]–[23] (per Lord Nicholls); [57]–[61] (per Lord Walker); [75]–[77] (per Lady Hale).

[112] See also *R (Amicus) v Secretary of State for Trade and Industry* [2004] EWHC 860 (Admin) [36]–[38]. Note that earlier English cases in which definitions of religion were attempted are not good authority for the scope of Art 9(1): eg *R v Registrar General, ex p Segerdal* [1970] 3 All ER 886; *Re South Place Ethical Society, Barralet v Attorney-General* [1980] 1 WLR 1565. Courts in many countries have taken a similar approach, eg the US Supreme Court in *United States v Seeger* 380 US 163 (1965); Supreme Court of Canada in *Syndicat Northcrest v Amselem* (2004) 241 DLR (4th) 1; High Court of Australia in *Church of the New Faith v Commissioner of Pay-Roll Tax (Victoria)* (1983) 154 CLR 120. Note by contrast the approach of the majority of the Supreme Court of India in *Commissioner of Police v Acharya Jagadishwarananda Avadhuta* [2005] 3 LRC 20.

[113] (1982) 4 EHRR 293. Note that the ECtHR held that a conviction under Art 2 Protocol 1 was not synonymous to opinion or ideas in Art 10 but rather akin to beliefs in Art 9.

and metaphor. Depending on the subject matter, individuals cannot always be expected to express themselves with cogency or precision. Nor are an individual's beliefs fixed and static. The beliefs of every individual are prone to change over his lifetime. Overall, these threshold requirements should not be set at a level which would deprive minority beliefs of the protection they are intended to have under the Convention.[114]

2.60 In some cases there has been a suggestion that the claimant has failed to meet the standard of proof required to establish their belief. However, it is not always clear in these cases what evidence is required to substantiate a belief.[115] The case law inevitably varies—some cases refer to reports and experts while others simply state that there is no conflict between state action and the belief of an individual.[116] Ultimately, the ECtHR is likely to defer to the fact-finding of the domestic courts in this regard.[117] The better approach as adopted by the House of Lords in *Williamson* is that if there is some evidence that the claimant genuinely holds a belief, however unreasonable, inconsistent or illogical (save where it infringes basic human dignity), then he should be given the benefit of the doubt.[118]

2.61 As Munby LJ said in *Sulaiman v Juffali*:[119]

> Although historically this country is part of the Christian west, and although it has an established church which is Christian, I sit as a secular judge serving a multi-cultural community of many faiths in which all of us can now take pride, sworn to do justice 'to all manner of people'. Religion—whatever the particular believer's faith—is no doubt something to be encouraged but it is not the business of government or of the secular courts. So the starting point of the law is an essentially agnostic view of religious beliefs and a tolerant indulgence to religious and cultural diversity. A secular judge must be wary of straying across the well-recognized divide between church and state. It is not for a judge to weigh one religion against another. All are entitled to equal respect, whether in times of peace or, as at present, amidst the clash of arms.

---

[114] [2005] UKHL 15 [23].

[115] *X v Germany*, Application 445/70 (1970) 37 Coll 119 (a light worshipper did not provide sufficient evidence of his beliefs or how they were infringed); *X v United Kingdom*, Application 7291/75 (1977) 11 DR 55 (claimant did not produce any facts to establish the existence of the Wicca religion).

[116] Eg in *Kokkinakis v Greece* (1994) 17 EHRR 397 the ECtHR referred to a report by the World Council of Churches in determining that proselytism was part of the 'essential mission' of all Christians, and said that improper proselytism was a 'corruption' of that mission, but in *X v United Kingdom*, Application 8231/78 (1982) 28 DR 5 the application was denied because the applicant did not substantiate his claim that Sikh leaders refuse to wear prison clothes for religious reasons, although no indication was given as to what evidence would have been acceptable.

[117] See *Kosteski v Macedonia*, Application 55170/00 (13 April 2006).

[118] This is also the position taken by the US Supreme Court in *Thomas v Review Board of the Indiana Employment Security Division* 450 US 707, 714 (1981) where the court expressly recognized that religious beliefs need not be 'acceptable, logical, consistent or comprehensible' to qualify for protection under the First Amendment.

[119] [2002] 1 FLR 479 [47]. See also *Premji Devraj Varsani v Jinabar Ranji Jesani* (Ch D, 31 July 2001) [11].

The second difficult area relates to the potential overlap between beliefs that are **2.62** protected under Article 9 and opinions that are protected under Article 10. The Commission and ECtHR have preferred not to set out any guidelines to delineate the two but have generally dealt with views that relate more to political opinion under Article 10 and those relating to world or transcendental views under Article 9. However, there are no strict guidelines.[120] In *Vereiniging Rechtswinkel Utrecht v Netherlands*,[121] it was stated that Article 9 does not cover purely idealistic or political goals, while in *Hazar v Turkey*,[122] a complaint by a member of the Communist party of adverse treatment was admissible under Article 9. Overall, it is preferable to adopt a flexible approach and either assess within the ambit of the right that more naturally fits or not to draw clear lines between the two but to deal with the case on the basis of whether there has been a justified interference in either case.[123]

Protection and freedom from religion

The terms of Article 9(1) suggest that it primarily relates to the positive right of **2.63** the individual to exercise a particular belief. However, it has also been referred to in connection with the protection of individuals from religion in cases of coerced religious education and worship, indoctrination or 'improper' proselytization.[124] This protection might be seen as an aspect of the *forum internum* but is generally not dealt with in this manner.[125] Although the cases do not expressly refer to freedom from religion, it is implicit in the reasoning that this is an aspect of Article 9 protection. As regards proselytization, there are a number of occasions on which the European courts have considered whether or not the expression of religious views amounts to improper proselytization or legitimate freedom of expression engaging Article 10.[126] The fear of coercion and indoctrination was bound up in part with the idea of protecting against totalitarianism in Europe exemplified by the then recent history of Nazi Germany and communist Eastern Europe. This is

---

[120] But note *Arrowsmith v United Kingdom* (1978) 3 EHRR 218.

[121] (1986) 46 DR 200.

[122] Application 16311/90 (1990) 72 DR 200.

[123] See also *Emek Partisi and Senol v Turkey*, Application 39434/98 (31 May 2005) (violation of Art 11 and therefore no need to examine same faith in the light of Arts 9, 10 and 14).

[124] See eg *Kokkinakis v Greece* (1994) 17 EHRR 397.

[125] See eg *Buscarini v San Marino* (1999) 6 BHRC 638 in which members of the Grand Council were required to take an oath on the Bible. The ECtHR considered this was contrary to Art 9 and that taking the oath was not necessary in a democratic society. It did not consider whether it was a case involving an interference with the *forum internum*. Similarly in *Valsamis v Greece* (1997) 24 EHRR 294, the ECtHR did not consider whether forcing children to attend a public parade could interfere with their private beliefs. Note that in *Riera Blume v Spain* (1999) 30 EHRR 632 the ECtHR was willing to find that the detention of adult children against their will in order to 'de-programme' them from their religious beliefs was a breach of the right not to be falsely imprisoned. Although Art 9 was raised the ECtHR did not expressly deal with it, finding that Art 5(1) had been violated.

[126] See further Chapter 3.

linked to the spread of ideas through a school education system and related to the protection under Article 2 Protocol 1.[127]

Manifestation of religion or belief

2.64 The right to manifest belief through 'worship, teaching, practice and observance' protects rituals, rites, acts of worship, and attempting to convert others. The Commission and ECtHR have tended to treat the categories as exclusive.[128] As the list itself is fairly broad, in principle this should not give rise to considerable difficulties so long as courts are prepared to give a wide meaning to each of the categories. However, the Strasbourg case law as to what amounts to a manifestation of a belief has been far from consistent.

2.65 The necessary link between an internal belief and the external manifestation of that belief was considered by the Commission in *Arrowsmith v United Kingdom*.[129] In that case a pacifist distributed a leaflet attempting to discourage soldiers from serving in Northern Ireland. The Commission held that Article 9(1) did not cover each act that was motivated or influenced by a religion or belief, but it did not make clear which acts were covered. It held that the leaflet was not provided to further pacifist views and did not constitute a manifestation of belief. By excluding actions that are merely motivated or influenced by belief, the Commission suggested that a very direct link is needed between the belief and the action if the action is to be considered a 'practice' under Article 9. This approach was followed by the ECtHR in *Valsamis v Greece*,[130] and has been interpreted as a type of 'necessity' test. Under this approach behaviour that is merely encouraged or permitted by a religion but not required by it is not protected by Article 9(1).[131]

2.66 The necessity test has not always been used. In *Knudsen v Norway*,[132] the Commission used a different test by asking whether the actions of the applicant 'give expression' to his or her religion or belief. And in *Hasan and Chaush v Bulgaria*,[133] the ECtHR stated that Article 9 protects acts that are 'intimately linked' to personal convictions and beliefs. In other cases the necessary link has simply been assumed once the claimant's religious beliefs are established without the need for the claimant to prove that the manifestation is a necessary aspect of their belief. In *Sahin v*

---

[127] See further Chapter 4.

[128] See M Evans (n 2 above) 298 and C Evans (n 97 above) 106.

[129] (1978) 3 EHRR 218.

[130] (1997) 24 EHRR 294; see also *Khan v United Kingdom* (1986) 48 DR 253.

[131] See also contrasting results in *Van Schijndel, Van der Heyden & Lennman v Netherlands*, Application 30936/96 (20 May 1998); *Van den Dungen v Netherlands*, Application 22838/93 (1995) 80-A DR 147. In *Pretty v United Kingdom* (2002) 35 EHRR 1, the ECtHR held at [82] that Mrs Pretty's claim to a right to assisted suicide did not involve a form of manifestation of religion or belief.

[132] Application 11045/84 (1985) 42 DR 247.

[133] (2002) 34 EHRR 55.

Turkey,[134] a case involving Muslim women wearing hijabs in educational institutions, no point was taken about whether the wearing of the hijab was required by their faith or not.

In *R (Williamson) v Secretary of State for Education and Employment*[135] it was stated **2.67** that a perceived obligation is not a prerequisite to manifestation of a belief in practice although the point was not in issue. The court thereby recognized that the necessity test is too rigid an approach. While there must be some close link between the belief and the manifestation which will certainly be satisfied in cases of a perceived obligation, there will be other acts that are not necessary to the belief but which are intimately linked with it that should also be protected. This will avoid the difficulty of subjective interpretation as to what amounts to a protected manifestation.[136] For example, there are many different views on whether it is necessary for religious adherents to wear particular head coverings such as the Muslim hijab, Sikh turban or Jewish yarmulke. For some it may be considered necessary, for others permissible but not necessary and for others not necessary at all, depending upon their perspective. It will also ensure that respect is maintained for manifestations that are directly inspired by belief even if they are unnecessary to that belief.[137]

It was also stated by Lord Bingham in *Williamson* that: **2.68**

> But when questions of 'manifestation' arise, as they usually do in this type of case, a belief must satisfy some modest, objective minimum requirements. These threshold requirements are implicit in article 9 of the European Convention and comparable guarantees in other human rights instruments. The belief must be consistent with basic standards of human dignity or integrity. Manifestation of a religious belief, for instance, which involved subjecting others to torture or inhuman punishment would not qualify for protection.[138]

In certain commercial and professional situations, Article 9(1) has been held by **2.69** the ECtHR not to constitute a manifestation at all. For example, advertising using

---

[134] (2005) 41 EHRR 8. But contrast the approach with that of the Commission in *Karaduman v Turkey*, Application 16278/90 (1993) 74 DR 93.

[135] [2005] UKHL 15 [33] (per Lord Bingham) citing *Syndicat Northcrest v Amselem* 241 DLR (4th) 1 [46]–[50].

[136] In this regard, the joint dissent of judges Thor Vilhjalmsson and Jambrek in *Valsamis v Greece* (1997) 24 EHRR 294 to the effect that the ECtHR should accept applicants' views of what their religious beliefs entail unless obviously unfounded and unreasonable would be a far more satisfactory approach. See also Judge Vedross in an Art 2 Protocol 1 claim in *Kjeldsen, Busk Madsen and Pedersen v Denmark* (1976) 1 EHRR 711 stating that the court had to respect the ideology of the applicants once that ideology had clearly been made out.

[137] Note the position of the US Supreme Court in *Thomas v Review Board of the Indiana Employment Security Division* (1981) 450 US 707 at 714 which recognized that 'Intrafaith differences . . . are not uncommon among followers of a particular creed, and the judicial process is singularly ill-equipped to resolve such differences in relation to the Religious Clauses . . .[T]he guarantee of free exercise is not limited to beliefs which are shared by all the members of a religious sect'.

[138] At [23].

religious content has been held not to be protected by Article 9. In a case involving an advertisement by the Church of Scientology for the E-meter, which was claimed to measure the electrical characteristics of the static field surrounding the body, the ECtHR held that this did not constitute a practice that manifested belief.[139] In another case pharmacists were convicted for refusing to distribute contraceptive pills. The case was declared inadmissible as the pharmacists in their professional/public capacity were not entitled to express their religious convictions in this manner.[140]

2.70 The difficulty with this approach is that it involves a decision as to the line between expression that is protected and expression that is not. Many religious organizations advertise and spread their beliefs in a variety of ways through the media. Given that Article 9 provides protection not only to individuals but also to religious organizations, it appears an arbitrary distinction to hold that religious expression through advertising is not covered by Article 9. Similarly the requirements of a profession or employment may obviously conflict with an individual's beliefs. A more logical and textually derived treatment would acknowledge that Article 9 is engaged and consider whether there is an inference and whether it is justified.[141]

Interference with Article 9(1)

Negative protection

2.71 It is uncontroversial that the state is under an obligation to refrain from taking actions that would amount to an unjustifiable interference. More recent European cases take a broader view of what amounts to an interference than some of the earlier cases. For example, in *Kalaç v Turkey*,[142] the compulsory retirement of a military officer with fundamentalist opinions on the basis of his conduct and attitude was not considered to be an interference with his rights under Article 9. In *Jewish Liturgical Association Ch'are Shalom Ve Tsedek v France*,[143] it was held that the right to religious practice and observance was not violated if such practice was made more difficult but not impossible by actions of the state. But in *Cyprus v Turkey*[144] the Grand Chamber found a violation where the Turkish government had imposed considerable restrictions on Greek Cypriots to travel to attend religious ceremonies and to access their monastery in Northern Cyprus. In *Metropolitan*

---

[139] *X and Church of Scientology v Sweden*, Application 7805/77 (1979) 16 DR 68. See also *X v Switzerland*, Application 7865/77 (1979) 16 DR 85 (right under Art 9 could not be enjoyed by a profit-making organization) and compare to the approach in *The Sunday Times v United Kingdom* (1980) 2 EHRR 245; *Autronic v Switzerland* (1990) 12 EHRR 48.

[140] *Pichon and Sajous v France* (2001) 12 EHRR CD 1017. See further 5.28 and 5.35 below.

[141] The case of employed professionals is considered further in Chapter 5.

[142] (1997) 27 EHRR 552.

[143] (2000) 9 BHRC 27.

[144] (2002) 35 EHRR 30 [243]–[246].

Church of Bessarabia v Moldova[145] it was held that a refusal to recognize a church violated Article 9 and that it was no answer for the state to assert that the same religious beliefs could be manifested in a different religious organization.[146]

In *Khan v Royal Air Force Summary Appeal Court*,[147] it was noted that there was a **2.72** shift in Strasbourg jurisprudence towards accepting that an interference had taken place that needed to be justified. At the domestic level, in two recent House of Lords decisions, the question of interference has been considered. In *R (Williamson) v Secretary of State for Education and Employment*,[148] the House of Lords stated that the test is whether there has been a material interference. It expressly doubted whether the ECtHR, by using the word 'impossible' in *Jewish Liturgical Association Cha'are Shalom Ve Tsedek v France*,[149] was intending to enunciate a less protective standard.

However, a far more restrictive approach was taken in *R (Begum) v Headteacher* **2.73** *and Governors of Denbigh High School*,[150] where the majority of the House of Lords found that there was no interference with Article 9 in a situation where a person voluntarily accepted a place at a school with knowledge of their uniform policy that did not permit the wearing of a jilbab (full length gown) and in a situation where they could have chosen to attend another school where the jilbab was permitted. In doing so they considered a number of cases from Strasbourg predominantly in the area of employment.[151] They acknowledged that the line of authority had been criticized by the Court of Appeal in *Copsey v WWB Devon Clays Ltd*[152] and that the 'impossibility' threshold had been questioned by the House of Lords in *Williamson*. Nevertheless, the majority stated that even if it were accepted that Strasbourg had erred on the side of strictness in rejecting complaints of interference, there remained a 'coherent and remarkably consistent' body of authority that supported their view.[153] Baroness Hale dissenting on this point held that there was an interference, noting that in reality parents imposed a choice of school on their children and that adolescents could not necessarily foresee all the consequences of a choice in any event.[154]

---

[145] (2002) 35 EHRR 13.
[146] See also *Salvation Army v Russia*, Application 72881/01 (5 October 2006) (removal of legal entity status of applicant by denial of reregistration was a breach of Art 11 read in the light of Art 9.
[147] [2004] HRLR 40 [95].
[148] [2005] UKHL 15 [39].
[149] (2000) 9 BHRC 29 [80].
[150] [2006] UKHL 15.
[151] At [23] (per Lord Bingham).
[152] [2005] EWCA Civ 932 [31]–[39], [44]–[66]
[153] At [24].
[154] At [92], Lord Nicholls also doubted the ease with which the applicant could move to another school and noted the disruption that this would cause to her education.

2.74 The decision in *Begum* is striking in that it elides the Strasbourg decisions relating to education with those relating to employment and professional situations. While on the one hand this is arguably a more principled approach, it is questionable whether the provision of state funded education can be so readily aligned with the situation of private employers. The majority based their decision ultimately on the free choice of Shabina Begum to attend another school, it not being alleged on the facts of the case that there was any substantial difficulty for her in so doing. However, the concept of free choice relating to both the areas of education and employment is not without difficulty. Following this decision, it will be necessary for an applicant bringing a case relating to freedom of religion to deal expressly with the issue of choice (if relevant) and explain why, in their particular case, it does not apply. A more satisfactory approach appears to lie in the approach of the minority in this case.[155]

Positive protection

2.75 A further controversial question relates to the issue of the extent to which the state has a positive obligation to create conditions in which freedom of religion can be exercised. As with other ECHR rights it appears clear that the right may involve imposing a positive obligation in certain circumstances. The positive duty was recognized in *Otto-Preminger-Institute v Austria*,[156] a case that involved the broadcast of a film that was said to be offensive to Christians. In that case the claim under Article 10 ECHR was rejected and the court recognized that the state had a positive duty to repress expression that was contrary to the spirit of tolerance. In a different area altogether in *Thlimmenos v Greece*,[157] it was expressly acknowledged in the context of discrimination that different categories of persons may need to be treated differently. In that case, an accountant who was a Jehovah's Witness had been prosecuted for failing to wear military uniform and was as a result of his conviction barred from entry to the accountants' profession. It was held that he was in a different position to prospective accountants who had no conscientious objection to military service and that the rules relating to entry to the profession needed to distinguish between the different situations.

2.76 This leads to the question of what circumstances will require a state to take positive steps to protect freedom of religion. Generally, it is an area where the ECtHR is likely to defer to the decision or assessment of the domestic courts. It may involve considerations of national budget and assessment of local situations, in which Strasbourg is unlikely to second-guess the decision of the national executive

---

[155] See also H Gilbert, 'Redefining Manifestation of Belief in Leyla Sahin v Turkey' [2006] EHRLR 308–326. See further 5.54 below.

[156] (1995) 19 EHRR 34.

[157] (2001) 31 EHRR 411.

as scrutinized by the domestic courts.[158] It is also likely in many cases to involve comparisons with the treatment of other religious groups within a society and, therefore, may entail claims under Article 14 ECHR. For example, where the state has provided for religious education for one group, it may be under an obligation to make appropriate provisions for another group. Depending on the circumstances of a particular case, simply ensuring that there are exemptions in place may not be sufficient.

Justification for an interference: Article 9(2)

The structure of the limitation clause in Article 9(2) is similar to that of other qualified rights in the ECHR. As with limitation clauses generally, the restriction must be prescribed by law with sufficient clarity, and must be necessary in a democratic society. The restriction must also be proportionate to its aim.   **2.77**

Legitimate aim

There are fewer limitations on Article 9 as compared to other articles and in particular there is no limitation on the grounds of national security as there are for other articles such as freedom of expression (Article 10) and freedom of association (Article 11). Despite this fact, the Commission and ECtHR have in some cases treated the Article 9(2) limitation clause in a broadly similar manner to other articles. For example, in the case of a man convicted for Nazi activities, the Commission referred to both Articles 9 and 10 and the state's actions being justified inter alia on the grounds of national security.[159] In other cases the Commission and ECtHR have properly drawn a distinction between the aims enumerated in Article 9(2) and other aims that are not listed. For example, they have ignored arguments by the state for upholding laws on the grounds that they support a tradition or historical links between the state and religion.[160]   **2.78**

It is important in an Article 9 case that the courts consider only the limitations listed in that provision. First, to accept other arguments undermines the principle   **2.79**

---

[158] See eg *Kjeldsen, Madsen & Pedersen v Denmark* (1976) 1 EHRR 711 [53] where the ECtHR said that the 'setting and planning of the [school] curriculum fall in principle within the competence of the Contracting States. This mainly involves questions of expediency on which it is not for the Court to rule and whose solution may legitimately vary according to the country and the era.'

[159] *X v Austria*, Application 1747/62 (1963) 13 CD 42, 326. Note that in practice of course national security concerns will be covered by the limitation relating to public safety and public order.

[160] In *Manoussakis v Greece* (1997) 23 EHRR 387 the state argued that the restrictions on building non-Orthodox temples had a legitimate aim partly due to the role of the Greek Orthodox Church in keeping alive the national conscience and patriotism during periods of foreign occupation. In *Buscarini v San Marino* (1999) 6 BHRC 638 the state argued that an oath of office had historical and social significance. The ECtHR did not address either argument expressly but did not find that either amounted to a legitimate aim.

of construing the limitations upon rights narrowly.[161] Secondly, the domestic courts have tended to be highly deferential towards claims by the state on the grounds of national security. This would effectively allow states to circumvent the scrutiny to which their claims might otherwise be subject. That said, if there is an issue of national security in the case, this will likely fall within the limitation on grounds of public safety and protection of public order.

Public safety and protection of public order

2.80 There is clearly a need to restrict manifestations of religion on this ground where religious individuals or groups may be involved in inciting or organizing acts of violence that threaten others. In *X v United Kingdom*,[162] it was held that free expression of belief does not include incitement to desert the army, murder officers and supply weapons to the IRA. There have been a number of prison cases relating to public order and safety. In *Childs v United Kingdom*,[163] the applicant was a multiple murderer who had given evidence against a number of other inmates. He was held in solitary confinement and not allowed to attend chapel services as the prison governor had determined that this would cause disruption. The Commission noted that the applicant was visited by the prison chaplain on a regular basis and upheld the restriction. But in other prison cases, less obvious justifications have been allowed to restrict freedom to manifest a belief.[164] Public order restrictions have also been upheld in relation to public planning in some cases.[165] At the European level, there does not always appear to have been strict adherence to the text of the ECHR, and at times a lower threshold test has been applied.[166] The decisions from Strasbourg often ultimately turn on the wide margin of appreciation granted to the state's arguments.[167]

---

[161] *Klass v Germany* (1979–80) 2 EHRR 214; *Sunday Times v United Kingdom* (1979–80) 2 EHRR 245.

[162] Application 6084/73 (1975) 3 DR 62. See also *Omkaranda and the Divine Light Zentrum v Switzerland*, Application 8118/77 (1981) 25 DR 105 in which the leader of a religious group was imprisoned and faced expulsion for leading the group to acts of criminal violence.

[163] (1983) 5 EHRR 513.

[164] In *X v Austria*, Application 1753/63 (1965) 8 YB ECHR 174, the refusal to let a prisoner grow a beard was based on a claim by the state about the need to identify him which was upheld by the ECtHR without any proper consideration of the issue.

[165] See eg *ISKCON v United Kingdom*, Application 20490/92 (1994) 76-A DR 90 (concern for residents near proposed site of Hindu temple). Note that in *United Macedonian Organisation Ilinden v Bulgaria*, Application 59491/00 (19 January 2006) the ECtHR held that a refusal to register a small cultural organization on the grounds of rights and freedoms of others and public order was not justified. It therefore found a breach of Art 11(2).

[166] In *Hakansson v Sweden*, [1982] 5 EHRR 297 the conviction of a man for loudly proclaiming the evils of alcohol was held necessary for the protection of public order even though it was only found that his actions had caused 'public indignation'.

[167] See further above at 2.65–2.67.

At the domestic level it is essential that a state's arguments on public order and safety **2.81** are subjected to proper scrutiny and not simply assumed to be valid, although deference will be accorded to decisions taken by public authorities in accordance with public law principles. It is important to draw a distinction between the natural and desirable tension within a plural society and the need to protect society. The tension caused by pluralism was recognized in *Serif v Greece*,[168] a case involving the prosecution of a man claiming to be the Mufti of a Muslim community and the potential for unrest arising out of two people who claimed this role, in which the ECtHR stated:

> Although the Court recognizes that it is possible that tension is created in situations where a religious or any other community becomes divided, it considers that this is one of the unavoidable consequences of pluralism. The role of authorities in such circumstances is not to remove the cause of tension by eliminating pluralism, but to ensure that the competing groups tolerate each other.

In this regard, it is worth noting that the United Kingdom has been prepared to **2.82** grant exemptions from generally applicable laws that are grounded in public safety and order.[169] This may suggest in other cases that limited exemptions for religious groups might be appropriate and outweigh the state interest in achieving full compliance by the population. On the other hand, there are good arguments for ensuring that laws of sufficient public importance such as the criminal laws and health and safety regulations in a state are adhered to by everyone. The balance will depend upon the nature of the provision and the particular circumstances.

Protection of health

This limb of the limitation clause gives rise to a number of questions about the **2.83** scope of protection. One issue is as to whether it is public health and the health of others that is protected or whether the health of the individual claimant is also protected. In practice the courts do not appear to have drawn a distinction and, given adults invariably have responsibility to others such as spouses and children, there are good policy reasons for protecting the consenting adult individual against self-harm where others such as dependants will be directly affected.[170] For example, the ECtHR has upheld a law requiring motor cycle helmets that have interfered with the right of the Sikh to wear the turban.[171] Another area

---

[168] Application 38178/97 (14 December 1999) [53].

[169] See eg exemption for Sikhs carrying the kirpan (ceremonial sword) from Criminal Justice Act 1988, s 139(5)(b), and from wearing motorcycle helmets while wearing the turban from Road Traffic Act 1988, s 17. See 7.09–7.12, 7.06–7.08 below.

[170] See J Fawcett, *The Application of the European Convention on Human Rights* (1987) in which it is argued that the protection is of public and not private individual health.

[171] *X v United Kingdom*, Application 7992/77 (1978) 14 DR 234. Note that the UK subsequently legislated to provide an exemption for Sikhs: see 7.06–7.08 below.

which has attracted considerable attention is the refusal of medication on religious grounds as in cases of the children of Jehovah's Witnesses or Christian Scientists. This relates to the question of protection of children from the religious beliefs of their parents. There have also been a number of cases relating to the health and safety of prisoners. In one case, for example, a prisoner was not permitted to have a religious book that included a section on martial arts due to the potential threat to the health and safety of others.[172]

2.84 In many instances, there will be some risk of harm to the health of the individual or to others. However, the risk must be of a sufficient level to justify the interference with a right. In *R (Begum) v Headteacher and Governors of Denbigh High School*,[173] the education authority argued that the restriction on the wearing of a long gown was justified inter alia on the grounds of protection of health. This argument was rejected by Bennett J in the administrative court and not pursued on appeal.[174]

Protection of morals

2.85 Unlike the protection of health, which gives rise to fewer definitional problems within the context of one society at least, the scope of protection of morals is harder to define. It is more obviously subject to competing claims about values within one society, and different religions invariably take differing stances on the issue of morality. Linked to this, the state's view of morality may well reflect the religious traditions or morals of the dominant or majority religion and may discriminate against the minority. In this regard the UN Human Rights Committee has stated that 'limitations on the right to manifest a religion or belief for the purposes of protecting morals must be based on principles not deriving exclusively from a single tradition'.[175] This issue was raised in a family case where a Protestant man from the Republic of Ireland claimed that the law prohibiting divorce infringed his freedom of religion.[176] The Commission decided the case under Article 12 (freedom to marry and have a family), holding that the law did not subvert the right to marry but regulated it in a manner consistent with the ECHR. In this area it is important to recognize the potential for highly subjective interpretation.

Protection of the rights and freedoms of others

2.86 At the heart of this is the need in a democratic society to reconcile the interests and respect the beliefs of the population as a whole, as was recognized by the ECtHR

---

[172] *X v United Kingdom*, Application 6886/75 (1976) 5 DR 100. See also *X v Austria*, Application 1753/63 (1965) 8 YB ECHR 174, in which a Buddhist prisoner was denied a prayer chain.

[173] [2006] UKHL 15.

[174] [2004] EWHC 1389 (Admin) [89]; [2005] EWCA Civ 199 [50].

[175] UNHRC General Comment No 22 on Article 18, para 8.

[176] *Johnston v Ireland* (1986) 9 EHRR 203.

in *Kokkinakis v Greece*.[177] A preliminary issue is whether this limitation is confined to the freedoms set out in the ECHR. Although in many cases it will be possible to point to such a right, this has not invariably been the case. In *ISKCON v United Kingdom*,[178] the application of restrictive planning laws to a Hindu temple was justified by reference to the rights and freedoms of those who lived nearby. In *R (Williamson) v Secretary of State for Education and Employment*,[179] the House of Lords expressly recognized that the rights of others were broader than the ECHR rights.

Another question relates to what evidence is required in order to demonstrate **2.87** that the rights and freedoms of others should prevail. How are their views to be ascertained in situations where they are not separately represented? In some cases reports are put before the courts. In some cases involving the public interest, the use of *amicus curiae* briefs to make representations on behalf of non-parties who may be affected by the outcome will benefit the court. In *R (Begum) v Headteacher and Governors of Denbigh High School*,[180] for example, the views of other pupils in the school were canvassed and presented in the form of a report which the judge took into account. In this context, where the rights of others who are not parties to the litigation are likely to be affected, an independent report as to their position is highly desirable.

Proportionality

The House of Lords in *R (Begum) v Headteacher and Governors of Denbigh High* **2.88** *School*[181] roundly rejected the procedural approach adopted by the Court of Appeal in that case. In assessing the question of proportionality, the court had to have regard to substance and decide for itself whether there was a violation of an ECHR right or not. Secondly, the court gave a clear indication that the issue of proportionality under the ECHR must 'go beyond that traditionally adopted to judicial review in a domestic setting'. In that context Lord Bingham noted:

> There is no shift to a merits review, but the intensity of review is greater than was previously appropriate, and greater even that the heightened scrutiny test adopted by the Court of Appeal in R v Ministry of Defence, ex p Smith [1996] QB 517, 554. The domestic court must now make a value judgment, an evaluation, by reference to the circumstances prevailing at the relevant time . . . Proportionality must be judged objectively, by the court (Williamson, above, para 51) . . . . [I]t is in my view clear that the court must confront these questions, however difficult. The school's action cannot properly be condemned as disproportionate, with an acknowledgement that on reconsideration the same action could very well be maintained and properly so.[182]

---

[177] (1994) 17 EHRR 397.
[178] (1994) 18 EHRR CD 133.
[179] [2005] UKHL 15 [80] (per Lady Hale).
[180] See decision of Bennett J at first instance [2004] EWHC 1389 (Admin).
[181] [2006] UKHL 15.
[182] Ibid [30].

2.89 The House of Lords cited the decision of the Grand Chamber in *Sahin v Turkey*[183] as recognizing the high importance of Article 9, the value of religious harmony and tolerance between opposing or competing groups and of pluralism and broadmindedness, the need for compromise and balance, the role of the state in deciding what is necessary to protect the rights and freedoms of others, the variation of practice and tradition among member states, and the permissibility in some contexts of restricting the wearing of religious dress.[184] Lord Bingham formed the view that in the situation whereby the school had taken advice, and had been told that its policy conformed with the requirements of mainstream Muslim opinion, the school was fully justified in acting as it did. He noted that the school had enjoyed a period of harmony and success to which the uniform policy was thought to contribute and that it was feared that acceding to the request to wear the jilbab would or might have significant adverse repercussions. In those circumstances it would be 'irresponsible of any court, lacking the experience, background and detailed knowledge of the headteacher, staff and governors, to overrule their judgment on a matter as sensitive as this'.[185]

2.90 Lord Nicholls also referred to *Sahin* which emphasized the margin of appreciation accorded to national authorities. He acknowledged that the doctrine as such had no application in a domestic setting but noted that, in the United Kingdom, Parliament had considered it right to delegate to individual schools the power to decide whether to impose requirements about school uniforms. It followed therefore that a domestic court should accept the decision of Parliament to allow individual schools to make their own decisions about uniforms and that the decision did not have to be made at a national level, and that national differences between Turkey and the United Kingdom were irrelevant.[186]

2.91 Baroness Hale adopted a more nuanced approach to the question of proportionality, recognizing at the outset that the question was more difficult in the case of a young girl than in the case of an adult who wished to manifest his religion in a particular form of dress.[187] However, she also acknowledged the task of schools as being to educate the young from many and diverse families and communities. It was also to 'promote the ability of people of diverse races, religions and cultures to live together in harmony'. To that end a school uniform could play an important

---

183 (2005) 41 EHRR 8.
184 Ibid [32].
185 Ibid [34].
186 Ibid [59]–[64]. See also [83] (per Lord Scott): '...[T]he direction to Shabina to attend school wearing the proper school uniform can only be attacked as an unlawful direction under domestic law if the school uniform rules that she was being required to obey were themselves so unreasonable as to be unlawful, or if the decision to insist upon Shabina observing the school uniform rules was similarly unreasonable. I regard both contentions as being virtually unarguable.'
187 Ibid [94].

role in easing ethnic, religious and social divisions. She also recognized a point that might have been taken in the case but was not aired, namely that the school was a good school which explained why Shabina Begum wanted to stay there. In that sense her choice may have been arguably constricted.[188] Ultimately she was of the opinion that the school was trying to achieve a balance between conflicting views and accommodate religious and cultural diversity in allowing girls to wear the shalwar khameez and the hijab.[189]

Margin of appreciation

The wide margin of appreciation granted by the Commission and ECtHR arises **2.92** from a number of factors. First, it relates to the recognition that there is no universal European approach to the relationship between state and church, and that states are themselves competent to determine the precise relationship and the place of religion in the public sphere. Secondly, it relates to the differing degree of importance accorded to religion within a society. Thirdly, it relates to the inherent difficulties of adjudication in the sphere of religion. In *Otto-Preminger-Institut v Austria*,[190] the ECtHR noted:

> As in the case of 'morals' it is not possible to discern throughout Europe a uniform conception of the significance of religion in society; even within a single country such conceptions may vary. For that reason it is not possible to arrive at a comprehensive definition of what constitutes a permissible interference with the exercise of the right to freedom of expression where such expression is directed against the religious feeling of others. A certain margin of appreciation is therefore to be left to the national authorities in assessing the existence and extent of the necessity of such interference.

The actual decision in that case is highly controversial and arguably would be decided **2.93** differently today. However, there are many examples of more recent decisions at the European level in cases involving religion, where the margin of appreciation has been specifically referred to. In *Murphy v Ireland*,[191] a case under Article 10, the ECtHR has acknowledged that a wider margin of appreciation applied to religious freedom of expression than other forms of expression. This related to the position of domestic authorities who were likely to be in a better position to assess what would be considered offensive in their own country than an international court.

---

[188] Ibid [97].
[189] Ibid [98].
[190] (1994) 17 EHRR 293 [50]. See also *Wingrove v United Kingdom* (1997) 24 EHRR 1. But in *Manoussakis v Greece* (1996) 23 EHRR 387 where the applicants had been prosecuted and convicted for having established a place of worship without prior authorization, the ECtHR did not refer to *Otto-Preminger-Institut v Austria* (1995) 19 EHRR 34 in considering the margin of appreciation but considered that the ECtHR should have regard to what was at stake, 'namely the need to secure true religious pluralism, an inherent feature of the notion of a democratic society'.
[191] Application 44179/98 (10 July 2003).

Overall, the ECtHR is likely to scrutinize cases more closely where criminal sanctions are imposed as opposed to civil or administrative penalties.[192]

Religious Discrimination: Article 14 ECHR

General comments

2.94   Article 14 provides:

> The enjoyment of the rights and freedoms set out in this Convention shall be secured without discrimination on any grounds such as sex, race, colour, language, religion, political or other opinion, national or social origin, association with a minority, property, birth or other status.

2.95   Article 14 ECHR does not prohibit all discrimination by the state but merely prevents states from discriminating in the way in which they guarantee the rights set out in the ECHR. It does not therefore provide a free-standing prohibition on discrimination.[193] Although Article 14 provides a common framework protecting against discrimination, there is no consensus as to the underlying rationale. There are a number of theories about the justification for non-discrimination measures referred to in academic writing. Article 1 UDHR refers to the belief in the inalienable equal dignity and worth of each human being. There are also ideas about equality of opportunity, a redistributive mechanism to adjust for the worst cases of inequality inherent in the system, and an attempt to level the playing field.[194]

2.96   The Strasbourg case law on Article 14 is highly problematic in many regards, not least because in so many cases the ECtHR has considered it unnecessary to deal with claims of discrimination where it has found a violation of another right.[195] This has effectively undermined the significance of equality legislation and prevented Strasbourg from developing a responsive line of jurisprudence to deal with both extant and newly emerging forms of discrimination. In this context

---

[192] For recent cases, see *Mehmet Agga v Greece (Nos 3 & 4)*, Applications 32186/02 & 33331/02 (13 July 2006); *Ulke v Turkey*, Application 39437/98 (24 January 2006) (ultimately decided on basis of Art 3 violation).

[193] A free standing prohibition is provided by Protocol 12 of the Convention, which is open to ratification as of 4 November 2000 and provides: '1. The enjoyment of any right set forth by law shall be secured without discrimination on any ground such as sex, race, colour, language, religion, political or other opinion, national or social origin, association with a national minority, property, birth or other status. 2. No one shall be discriminated against by any public authority on any ground such as those mentioned in paragraph 1.' The UK has not signed or ratified this Protocol due to concerns about its broad wording and potential application.

[194] See generally A McColgan, *Discrimination Law: Text, Cases and Materials* (Hart Publishing, 2005).

[195] See eg *Cyprus v Turkey*, Application 25781/94 (10 May 2001).

landmark decisions such as *Nachova v Bulgaria*[196] are to be welcomed as isolated examples of the ECtHR taking these issues seriously.

Approach to Article 14

The traditional approach of the domestic courts in cases of discrimination under **2.97** Article 14 was to consider the case by reference to five questions.[197] However, Baroness Hale in the House of Lords judgment in *Ghaidan v Godin-Mendoza*[198] stated that these were not necessarily to be treated as rigidly formulaic and there was potential for overlap between the relevant considerations. The questions were:

(1) Is there an act of discrimination falling within the ambit of a substantive ECHR right?
(2) Is there a difference of treatment in comparison to other persons?
(3) Is the difference based upon one of the grounds prescribed by Article 14 (here 'religion')?
(4) Are the chosen comparators in a relevantly similar situation to that of the complainant?
(5) Does the difference in treatment have an objective and rational justification?

In *R (Carson) v Secretary of State for Work and Pensions*,[199] the House of Lords **2.98** expressly referred to their preference for keeping the formulation of the relevant issues as simple and non-technical as possible. Lord Nicholls stated:

> Article 14 does not apply unless the alleged discrimination is in connection with a Convention right and on a ground stated in article 14. If this prerequisite is satisfied, the essential question for the court is whether the alleged discrimination, that is, the difference in treatment of which complaint is made, can withstand scrutiny. Sometimes the answer to this question will be plain. There may be such an obvious, relevant difference between the claimant and those with whom he seeks to compare himself that their situations cannot be regarded as analogous. Sometimes, where the position is not so clear, a different approach is called for. Then the court's scrutiny may best be directed at considering whether the differentiation has a legitimate aim and whether the means chosen to achieve the aim is appropriate and not disproportionate in its adverse impact.[200]

---

[196] (2004) 39 EHRR 37. See also *Timishev v Russia*, Application 55762/00 (13 December 2005).
[197] See *Wandsworth LBC v Michalak* [2002] EWCA Civ 271 *R (Carson) v Secretary of State for Work and Pensions* [2003] EWCA Civ 797; *Ghaidan v Godin-Mendoza* [2001] EWCA Civ 1533.
[198] [2004] UKHL 30 [133]–[134] (per Lady Hale).
[199] [2005] UKHL 37 [3].
[200] Ibid, see also [28]–[33] where Lord Nicholls further criticizes the list of questions formula.

Scope of Article 14

Act of discrimination

2.99 Article 14 has no independent existence and there must be discrimination in the enjoyment of a substantive ECHR right. Article 14 can also apply to rights that a state chooses to guarantee even if it is not obliged to do so.[201] There need not be an actual violation of another substantive article.[202] The ECtHR has referred to a number of expressions to describe how an act of discrimination might come into play. These include where the measures complained of are 'linked to the exercise of the right guaranteed'[203] or where a 'clear inequality of treatment in the enjoyment of the right in question is a fundamental aspect of the case'.[204] It has been suggested that even the most tenuous link with another provision of the ECHR will suffice.[205]

2.100 There are good arguments for providing a generous interpretation of this requirement as this would accord with the strong international consensus against discrimination, the principle of effective protection, and the nature of the ECHR as a living instrument. This would treat cases as falling within Article 14 where the act complained of impinges on some ECHR right that falls short of an interference, involves the state's implementation of a right, and has a practical impact on an aspect of the life of the claimant subject to ECHR protection.

2.101 There is no doubt that directly discriminatory acts are covered. The more important question is in what circumstances Article 14 covers acts of indirect discrimination. There is some inconsistency in the European cases, although in principle it is accepted that Article 14 prohibits indirect discrimination. In *Belgium Linguistic Case (No 2)*,[206] the ECtHR suggested that Article 14 was concerned with 'aims and effects' of challenged measures. In *Thlimmenos v Greece*,[207] the ECtHR found discrimination under Articles 14 and 9 where a man, who had been prosecuted because of his refusal as a Jehovah's Witness to wear a military uniform during compulsory military service, was refused admission as a chartered accountant because of the conviction under a neutral and generally applicable regulation. This case contains the important principle, therefore, that Article 14 may require different cases to be treated differently, as well as like cases alike.

---

[201] *Belgium Linguistic Case (No 2)* (1968) 1 EHRR 252.

[202] Ibid [9].

[203] *Petrovic v Austria* (1998) 33 EHRR 307. Cited with approval by the House of Lords in *Ghaidan v Godin-Mendoza* [2004] UKHL 30 [10].

[204] *Airey v Ireland* (1979) 2 EHRR 305 [30].

[205] See S Grosz, J Beatson & P Duffy, *Human Rights* (Sweet & Maxwell, 2000) C14-10. Cited in *Ghaidan v Godin-Mendoza* [2001] EWCA Civ 1533 [9] and referred to by the House of Lords [2004] UKHL 30 [11], but see *R (Douglas) v North Tyneside Metropolitan Borough Council* [2003] EWCA Civ 1847.

[206] (1968) 1 EHRR 252.

[207] (2001) 31 EHRR 411.

More recently in *Jordan v United Kingdom*,[208] the ECtHR stated: **2.102**

> Where a general policy or measure has disproportionately prejudicial effects on a
> particular group, it is not excluded that this may be considered as discriminatory
> notwithstanding that it is not specifically aimed or directed at that group.

However, in an earlier decision in *Abdulaziz, Cabales and Balkandali v United*   **2.103**
Kingdom,[209] the applicants claimed indirect discrimination in the immigration
rules (which required that fiancés had previously met) against persons from the
Asian sub-continent (who were more likely to contract arranged marriages). The
ECtHR, without considering the point about indirect discrimination, simply stated
the requirement 'cannot be taken as an indication of racial discrimination: its main
purpose was to prevent evasion of the rules by means of bogus marriages or engage-
ments'. The better view of this case is that no finding was made one way or the
other relating to indirect discrimination. It is also inconsistent with the approach
taken in *Thlimmenos v Greece* and *Jordan v United Kingdom* referred to above.

As regards domestic law, it is also accepted that both direct and indirect discrimi- **2.104**
nation are covered by Article 14. In *R (Smith) v Secretary of State for Defence*,[210] the
court considered the effect of pension-sharing orders on divorce under the armed
pensions scheme. The scheme allowed for members to receive payments for
pensions before 50, whereas the member's divorced spouse was not so allowed.
The court in this case held that this amounted to indirect sex discrimination.
Similarly in *R (L) v Manchester City Council*[211] it was accepted that a claim of
indirect discrimination was available.[212] With the express protection of indirect
discrimination contained in the EC Directives and the Equality Act 2006, the
areas in which Article 14 alone will be applicable have been considerably reduced.

Plainly, it is essential in the light of the principle of effective protection that   **2.105**
both types of discrimination are covered by Article 14. First, in the present day
relatively few laws are likely to discriminate overtly between religious groups.[213]
But many laws and administrative practices will reflect and favour the traditions,
customs and practices of the majority, such as working hours and days, school
timetables, and health and safety regulations. Secondly, a failure to recognize that

---

208 (2003) 37 EHRR 2. See also *Stedman v United Kingdom* (1997) 23 EHRR CD 168; *McShane
v United Kingdom* (2002) 35 EHRR 593; *McKerr v United Kingdom* (2002) 34 EHRR 553; *DH v
Czech Republic*, Application 57325/00 (7 February 2006).
209 (1985) 7 EHRR 471 [85].
210 [2004] EWHC Admin 1797.
211 [2002] 1 FLR 43 [91].
212 But see the earlier decision of *R (Barber) v Secretary of State for Work and Pensions* [2002] 2
FLR 1181 [39]–[40] where the court expressed some doubt as to whether indirect discrimination
was covered.
213 The obvious exception is where exemptions from generally applicable laws are granted for
certain minority groups. But these are not likely to be challenged by the majority who have voted in
favour of the general rule.

these apparently neutral laws may give rise to unlawful discrimination will considerably weaken the protection afforded to minorities and may render protection nugatory. Thirdly, the recognition of interference by generally applicable laws and practice has already happened in many jurisdictions including the United Kingdom by the enactment of exemptions for certain categories of religious adherent. In short, recognition of indirect discrimination reflects the fundamental rationale behind anti-discrimination laws, the reality of the European situation where forms of discrimination are frequently disguised, and give proper protection to minorities.[214] The more difficult question is the degree of scrutiny that the relevant provision should be subject to in a case and in particular a case of indirect discrimination. This is dealt with in the context of justification below.

Difference in treatment

2.106 There are three issues that are important here. First, the applicant must show that he has been treated substantively differently and less favourably than others; secondly, he must show that the different treatment is based on one of the proscribed grounds, namely religion in the present context; thirdly, the applicant must show that the chosen comparator is analogously situated.

Difference of treatment on grounds of religion

2.107 The requirement that the applicant demonstrate that he has been subjected to less favourable treatment and that it is on the grounds of religion does not usually cause difficulties in this area.

Analogous situation

2.108 Some difficulty arises in relation to identifying the relevant comparator group in relation to a case concerning religious discrimination. The general approach of the courts has been to ask whether the respective situations are analogous or relevantly similar.[215] This has not been dealt with consistently by the Commission and ECtHR and there appears to be some confusion as to what this means in practice. As regards religious discrimination, the question is whether the claimant representative of a minority should be compared to other minority religions, to the majority religion, or to the religious population as a whole. In *Ahmed v United Kingdom*,[216] in which a Muslim teacher was refused time off work to attend his mosque, the court took a very narrow approach to the issue of discrimination. It stated that the relevant

---

[214] See also S Stavros, 'Freedom of Religion and Claims for Exemption from Generally Applicable, Neutral Laws: Lessons from Across the Pond?' [1997] EHRLR 607.

[215] See *Van der Mussele v Belgium* (1984) 6 EHRR 163 (trainee barrister could not be compared to members of other professions and trained legal professionals); *Johnston v Ireland* (1986) 9 EHRR 203 (foreign domiciliaries not in analogous position to residents in relation to divorce law).

[216] (1981) 4 EHRR 126.

comparator was other minority religions rather than the majority religion and that because these religions were treated equally there was no violation of Article 14. This argument ignored the fact that the policy adversely affected Muslims but not Christians. If the comparator is taken to be other minority religions then the favoured position of the majority religion will not be challenged in very many cases. In *Thlimmenos v Greece*,[217] the ECtHR considered the position of a people who conscientiously objected to engagement in the military on the grounds of conscience in comparison to people who did not object.

There is a link between identifying the comparator and the question of justification. **2.109** Often the justification will depend upon showing that the positions of the two comparators are not analogous. This has led to case law that is difficult to reconcile in terms of underlying principles. It has been suggested in domestic case law that the test should be reformulated as a single question: 'is there enough of a relevant difference between X and Y to justify different treatment?'[218] A flexible approach is to be preferred. In many cases it will be most appropriate for the comparator to be religious adherents in general, including those of the majority religion.

Justification for difference in treatment

Unlike other provisions in the Convention, Article 14 ECHR does not contain a **2.110** clause that expressly sets out grounds of justification. Not every difference in treatment will amount to a violation of Article 14. In *Belgium Linguistic Case (No 2)*[219] the ECtHR held that the principle of equality of treatment is violated if there is no reasonable and objective justification for the treatment. The court stated: 'this existence of such justification must be assessed in relation to the aims and effects of the measure under consideration, regard being had to the principles which normally prevail in a democratic society'.

In addition to pursuing a legitimate aim, differential treatment must also be **2.111** proportionate to the aim sought to be realized. Where the treatment conforms to a common European standard, it is less likely to be challenged at the European level. However, in the area of religion there are no general European standards due to the acceptance by the European Union of differing church and state relationships. This means that a wider margin of appreciation is likely to be accorded to states in this area.

However, the issue of the degree of scrutiny must be explored. It is accepted that **2.112** discrimination on certain grounds such as race and sex must be subjected to

---

[217] (2001) 31 EHRR 411.
[218] *R (Carson) v Secretary of State for Work and Pensions* [2005] UKHL 37 [31] (per Lord Hoffmann).
[219] (1968) 1 EHRR 252 [34].

particular scrutiny. This was considered recently by Lord Walker in *Carson* where he said:

> The proposition that not all possible grounds of discrimination are equally potent is not very clearly spelled out in the jurisprudence of the Strasbourg Court. It appears much more clearly in the jurisprudence of the United States Supreme Court, which in applying the equal protection clause of the 14th Amendment has developed a doctrine of 'suspect' grounds of discrimination which the court will subject to particularly severe scrutiny. They are personal characteristics (including sex, race and sexual orientation) which an individual cannot change (apart from the wholly exceptional case of transsexual gender reassignment) and which, if used as a ground for discrimination, are recognized as particularly demeaning for the victim.[220]

2.113 As regards religion, Lord Walker noted that the judgments of the ECtHR often referred to 'very weighty reasons' being required to justify discrimination on the grounds of race or sex. In referring to the authorities and writing on the subject he concluded that religion, nationality and sexual orientation had been added.[221] The contention that religious discrimination required particular scrutiny was challenged in *R (Baiai) v Secretary of State for the Home Department*[222] on the grounds that the only case relating to religion cited by Lord Walker in *Carson* was *Hoffmann v Austria*.[223] However, Silber J in *Baiai* affirmed Lord Walker's position on three grounds: (1) that the wording in that paragraph was significant and agreeing with the citation of Pannick and Lester; (2) that it was not easy to understand why there should be a different approach towards religion as opposed to race and sex; (3) it would be strange to differentiate between religion and race as there was an obvious and frequent factual overlap between these two forms of discrimination; and (4) there was no sound reason for distinguishing between religion and nationality.[224] He expressly noted that in forming this conclusion he had not overlooked the weight that should be accorded to the historical position of church and state in society.[225]

2.114 As regards specific examples of justification relating to discrimination on religious grounds, in *Hoffmann v Austria*,[226] the ECtHR held that Articles 9 and 14 had been breached where a mother was refused custody of her children because she was a Jehovah's Witness, her husband and children being Catholics. In *Thlimmenos v Greece*,[227] the claimant was denied access to the accountancy profession because his conscientious objection to military service as a Jehovah's Witness had led to

---

[220] At [55].
[221] At [58].
[222] [2006] EWHC 823 (Admin).
[223] (1994) 17 EHRR 293.
[224] Ibid [130]. See *Secretary of State for the Home Department v Elias* [2006] EWCA Civ 1293 and *R (Al Rawi) v Secretary of State for Foreign and Commonwealth Affairs and Secretary of State for the Home Department* [2006] EWCA Civ 1279 for two recent decisions on nationality discrimination.
[225] Ibid [131].
[226] (1994) 17 EHRR 293.
[227] (2000) 31 EHRR 411.

a criminal conviction. The ECtHR found Articles 9 and 14 had been breached, and stated that the criminal record had no proper bearing on his fitness to be an accountant. In *Canea Catholic Church v Greece*,[228] the applicant claimed breaches of Article 14 and 6 on the basis that it was prohibited from taking domestic proceedings to protect its property while the Orthodox Church and Jewish synagogues had legal personality. The ECtHR held there was no objective and reasonable justification for the difference in treatment. In *Kjeldsen, Madsen and Pedesen v Denmark*,[229] the ECtHR held that sex education had a valuable purpose in a democratic society and that there was no breach of Articles 9, 2 Protocol 1 and 14 in refusing to grant pupils an exemption from sex education.

Margin of appreciation

In practice states enjoy a wide margin of appreciation in assessing whether differences in otherwise similar situations justify different treatment.[230] The fact that the state might seek alternative solutions such as granting exemptions to certain religious groups from generally applicable laws, is not of itself likely to be determinative.[231] **2.115**

The wide margin of appreciation granted in relation to Article 9 and 14 cases has been the subject of considerable criticism.[232] It is easy to criticize the decisions of the Commission and ECtHR relating to religion on other grounds—sketchy reasoning, failure to deal adequately or at all with Article 14 claims in relation to Article 9, lack of a systematic approach in many cases, and the apparent substitution of the subjective views of judges relating to the issue of beliefs and manifestations of those beliefs. But it is important to note that the decisions of the European organs are not binding on the domestic courts in other cases, although they are persuasive and should be regarded as important guidelines. The very sensitive and controversial nature of the rights and freedoms involved in cases concerning religion requires a close scrutiny at the domestic level. Situations and needs may vary considerably between EU Member States and parties to the Council. What is important is that the domestic courts and state authorities are clear on what the minimum content of the right entails and are able to apply the law in a systematic and coherent fashion. **2.116**

---

[228] (1999) 27 EHRR 521.
[229] (1976) 1 EHRR 711 [56].
[230] See *DH v Czech Republic*, Application 57325/00 (7 February 2006).
[231] See *Inze v Austria* (1987) 10 EHRR 394 [44]; *Rasmussen v Denmark* (1984) 7 EHRR 371 [41].
[232] See P Edge, *The European Court of Human Rights and Religious Rights* (1998) 47 ICLQ 680, 684–5.

3

THE BALANCE OF COMPETING INTERESTS

Introduction

The primary focus of the qualified right to freedom of religion is the striking of a **3.01** balance between the rights of the victim for European Convention on Human Rights ('ECHR') purposes, against the obligations and interests of the state. However, an important aspect underlying many cases is the need to strike a balance between the competing interests of parties other than the state—whether those of child and parent, the individual and others, the individual and a religious organization, or a minority religion and the majority. In this chapter some of the underlying issues relating to competing interests are considered more closely. First, the issue of balancing competing rights generally is considered. Secondly, the interests of the individual as opposed to the religious group are examined; followed by consideration of the competing interests of children and parents. Finally, the issue of the interests of minority religions as opposed to those of the majority religion is examined.

Balancing Competing Rights

General comments

In some cases there will be ECHR rights or rights of parties other than the state that are **3.02** in competition. This is of course not a feature that is specifically confined to Article 9.

Sometimes the competing interests in a case will be separately represented but this is not always the case. There are in principle two different scenarios: first, where competing rights are relied upon by private parties in domestic proceedings, and secondly, at the European level where the issue is one of justification for interference on grounds of protection of rights and freedoms of others. The ECHR as such does not contain specific guidance on how to deal with competing interests and it is primarily the role of the domestic courts to strike a balance in any case.

3.03   There are a number of areas where there will be competition between substantive rights. The balance in a society of freedom of religion (Article 9) may involve considering other competing ECHR rights including freedom of expression (Article 10), freedom of association (Article 11), right to peaceful enjoyment of possessions (Article 1 Protocol 1), privacy and family life (Article 8), right to marriage (Article 12), and freedom from torture (Article 3). There may be a tension between the right of organized religions to establish places of worship and to act in accordance with religious doctrine, and the right of the local community as a whole to peaceful enjoyment of property. The ringing of church bells, the call to prayer broadcast through speakers from the minarets of mosques, and the celebration of religious festivals may all interfere with the rights of local residents to peaceful enjoyment of their homes.

3.04   In cases concerning religious freedom, the balancing exercise may be affected by the relative importance ascribed to the particular religion in question within society. It may, therefore, depend partly on the church and state divide and the position of religion within the public sphere. To that end it might be thought that greater weight may be placed upon religious freedom in a state which acknowledges the role of religion in public, as opposed to a totally secular state. However, even in cases involving a state with an established church, there is no presumption in the Strasbourg jurisprudence that Article 9 supersedes other rights, despite Strasbourg stressing the fundamental importance of the right.[1] In practice, decisions in particular cases are highly fact specific and turn upon a number of factors including the position of religion in society as a whole, the nature of the competing interests, the relative numbers of individuals affected on each side of the equation, and the extent of interference in the rights on respective sides.

3.05   One area where the balance is frequently engaged is between the right to freedom of religion and to freedom of expression.[2] This is pertinent both to civil and criminal law.[3] The cases may in some instances be seen as balancing two aspects of

---

[1]   See *Wingrove v United Kingdom* (1997) 24 EHRR 1.

[2]   For general consideration of freedom of expression see J Beatson & Y Cripps (eds), *Freedom of Expression and Freedom of Information* (OUP, 2000); R Clayton & H Tomlinson, *Privacy and Freedom of Expression* (OUP, 2001). See 2.16–2.17 above.

[3]   For a brief consideration of criminal law sanctions relating to the expression of religious views see 2.12–2.17 above.

freedom of religion, namely the right to preach and express views, as against the right to be free from religion, ie not to be subjected to improper proselytization. This issue has been the subject of widespread debate recently throughout the EU and Council of Europe Member States. In the Netherlands, a Dutch film maker was shot dead for a film which criticized the treatment of women in Islam, prompting a debate about the extent to which freedom of expression should prevail. In the United Kingdom, the Salman Rushdie affair provoked widespread anger among a vociferous group of Muslims. More recently, a theatre in the United Kingdom closed a production written by a Sikh woman that portrayed the Sikh community in a negative light, for fear of public order reprisals.[4] As such there is no ECHR right not to be shocked or offended although it is arguably implicit in Article 9 that one may have a right not to be insulted in one's religious feelings.[5] Detailed consideration of this area is beyond the scope of this book, but there have been a number of cases brought against Turkey in particular in this area.[6]

As regards a case involving one or both of these rights there is a question as to **3.06** whether and how ss 12 and 13 of the Human Rights Act 1998 ('HRA 1998') affect the balancing exercise. Section 12 HRA 1998 applies when a court (other than a criminal court) considers a case involving freedom of expression. It requires that the court must have 'particular regard' to the importance of the right to freedom of expression.[7] However, the House of Lords has made it clear in *Re S (A Child)*,[8] a case involving Articles 8 and 10, that the section did not disturb the balance between the ECHR rights. Further, it has been doubted whether s 13 HRA 1998, which provides that a court must have particular regard to the importance of Article 9 if the court's determination of a case might affect the exercise by a religious organization of its Article 9 rights, adds anything.[9] In practice, it seems unlikely that the balancing exercise itself in cases involving Articles 9 and 10 or Article 9 and another ECHR right, will be affected by either ss 12 or 13.

Domestic law

A number of cases have made reference to the need to strike a fair balance in cases **3.07** concerning ECHR rights between the right of the individual on the one hand and

---

[4] See 2.16 above.

[5] See *R (ProLife) v British Broadcasting Corporation* [2003] UKHL 23 [123] (per Lord Walker: 'a citizen has a right not to be shocked or affronted by inappropriate material transmitted into the privacy of his home' leaving open whether it was covered by Art 8 and citing *Chassagnou v France* (1999) 29 EHRR 615). See also P Elias & J Coppel, 'Freedom of Expression and Freedom of Religion: Some Thoughts on the Glen Hoddle Case' in Beatson & Cripps (n 2 above).

[6] See eg *Karademirci v Turkey*, Applications 37096/97 & 37101/97 (25 January 2005). See also *Paturel v France*, Application 54968/00 (22 December 2005).

[7] HRA 1998, s 12(4).

[8] *Re S (A Child)* [2004] UKHL 47 [16]–[17] (per Lord Steyn).

[9] See 2.38–2.39 above.

the general interests of the community on the other.[10] The position in a case where there are competing rights has recently been considered by the House of Lords in *Re S (A Child) (Identification: Restrictions on Publication),*[11] in the context of a balance between a child's right to respect for privacy and the right of the press to freedom of expression.[12] In that case Lord Steyn said:

> [N]either Article has as such precedence over the other. Secondly, where the values under the two Articles are in conflict, intense focus on the comparative importance of the specific rights being claimed in the individual case is necessary. Thirdly, the justifications for interfering with or restricting each right must be taken into account. Finally, the proportionality test must be applied to each. For convenience, I will call this the ultimate balancing test.[13]

3.08   There have been a number of recent cases where the courts have held that the relevant balancing exercise is inherent in domestic statutory provisions such that ECHR rights, save in the most exceptional circumstances, will not affect the outcome. These to date have predominantly concerned areas of the law involving private and family life where considerations of family life are central to the statutory framework.[14] It is less obvious that the balance will be inherent in statutory provisions where Article 9 is at stake unless the legislation itself is concerned with religious rights.[15]

3.09   In *R (Begum) v Headteacher and Governors of Denbigh High School,*[16] the House of Lords had to consider competing rights in a case involving the right of the claimant school girl to wear a jilbab (full length gown) to her state school. In that case, on the issue of justification for interference, there was evidence from the headteacher as to the interests of other pupils in the school to the effect that they were concerned that if the claimant were allowed to wear the jilbab, they may be

---

[10] See eg *Wilson v First County Trust Ltd* [2001] EWCA Civ 633 [9].

[11] [2004] UKHL 47.

[12] See also *Campbell v MGN Ltd* [2004] UKHL 22; *Green Corns Ltd v Claverley Group Ltd* [2005] EWHC 958 (QB); *A Local Authority v (1) PD (2) GD (By her guardian Cathy Butcher)* [2005] EWHC 1832 (Fam).

[13] At [17].

[14] See eg *Secretary of State for Work and Pensions v M* [2006] UKHL 11 [87] (per Lord Walker where he accepted that the complicated formulae employed by the Child Support Act 1991 and the Child Support (Maintenance Assessments and Special Cases) Regulations 1992, SI 1992/1815 were intended to strike a fair balance between the competing demands of the children and the new household); *R (Razgar) v Secretary of State for the Home Department* [2004] UKHL 27 [20] (per Lord Bingham where he stated that decisions taken pursuant to the lawful operation of immigration control will be proportionate in all save a small minority of exceptional cases, identifiable only on a case-by-case basis).

[15] But note *R (ProLife Alliance) v British Broadcasting Corporation* [2003] UKHL 23 [16] (per Lord Nicholls stating that Parliament had decided where the balance should be held between the requirements of freedom of political speech and the protection of the public from being unduly distressed in their own homes).

[16] [2006] UKHL 15.

pressurized by their family and by more conservative members of the community to do the same. Bennett J in the Divisional Court had regard to their interests in striking the balance in the case, notwithstanding the fact that there was no first hand evidence from these other pupils, and they were not formally represented in the litigation.[17] On appeal to the House of Lords Lord Bingham said:

> On the agreed facts, the school was in my opinion fully justified in acting as it did. It had taken immense pains to devise a uniform policy which respected Muslim beliefs but did so in an inclusive, unthreatening and uncompetitive way. The rules laid down were as far from being mindless as uniform rules could ever be. The school had enjoyed a period of harmony and success to which the uniform policy was thought to contribute. On further inquiry it still appeared that the rules were acceptable to mainstream Muslim opinion. It was feared that acceding to the respondent's request would or might have significant adverse repercussions. It would in my opinion be irresponsible of any court, lacking the experience, background and detailed knowledge of the head teacher, staff and governors, to overrule their judgment on a matter as sensitive as this. The power of decision has been given to them for the compelling reason that they are best placed to exercise it, and I see no reason to disturb their decision.[18]

In *R (Amicus) v Secretary of State for Trade and Industry*,[19] Richards J noted that it **3.10** was inherent in any case involving competing rights that a fair balance had to be struck between the competing interests. As regards a situation where religious rights were at stake, he stated:

> Religion is an area where the principle of non-discrimination on grounds of sexual orientation may conflict very obviously with other important rights which are themselves recognised by the Convention and by the Directive. At the same time it should be noted that the weight to be given to religious rights may depend upon how close the subject-matter is to the core of the religion's values or organisation. X v Denmark concerned a clergyman. Hasan v Bulgaria concerned executive interference in the appointment of the Chief Mufti of the Bulgarian Muslims. The statements of principle in those cases must be read in context . . . . [Mr Singh] submits that the greater the degree of intrusion into the rights of others, the more likely it is that those other rights will have to prevail. Such considerations are plainly relevant to whether the impugned regulations strike an appropriate balance or enable an appropriate balance to be struck.[20]

---

[17] [2004] EWHC 1389 (Admin) at [90] where he stated: ' . . . it is clear from the evidence that there are a not insignificant number of Muslim female pupils at Denbigh High School who do not wish to wear the jilbab and either do, or will feel pressure on them either from inside or outside the school. The present school uniform policy aims to protect their rights and freedoms.'

[18] [2006] UKHL 15 [34].

[19] [2004] EWHC 860 (Admin).

[20] At [44]. See also *Church of Jesus Christ of Latter Day Saints v Price* [2004] EWHC 3245 (Admin) where the corresponding rights of a preacher and those of residents and local churchgoers were considered under the law of tortious nuisance and unlawful harassment.

ECHR law

3.11 The Strasbourg case law is concerned primarily with the question of whether a state has breached its obligations under the ECHR. However, in cases where a qualified right such as Article 9 is engaged, and where the justification for the interference is based upon the rights of others, the European Court of Human Rights ('ECtHR') will examine whether the interference is in pursuit of a legitimate aim and proportionate to that aim. The test of proportionality will require some form of assessment as to the nature of the balance of rights. However, it is evident that while the ECtHR is concerned that the domestic authorities have performed a proper balancing exercise, it grants a wide margin of appreciation as regards the result reached by the domestic courts. In some cases, however, the ECtHR has been prepared to intervene.[21]

3.12 In *Müslüm Gündüz v Turkey*,[22] a line was drawn between the legitimate exercise of freedom of expression on the one hand, and expression aimed at spreading, inciting or justifying hate-based intolerance on the other, which was not protected by Article 10. The applicant in that case was the director of an organization with extremist Islamic views who had been convicted for his views following a live television debate. The ECtHR noted that it was difficult to declare one's respect for democracy and human rights while at the same time supporting a regime based on Shar'ia. However, it found that the simple act of defending Shar'ia, without calling for violence to achieve it, did not constitute hate speech. The court also stressed the very particular context of the case which was important to the outcome—namely that the aim of the programme was to present the views of the sect, his extremist ideas were already known to the public and were counterbalanced by views of others as part of a pluralist debate. It concluded that the criminal conviction was unjustified and violated Article 10.[23]

3.13 In *Otto-Preminger-Institut v Austria*,[24] the ECtHR considered an application by a non-profit association that had been prevented from showing a satirical film set in heaven due to concerns about offending Christians, especially Roman Catholics. The applicable Austrian legal provisions required a balancing exercise between freedom of artistic expression and the rights of others including respect for religious beliefs. The ECtHR held that it was primarily for national authorities, notably courts, to interpret and apply national law and could find no grounds for holding that the law had been wrongly applied. It noted that those holding religious beliefs

---

[21] See eg *Öllinger v Austria*, Application 79600/01 (29 June 2006) for a recent case involving a rigorous examination of the balance between rights. Note that the ECtHR decided the case under Art 11 although Art 9 was raised.
[22] Application 35071/97 (4 December 2003).
[23] See also 3.05 above.
[24] (1995) 19 EHRR 34.

cannot reasonably be expected to be exempt from all criticism but that the manner in which such beliefs are opposed or denied is a matter that may engage the responsibility of the state to ensure the peaceful enjoyment of the right contained in Article 9 ECHR. Ultimately as the application was made under Article 10, the ECtHR considered whether the need for a restriction of freedom of expression was established, but in doing so it recognized the need for a wide margin of appreciation in relation to a case concerning the significance of religion in society.[25]

In *Kokkinakis v Greece*,[26] the ECtHR was concerned with the fine line between **3.14** proper and improper proselytization. In that case a Jehovah's Witness had been arrested over 60 times and convicted and imprisoned on several occasions for proselytism. It accepted that Greek criminal laws prohibiting proselytism had the legitimate aim of protecting the rights and freedoms of others. Although it did not expressly spell out those rights, it is understood that the right to be free from improper preaching is an aspect of freedom of religion and belief. In the context of that case, the ECtHR did not interfere with the distinction drawn by Greece despite the fact that Judge Pettiti noted that proselytism is the main expression of freedom of religion and that attempting to make converts is not in itself an attack on the freedom and beliefs of others. However, the ECtHR found a violation of Article 9, as it was not shown that the applicant's conviction was justified in the circumstances of the case by a pressing social need. As such, the decision does not shed much light on the approach to the balancing exercise.

In *ISKCON v United Kingdom*,[27] the application of restrictive planning laws to a **3.15** Hindu place of worship was justified in part by reference to the rights and freedoms of those who lived in the nearby village in a greenbelt area. The number of attendees had begun to exceed greatly the number for which the temple had originally been given permission to operate and the influx of people was beginning to cause problems in the village. The government argued the case on the basis of the need to protect the rights and freedoms of others. The Commission noted that the Secretary of State had given sufficient weight to the position of ISKCON. In particular it stated that the ECHR could not be used to circumvent existing planning legislation, provided that adequate weight is given to freedom of religion in proceedings under the legislation. Accordingly, it found no violation of Article 9.

---

[25] At [45]–[50]. Note that the three judges dissenting considered that the seizing of the film was not proportionate to the legitimate aim pursued, taking into account that the applicant had acted reasonably to limit the possible harmful effects of showing the film by its announcement of the film which enabled the religiously sensitive to make an informed decision to stay away. It also noted that the announcement made it clear that viewers had to be 17 and over. See also *Wingrove v United Kingdom* (1997) 24 EHRR 1 (UK blasphemy laws were held not to be incompatible with the European concept of freedom of expression). See for a recent case *Klein v Slovakia*, Application 72208/01 (1 November 2006).

[26] (1994) 17 EHRR 397.

[27] Application 20490/92 (1994) 76-A DR 90.

3.16   In *Chappell v United Kingdom*,[28] a group of Druids lodged a claim in the ECtHR based on access to the ancient archaeological site of Stonehenge on the solstice. The Druids claimed that this interfered with their freedom of worship. The Commission held in this case that, if Druidism were a religion, the regulations that prevented them from carrying out their midsummer solstice rights were a justified limitation on their freedom of religion. It noted that the relevant authorities were under a duty to protect Stonehenge and the surrounding area and had tried to find a solution to the problem. It concluded that in view of the absence of a suitable site for the festival and the risk of harm to the public through disruption, the decision to close the area was a necessary public safety measure. Accordingly, any implied interference was necessary in a democratic society in the interests of public safety, for the protection of public order, or for the rights and freedoms of others.

3.17   The cases cited above deal with a variety of areas of law. From these it can be seen that it is not always clear in the Strasbourg jurisprudence, particularly in the cases concerning both freedom of expression and religion, what the underlying rationale of the decision is and there is not always a clear methodical approach to the balancing exercise. However, the ECtHR is primarily concerned in each case to ensure that a fair balance has been struck between the competing interests by the domestic authorities, and that any interference is proportionate to the legitimate aim sought. In this context, as the domestic courts are in a much better position to judge the balance, a wide margin of appreciation is likely to be granted at the European level. As the ECtHR has repeatedly said in a number of cases, it is not a court of fourth instance.

Individual and Group Rights

General comments

3.18   The ECHR is mainly concerned with the rights of individuals although it is accepted that groups such as religious organizations are also capable of being victims for the purposes of the HRA 1998.[29] In many contexts, freedom of religion, as with other ECHR rights, may be more naturally or better articulated as a group right. A claim by the group may be a more practical and cost effective way of litigating and may be the only realistic option in cases where individuals do not want to shoulder the costs of litigation. It is a logical approach where the issue concerns a wider religious community, such as a challenge to the refusal of planning permission for a religious place of worship, refusal of registration of a particular group, or

---

[28] (1988) 10 EHRR CD 510.
[29] See 1.16–1.17 and 2.56 above.

respect for practices that are adhered to by a majority within the religious group, but which are unlawful under domestic legislation. It may also strengthen a claim if it can be shown that it has broad-based grass roots support.[30]

One view of group rights regards the group as important in itself, and not simply as the collective of individual rights.[31] Recognition is based on the fact that groups in a society are an important aspect of individual self-identification. Most individuals are members of a variety of different groups—local community, religious, education, sport, and others—and these groups themselves have an important role to play in society. Recognition can and should be given to groups in so far as they represent important social markers. Just as the Church of England was at one time an important group marker for most local communities across the country, so now there is a multitude of different religious groups that fulfil essential functions among their respective communities. **3.19**

Conceptually there need not be a difficulty in a state recognizing an aspect of group rights at the same time as advancing individual rights under the umbrella of the human rights framework.[32] There are cases, however, where the interests of the group as articulated by the leadership of the organization may conflict with the rights of individual members. The rationale of individual protection for freedom of religion is to protect religious pluralism, dissenters and those whose beliefs do not fall within the orthodoxy of the group. The rights of women and children are of particular concern as the major religions tend to be dominated by men, masculine values, and a patriarchal hierarchy. Many religious groups prevent women from holding the highest offices within the religious organization. In such a case there is an obvious tension between the right of the individual whose own interpretation of religion may include being able to hold such an office, and the right of the religious organization as a whole to self-determine. **3.20**

Many liberal democratic societies are, in theory at least, unwilling to intervene in the internal organization of religious groups. An extreme form of liberalism would suggest that they should self-determine to the extent that they do not physically harm individual members and there is a right of exit.[33] This solution has **3.21**

---

[30] See N Lerner, *Group Rights and Discrimination in International Law* (Martinus Nijhoff, 1990); M Weller (ed), *The Rights of Minorities: A Commentary on the European Framework Convention for the Protection of National Minorities* (OUP, 2005); D Fottrell & B Bowring, *Minority and Group Rights in the New Millenium* (Martinus Nijhoff, 1999).

[31] See B Bowring, 'Multicultural Citizenship: A More Viable Framework for Minority Rights?' in Fottrell & Bowring (n 30 above) 1–23.

[32] See J Packer, 'Problems in Defining Minorities' in Fottrell & Bowring (n 30 above) 223–73.

[33] See *Bahamas District of the Methodist Church in the Caribbean and the Americas v Symonette* (2002–2003) 5 International Trust and Estate Law Reports 311 (PC) (per Lord Nicholls: 'If some members of a church, be they many or few, wish to depart from the church's constitution and set up their own church, they are at liberty to do so').

many advantages for a state that does not wish to entangle itself with religious matters too deeply. But it ignores the fact that religious groups are employers for both religious posts and non-religious posts, involved in education and the provision of other public services. It also ignores the fact that the right of exit may not be a realistic option where the organized group is powerful, wealthy, and has numerous benefits bestowed upon it.[34]

3.22   As such the issue as to when and in what circumstances a secular authority should intervene in the exercise of power by the religious organization over its own members is fundamental. It is directly linked to the relationship between church and state and the view of liberalism taken by the state. At one end of the spectrum are cases where individuals are at direct risk of harm, in which case the state will readily intervene and criminal law sanctions can be invoked. At the other end of the spectrum are the day-to-day administrative decisions taken by religious groups or theological questions of doctrine in which the state has no or little interest. The far more difficult cases are those in between that affect the rights of individuals but fall short of criminal offences.[35]

Domestic law

3.23   Following the introduction of the HRA 1998, an important consideration is whether a religious organization should be considered a public authority within the meaning of s 6 HRA 1998. If it is a core public authority it would be bound to respect ECHR rights in carrying out all of its activities, if it is a 'hybrid' authority it would be bound to respect ECHR rights in the exercise of its public functions, save where its acts are purely private. This will impact on whether a religious organization can be a victim for the purposes of the ECHR and the type of remedies that may be available to a claimant. In *Aston Cantlow and Wilmcote with Billesley Parochial Church Council v Wallbank*,[36] the House of Lords considered that the Church of England was primarily a religious organization, even though some of the emanations of the church carried out functions which might be regarded as governmental. It held specifically that parochial church councils were not public authorities within the meaning of s 6 HRA 1998.[37]

3.24   A secondary question will be whether the decisions of a religious organization will be amenable to judicial review or whether the dispute in question is an internal matter for the hierarchy of the particular religious organization. This impacts on the requirement to exhaust domestic remedies for the purposes of an application

---

[34] See 1.28 and 1.33–1.35 above.
[35] See 1.24 above.
[36] [2003] UKHL 37.
[37] At [13], [16]; see further 2.33–2.34 above.

to the ECtHR. The Church of England as the established church is in a special position and has been granted considerable autonomy in regulating its organizational affairs. The General Synod of the Church of England has the power to propose legislation (Measures) relating to the government and organization of the church to Parliament's Ecclesiastical Committee made up of Members of both Houses. The committee examines the Measure and puts a report before the legislative committee of the Synod. If Synod agrees, the report and the Measure can then be laid before Parliament. Motions need to be passed by both Houses before the Measure can be presented for Royal Assent. In practice neither Parliament nor the monarchy generally challenges the Measure passing through.[38]

3.25 As regards other religious groups, there is no requirement that matters relating to their religious organization should be sanctioned by Parliament or Royal Assent. There is equally no specific legislation that protects their internal and spiritual affairs from being the subject of attention by the ordinary civil courts. But, many organized religions have established their own religious tribunals or courts to determine such issues, for example the Jewish Beth Din.[39] Consistent with the treatment of the Church of England, and the legal protections against discrimination and freedom of religion, it is likely that generally the actions of religious organizations as regards religious matters will not be judicially reviewable.

3.26 This approach was endorsed in *R v Chief Rabbi, ex p Wachmann*,[40] in which Simon Brown J stated that 'the court would never be prepared to rule on questions of Jewish law'. He further said that in relation to the question of whether a person was morally and religiously fit to carry out the spiritual and pastoral duties of his office, the court 'must inevitably be wary of entering so self-evidently sensitive an area, straying across the well recognised divide between church and state'.[41]

3.27 A further question is as to whether an English civil court would recognize or give effect to an order made by a religious court. As regards civil disputes that have been determined by way of arbitration, in so far as an award is enforceable under the Arbitration Act 1996, the fact that it is made by a religious court or religious arbitrators is not in principle a barrier.[42] For example, the London Beth Din of Federation of Synagogues in its capacity as Court of the Chief Rabbi deals with all

---

[38] See generally M Hill, *Ecclesiastical Law* (2nd edn, OUP, 2001).

[39] See 1.35 above.

[40] [1992] 1 WLR 1036.

[41] Ibid, at 1042G–1043A. See also *R v Provincial Court of the Church in Wales, ex p Williams* [1999] COD 163 (The Church in Wales was a body whose legal authority arose from consensual submission to its jurisdiction, with no statutory or governmental function. It was analogous to other religious bodies which were not established as part of the state); and *R v London Beth Din, ex p Bloom* [1988] COD 131; *R v Imam of Bury Park Jame Masjid Luton, ex p Sulaiman Ali* [1994] COD 142.

[42] See generally A Tweeddale & K Tweeddale, *Arbitration of Commercial Disputes: International and English Law and Practice* (OUP, 2005).

questions of Jewish Law. Arbitration awards made by the Beth Din have been enforced by the civil courts.[43] However, in a case involving a judgment of the Islamic Council of Great Britain, the Commercial Court held that it was not an arbitration award for the purposes of the Arbitration Act 1996 and was not enforceable in the English courts.[44]

3.28 As regards other areas of law, the English courts are not bound to enforce any order made by a religious court within the United Kingdom other than orders made by the courts of the Church of England. In the area of family law, the courts have been prepared in some instances effectively to give recognition to some religious orders or decrees made by religious organizations in the circumstances of the case. This subject is, however, beyond the scope of this book.[45] To date proposals to have a system of separate religious courts for the Muslim community with jurisdiction to hear a wide range of disputes between members of the community, for example family law issues such as child custody, in England have been rejected.[46]

3.29 Many religions discriminate on the basis of sex and sexual orientation in appointments to positions in the religious organization. There are statutory exceptions in the Employment Equality (Religion or Belief) Regulations 2003 and the Employment Equality (Sexual Orientation) Regulations 2003 to allow religious organizations to discriminate on the basis of sex and sexual orientation.[47] The United Kingdom has also tried to ensure by way of s 13 HRA 1998 that the ECHR would not affect the ability of religious organizations to discriminate in terms of religion and sex in their choice of leader.[48]

3.30 In *Percy v Church of Scotland Board of National Mission*,[49] the House of Lords considered two main issues. The first was whether Ms Percy's relationship with the church constituted 'employment' as defined in s 82(1) of the Sex Discrimination Act 1975.[50] The second issue, to be considered in this section, was whether Ms Percy's discrimination claim constituted a spiritual matter within s 3 of the Church of

---

[43] See *Cohen v Baram* [1994] 2 Lloyd's Rep 138; *Kastner v Jason* [2004] EWCA Civ 1599.

[44] *Al-Midani v Al-Midani* [1999] 1 Lloyd's Rep 923.

[45] See C Hamilton, *Family, Law and Religion* (Sweet & Maxwell, 1995); D Pearl & W Menski, *Muslim Family Law* (Sweet & Maxwell, 1998); A Bradney, *Religions, Rights and Laws* (Leicester University Press, 1993).

[46] Note that in Canada the head of Ontario province rejected a proposal by the Attorney General to allow family law and other disputes between Muslims to be settled by Shar'ia courts. See BBC report, 12 September 2005.

[47] SI 2003/1660 and SI 2003/1661 respectively. See *R (Amicus) v Secretary of State for Trade and Industry* [2004] EWHC 860 (Admin).

[48] See 2.38–2.39 above and 5.21 below.

[49] [2005] UKHL 73.

[50] See Chapter 5 below.

Scotland Act 1921 and, as such, was within the exclusive cognizance of the Church of Scotland and its own courts. The relevant Declaratory Article preserved the right of the church to legislate, and to 'adjudicate finally in all matters of doctrine, worship, government and discipline in the Church, including the right to determine all questions concerning membership and office in the Church'. The majority of the House of Lords held that a sex discrimination claim based upon a contract of employment was not a spiritual matter.[51]

ECHR law

At the Strasbourg level, the ECtHR and Commission have considered in a number **3.31** of cases whether religious organizations are carrying on governmental functions. This is important to the question of whether they may be victims for the purpose of the ECHR but it is important to note that it is a different test to that contained in s 6 HRA 1998.[52]

In *Holy Monasteries v Greece*,[53] the applicants were challenging legislation which **3.32** provided for the transfer of monastic property to the Greek state. The government argued that the monasteries were not non-governmental organizations as they were integrated into the organic structure of the Greek Orthodox Church and that the church and its institutions which played a direct and active part in public administration were subject to review by the administrative court. The ECtHR rejected this submission, noting that the monasteries did not exercise governmental powers and that their objectives were primarily ecclesiastical and spiritual, as well as cultural and social.

As regards consideration of cases involving conflict between the internal workings **3.33** of religion, Strasbourg is concerned principally with the obligations on the state to secure ECHR rights. In *Supreme Holy Council of the Muslim Community v Bulgaria*,[54] the ECtHR considered a claim by one of two rival groups claiming leadership of the Muslim community in Bulgaria. The claimant argued that its Article 9 rights inter alia had been violated by the intervention of the Bulgarian authorities into the affairs of the Muslim community by manipulating a Muslim conference in support of the rival faction. The ECtHR held that there had been a violation as the state actions had the effect of compelling the divided community to have a single leadership against the will of one of the two factions. It stated that the role of the authorities in a situation of conflict between or within religious

---

51 [2005] UKHL 73 [40]. This is to be contrasted with the exercise of disciplinary powers which would be regarded as spiritual matter for the jurisdiction of the church courts: see *Logan v Presbytery of Dumbarton* (1995) SLT 1228.

52 See 2.33–2.37 above.

53 (1995) 20 EHRR 1. See also *Hautaniemi v Sweden* (1996) EHRR CD 156.

54 Application 39023/97 (16 December 2004).

groups was not to remove the cause of tension by eliminating pluralism, but to ensure that the competing groups tolerated each other. State measures favouring a particular leader of a divided religious community would constitute an infringement of freedom of religion.[55]

3.34   In *Hasan and Chaush v Bulgaria*,[56] the ECtHR recognized the importance of self-determination of internal matters within religious organizations linking Article 9 with Article 11. The applicants were Bulgarian Muslims who complained of violations of Articles 6, 9, 11 and 13 in that there had been an unlawful and arbitrary interference with their religious liberties and the rights of the religious community to govern its own affairs and choose a leader. There was a rift within the Muslim community as to the position of a Chief Mufti with two factions each supporting their own leader. The responsible government agency, the Directorate of Religious Denominations, registered a new leader along with the Supreme Holy Council, but subsequently registered a new leadership. In finding a violation of Article 9, the ECtHR stated:

> Where the organisation of a religious community is at issue, Article 9 had to be inter-preted in light of Article 11, which safeguarded associative life against unjustified state interference. Seen in this perspective, the believer's right to freedom of religion encompasses the expectation that the religious community will be able to function peacefully, free from arbitrary state intervention. Indeed the autonomous existence of religious communities is indispensable for pluralism in a democratic society and is thus an issue at the very heart of the protection which Article 9 affords. It directly concerns not only the organisation of the community as such but also the effective enjoyment of the right to freedom of religion by all its active members.[57]

3.35   There is a clear line of principle emerging from the European decisions that the state should not interfere in the internal affairs of religious groups. However, in any case where there were issues of physical harm to individuals or criminal sanctions imposed, a more rigorous scrutiny of the obligations on the state would be inevitable.[58]

Parental and Child Rights

General comments

3.36   As a matter of international, European and domestic law, there is legal recognition that children have interests and rights that may conflict with the rights of parents,

---

[55] See also *Mehmet Agga v Greece (Nos 3 & 4)*, Applications 32186/02 & 33331/02 (13 July 2006).
[56] (2002) 34 EHRR 55. See also *X v Denmark*, Application 7374/76 (8 March 1976).
[57] Ibid [62].
[58] See 2.92–2.93 above.

and which should be taken into account in any case. Despite this de facto recognition, the rights of the child contained in international law instruments are not directly incorporated into English law. However, the courts may have regard to other international human rights instruments when interpreting the ECHR and domestic provisions.

At the international level, the Universal Declaration of Human Rights, the **3.37** International Covenant on Civil and Political Rights ('ICCPR') and the International Covenant on Economic, Social and Cultural Rights all characterize the family as the basic unit of society.[59] This has contributed to the slow recognition that children may have separate rights to self-determination and autonomy. The most significant step relating to recognition of the rights of children is the UN Convention on the Rights of the Child 1989 ('CRC').[60] It is almost universally accepted and imposes limitations on adult power and state discretion.[61] A child for the purposes of the CRC is 'every human being below the age of eighteen years unless under the law applicable to the child, majority is attained earlier'.[62] Article 30 CRC reiterates Article 27 ICCPR in its protection of minority culture but also extends protection to indigenous children as well as to children of minorities. It formulates a negative right that children should not 'be denied the right' in community with others to enjoy their own language, religion and culture. It should also be noted that the children of minorities may be doubly affected both as minors and as a minority.[63] The CRC recognizes the principle of acting in the best interests of the child in any case concerning children.[64] It also recognizes the right of children to express views freely on matters affecting them.[65]

Although some regional treaties expressly recognize the rights of the child, the **3.38** ECHR does not expressly provide protection to children as a separate group or

---

[59] See G Van Bueren, 'The International Protection of Family Members' Rights as the 21st Century Approaches' (1995) 17 HRQ 733–5; J Fortin, 'Accommodating Children's Rights in a Post Human Rights Act Era' (2006) 69(3) MLR 299–326.

[60] See generally G Van Bueren, *The International Law on the Rights of the Child* (Martinus Nijhoff, 1995); C Breen, *The Standard of the Best Interests of the Child: A Western Tradition in International and Comparative Law* (Martinus Nijhoff, 2002); D Fottrell (ed), *Revisiting Children's Rights: 10 Years of the UN Convention on the Rights of the Child* (Kluwer Law International, 2000); P Alston (ed), *The Best Interests of the Child: Reconciling Culture and Human Rights* (Clarendon Press, 1994).

[61] It was ratified by the UK in 1991. Note that the first Declaration of the Rights of the Child 1924 was drafted following treaties prohibiting child trafficking and exploitation.

[62] Art 1 CRC.

[63] G Van Bueren, 'Of Minors and Minorities' in Fottrell and Bowring (n 30 above) 80.

[64] Art 3 CRC.

[65] See Art 12(1) CRC. Note in this regard there has been international criticism of the unilateral right of parents to withdraw from education without regard to child's views: Concluding Observations of the UN Committee on Rights of the Child: UK (15 February 1995, UN Doc CRC/C/15/Add 34) para 14 and (9 October 2002, UN Doc CRC/C/15/Add 188) para 29.

recognize the rights of the child per se.[66] It does however make provision for the protection of children in certain specific areas. One area in which children are mentioned specifically relates to education and religious convictions. The rights of the parent to have their religious beliefs respected in relation to their child's education are enacted in Article 2 Protocol 1.[67] This right proved to be so controversial that the text could not be agreed upon in time for inclusion in the main body of the ECHR. The underlying rationale in this provision was to protect against state indoctrination of the type associated with the totalitarian regimes in Germany and many Eastern European countries at the time of drafting. But the respect for parental beliefs may not necessarily coincide with the best interests of the child in a case involving Article 2 Protocol 1.[68] In fact as ECHR rights apply to all human beings regardless of age, children in principle are protected generally under the ECHR.

3.39 A question that may arise in a case relates to the age at which a person can enjoy the right to freedom of religion. Some rights may be exercised by parents on behalf of their children such as freedom of religion and the right to education. The Commission and ECtHR have not attempted to identify a specific point at which children can be said to enjoy ECHR rights. This has been left to the nature and importance of the right in question and the circumstances of the particular case.[69] The ECtHR is likely to exercise considerable deference to the decision-making of domestic authorities on this point.

3.40 Religious questions and in particular religious education may give rise to some tensions between the parental right to bring up children in accordance with a particular set of beliefs and the rights of the child to be protected from harm and not to be indoctrinated. There is a strong presumption contained in Article 2 Protocol 1 that parents in the first place are primarily responsible for the education and upbringing of their children. But parental religious or philosophical beliefs may have negative effects on their children both physically and mentally. There are some religious adherents, most notably Christian Scientists and Jehovah's Witnesses, who reject the intervention of modern medicine including a blood transfusion necessary to save a child's life. In other instances the religious beliefs of parents may lead to physical harm falling short of threatening life, such as corporal punishment.

---

[66] See U Kilkelly, *The Child and the European Convention on Human Rights* (Ashgate, 1999); P Naskou-Perraki & P Papapaschalis, *Child Protection in the Framework of the Council of Europe* (Ant. N. Sakkoulas, 2002) for an overview.

[67] See further Chapter 4 for a fuller discussion.

[68] Note the best interests of the child are also reflected in Art 5 Protocol 7 ECHR which guarantees parental equality during marriage and in the event of its dissolution and provides for the state to take measures in the best interests of the child. Article 5 ECHR also permits the detention of a minor for the purpose of educational supervision or for bringing him before the competent legal authority, thereby providing for his protection from harm.

[69] See Kilkelly (n 66 above) 19.

The education system is a complex area potentially involving competing rights of   **3.41**
children and parents. Rights may be engaged in not only religious education but
also other areas such as sex education, physical education and school uniform
requirements that parents may wish their children to be exempted from on religious grounds.[70] These areas may not affect a child in actual physical terms but give
rise to other important arguments about fulfilment, development and opportunity
for the individual child. They may be linked to the issue of the right to exit a community, and equal opportunity. An education which accords with parental beliefs
may in fact affect a child's opportunity to integrate into the wider community and
may preclude certain subjects such as sports classes from being attended or may
prevent the child from accessing higher education and therefore professions.

Domestic law

At the domestic level, the most important statute is the Children Act 1989.   **3.42**
The overriding criterion is that all decisions should be based on the child's best
interests, the so-called 'welfare principle'.[71] The 1989 Act introduced comprehensive
reforms of both private and public law affecting children. In private law, the concept
of parental rights was replaced with the concept of parental responsibility. Where
the court is considering the upbringing of a child or the administration of a child's
property, the child's welfare is the court's paramount consideration.[72]

At common law the rights of parents derive from their duties to children. There   **3.43**
comes a time when a child will be able to decide for himself what his best interests
are. This age was originally set at 16 by statute as regards wardship jurisdiction and
applied to other areas by case law.[73] The precise meaning of child's best interests is
inevitably open to considerable scope in interpretation. But there has been a shift
in more recent times to having regard to the views of the child himself. In *R (Axon)
v Secretary of State for Health*,[74] the Court of Appeal noted that in order to decide
whether parents have 'the right to parental authority over a child' it was of critical
importance to have regard to the age and maturity of the young person.[75]
Specifically in that case (in the context of whether a doctor may give advice and

---

[70] See Chapter 4 for considerations of these and other issues.

[71] See generally M Hayes, *Family Law* (OUP, 2005); J Black, *A Practical Approach to Family Law*
(OUP, 2004); B Hale, *Family, Law & Society* (OUP, 2005).

[72] Children Act 1989, s 1. See *R (Axon) v Secretary of State for Health* [2006] EWHC 372
(Admin) [73] for a recent restatement of this. See also *Re U (A Minor) (Specific Issue Orders: Muslim
Upbringing and Circumcision)* (2000) 1 FLR 571.

[73] *R v Howes* (1860) 1 E & E 332, 336–7. For a recent case see *Gillick v West Norfolk and Wisbech
Area Health Authority* [1986] 1 FLR 224; *R (Axon) v Secretary of State for Health* [2006] EWHC 372
(Admin).

[74] [2006] EWHC 372 (Admin).

[75] Ibid [129].

treatment on sexual matters to young people under 16 without parental consent)
the court said:

> As a matter of principle, it is difficult to see why a parent should still retain an article 8
> right to parental authority relating to a medical decision where the young person
> concerned understands the advice provided by the medical professional and its
> implications. Indeed, any right under article 8 of a parent to be notified of advice or
> treatment of a sexual matter as part of the right claimed by Mr Havers must depend
> on a number of factors, such as the age and understanding of their offspring.[76]

3.44 As regards cases where parents of children withhold consent to necessary medical
intervention based on religious grounds, the state has had little difficulty in overriding the views of the parents. In *Re O*[77] the court was asked to authorize blood
transfusions in a case where parents refused consent on the basis of their beliefs as
Jehovah's Witnesses. It should be noted that the courts have gone further and
authorized medical treatment in cases where a competent child also declines intervention.[78] The courts have also considered cases where one parent has requested
that the child be circumcised on religious grounds. In *Re S (Specific Issue Order:
Religion: Circumcision)*[79] the court considered an application by a Muslim mother
that her children become practising members of the Islamic faith and that her eight
year old son be circumcised. The application was challenged by the father who
practised the Jain religion and wished the children to continue to experience both
faiths so that they would later be free to choose, and who opposed circumcision
regarding it as mutilation. The court held that the children had a mixed cultural
heritage and were of an age when they knew life both in a Jain and in a Muslim
household and that it was in their best interests to continue life as before.[80]

3.45 The decision of the House of Lords in *R (Williamson) v Secretary of State for
Education and Employment*[81] concerned the ban on corporal punishment in
schools under s 548 of the Education Act 1996 and the desires of certain Christian
parents that their children should receive such punishment in accordance with the
religious view of those parents. Interestingly, the case was apparently argued without separate representation of the interests of the children. This was expressly
noted in the judgment of Baroness Hale who referred to the international legal
standards contained in the CRC, the recommendations of the UN Committee on

---

[76] Ibid [130].
[77] [1993] 2 FLR 149. See also *Prince v Massachusetts* 321 US Rep 158 (1944).
[78] See *Re R (A Minor) (Wardship: Medical Treatment)* [1991] 4 All ER 177; *Re W (Wardship)
(Medical Treatment: Court's Jurisdiction)* [1992] 4 All ER 627 in which the judges relied on some
evidence of incapacity of the child to override their wishes. But in *Re E (A Minor) (Wardship:
Medical Treatment)* [1993] 1 FLR 386 the court ordered medical treatment on an intelligent and
competent 15 year old.
[79] [2004] EWHC 1282 (Fam).
[80] See also *Re U (A Minor) (Specific Issue Orders: Muslim Upbringing and Circumcision)* (2000)
1 FLR 571.
[81] [2005] UKHL 15.

the Rights of the Child and to the paradox of a case about children in which the separate rights of the children were not considered. Baroness Hale stated:

> This is, and has always been, a case about children, their rights and the rights of their parents and teachers. Yet there has been no-one here or in the courts below to speak on behalf of the children. No litigation friend has been appointed to consider the rights of the pupils involved separately from those of the adults. No non-governmental organisation, such as the Children's Rights Alliance, has intervened to argue a case on behalf of children as a whole. The battle has been fought on ground selected by the adults. This has clouded and over-complicated what should have been a simple issue.[82]

In the field of family law, there are a number of cases involving children, adoption **3.46** and custody where the religion of the parents and children is considered in contexts which fall short of actual physical harm. This area is beyond the scope of this book.[83]

ECHR law

At the European level, although the rights of the child are not expressly protected, **3.47** the Court and Commission have in some cases been concerned both indirectly and directly about the interests of the child that have conflicted with the rights of parents. In doing so they have considered that the best interests of the child should be considered, despite the fact that the child may not be formally represented. In more recent cases and particularly those after the ratification of the CRC, there is a trend towards expressly considering the best interests of the child.[84]

There have been a number of cases before the Commission and ECtHR relating **3.48** to corporal punishment of children. In *Campbell and Cosans v United Kingdom*[85] parents lodged applications on behalf of themselves and their children arguing that the application of corporal punishment in state schools was contrary inter alia to Article 2 Protocol 1. The ECtHR found that both the rights of the parents had been violated (as regards the second sentence of Article 2) and the rights of the

---

[82] Ibid [71]. See E Craig, 'Accommodation of Diversity in Education—A Human Rights Agenda?' [2003] 15(3) CFLQ 279 suggesting ways in which a child's views should be canvassed by schools before acceding to parental requests. See also *Wisconsin v Yoder* 406 US 205 (1972) where the US Supreme Court considered a claim by the Amish community to have their children exempted from the final two years of compulsory public school education on grounds that the numbers in the community were depleting as children entered college and decided to exit the community. In a controversial decision in which the children were not separately represented the court upheld the claim of the Amish elders. The partly dissenting judge in the case noted that the interests and views of the children had not been separately addressed and suggested that the case should be sent back to the lower court and a report put before the court as to their interests.

[83] See n 71 above.

[84] In *Marckx v Belgium* (1979) 2 EHRR 330 the ECtHR referred to the Convention on the Legal Status of Children born outside Wedlock 1975; in *Kjeldsen, Madsen & Pedersen v Denmark* (1976) 1 EHRR 711 the Commission referred to the Declaration on the Rights of Children 1959; and in *Costello-Roberts v United Kingdom* (1995) 19 EHRR 112 the ECtHR referred to the CRC. See also Kilkelly (n 66 above) 15.

[85] (1982) 4 EHRR 293.

child (as regards the first sentence). It is worth noting that in that case the rights of parents and child did not conflict unlike in the case of *R (Williamson) v Secretary of State for Education and Employment*.[86]

3.49 However, in many cases involving children, the children are not separately represented and the ECtHR does not specifically consider whether they have separate interests that should be taken into account. In *Kjeldsen, Madsen, Pedersen v Denmark*,[87] the ECtHR considered a claim by three sets of parents who objected to the compulsory sex education that was an integrated part of the curriculum and taught through a number of subjects at a public school in Denmark. They claimed it was contrary to the beliefs they held as Christian parents and a violation of Article 2 Protocol 1. The ECtHR might have considered the balance between the right of the children to education on the one hand as opposed to the right of parents to have their beliefs respected. The majority did not view the case this way and simply held there was no violation of Article 2 Protocol 1, noting that there was a private school system in place. However, the concurring judgment noted that the children's best interests should be taken into account. Although the majority decision in the case may well be sound as a matter of principle, it is problematic as regards the legal reasoning. It rejects out of hand that the parents' religious beliefs could have been infringed in any way. It did however consider the state interest in imparting information about sex education although it did not consider the position from the children's perspective as the children were not parties to the litigation.

3.50 There does not appear to be a common approach taken to this issue. Many Strasbourg cases were decided before the CRC came into effect and the consideration of children's rights may be given greater weight now.[88] There is increasing reference to the CRC in the jurisprudence from the ECtHR.[89] In addition because the Strasbourg case law is focusing on the obligations of states to secure rights in their respective territories and is concerned chiefly with the balance of the rights as articulated in the case, it does not necessarily involve itself in asking questions as to the positions of unrepresented parties.

Minority and Majority Rights

General comments

3.51 Minority views are likely to need greater protection than majority views under a constitutional democracy in that they may not be able to gain the necessary protection

---

[86] See 3.45 above.
[87] (1976) 1 EHRR 711.
[88] Van Beuren (n 60 above) 82.
[89] Kilkelly (n 66 above) 15.

through the normal channels. However, certain minority views may be considered by the majority as conflicting directly with democratic values, such that it is argued that no recognition should be given to those views. It is clear from a number of decisions from Strasbourg that one of the underlying principles of the ECHR is to ensure pluralism in society, which will entail support and respect for minorities. Therefore, in some decisions, even where discrimination is not raised as an issue, it will be possible to discern in the judgment the need to support a vulnerable or politically weak group in society against more powerful interests.[90]

Domestic law

The protections afforded in the HRA 1998 to minorities will inevitably be balanced **3.52** in a case against the views of the majority. In some cases the courts have referred directly to the vulnerable position of groups within society, although this is not invariably the case. In *R (Countryside Alliance) v Attorney General*,[91] Sir Anthony Clarke MR approved the judgment of the Divisional Court to the effect that a measure is not necessary in a democratic society only because the democratically elected majority of the legislature enacts it.[92] In *Singh v Entry Clearance Officer, New Delhi*,[93] Munby LJ made reference to the pluralistic nature of British society and the need for the courts to reflect this in their decision making. His speech is worth reading in full for its insight into the role of the judiciary in considering the customs of religious minorities.[94] He stated:

> We live, or strive to live, in a tolerant society increasingly alive to the need to guard against the tyranny which majority opinion may impose on those who, for whatever reason, comprise a weak or voiceless minority. Equality under the law, human rights and the protection of minorities have to be more than what Brennan J in the High Court of Australia once memorably described as 'the incantations of legal rhetoric'.[95]

In the discrimination law context, Keene LJ in the Court of Appeal in *Ghaidan v* **3.53** *Godin Mendoza*[96] stated:

> Where discrimination against a minority is concerned, amounting on the face of it to a breach of article 14 rights, the courts are entitled to require to be satisfied that a proper and rational justification for the difference in treatment has been made out. It is, as Buxton LJ has emphasised, a matter involving rights of high constitutional

---

[90] See generally Weller (n 30 above); Fottrell & Bowring (n 29 above); R Jones & W Gnanapala, *Ethnic Minorities in English Law* (Trentham Books, 2000).

[91] [2006] EWCA Civ 1677.

[92] Ibid [124].

[93] [2004] EWCA Civ 1075.

[94] See 2.05 above.

[95] [2004] EWCA Civ 1075 [67]. See also *Re T (Minors) (Custody: Religious Upbringing)* (1975) 2 FLR 239.

[96] [2001] EWCA Civ 1533 [44]. The decision was upheld by the House of Lords: [2004] UKHL 30.

importance where the courts are equipped to arrive at a judgment. It is indeed a classic role of the courts to be concerned with the protection of such minority rights. That being so, this court is entitled to ask whether there is any rational and proportionate basis for the distinction. For my part, I am not satisfied that any such basis has been established.

ECHR law

3.54 The ECtHR on a number of occasions has made reference to the particular need to protect minorities. In *Connors v United Kingdom*,[97] the ECtHR made reference to the vulnerable position of Gypsies as a minority which meant that some special consideration should be given to their needs and their different lifestyle, both in the relevant regulatory framework and in reaching decisions in particular cases. To that extent it was held that there was a positive obligation imposed on contracting states under Article 8 to facilitate the Gypsy way of life.[98] In *Chapman v United Kingdom*,[99] the ECtHR noted that there was an emerging international consensus recognizing the special needs of minorities and an obligation to protect their security, identity and lifestyle, although it was not persuaded that the consensus was sufficiently concrete for it to derive any guidance as to the conduct or standards which contracting states considered desirable in any particular situation.[100]

3.55 As such, the ECHR having as its basis the protection of individual rights, does not discriminate in its protection of rights depending on whether they are claimed by a large or a small group in society. In practice of course no court can ignore such matters, not least because they may be relevant to the competing relative interests and to the justifications for interference in qualified rights such as Article 9. Therefore, although domestic and Strasbourg jurisprudence does not always articulate a point about the relative bargaining position of the parties in question, it is worth considering some of the case law from this angle.

3.56 In *Kokkinakis v Greece*,[101] the claimant was a member of a minority religion, namely Jehovah's Witnesses. In that case, the vast majority of the population belonged to the majority Greek Orthodox Church. It was noted in the case that had a Greek Orthodox person sought to articulate their views, they would not likely have been subject to any form of penalty. Regard was also had to the relative positions of the two religions and the argument that the complainant in the case needed protection from the views of the claimant was rejected.

---

[97] (2005) 40 EHRR 9.
[98] Ibid [84].
[99] (2001) 33 EHRR 18 [83].
[100] See also *G and E v Norway* (1983) 35 DR 30.
[101] [1996] 17 EHRR 397.

Ultimately the Strasbourg court is at pains to stress the underlying importance of   **3.57**
pluralism in society and the need to protect the rights of the variety of groups and
individuals in society. On a number of occasions the ECtHR has said that state
measures favouring a particular leader or group in a divided religious community
or seeking to compel the community, or part of it, to place itself under a single
leadership against its will would constitute an infringement of Article 9.[102]
The obligation of the state in a situation of conflict between or within religious
groups is not to remove the cause of tension by eliminating pluralism, but to
ensure that the competing groups tolerate each other.[103]

---

[102] See eg *Mehmet Agga v Greece (Nos 3 & 4)*, Applications 32186/02 & 33331/02 (13 July 2006);
Supreme Holy Council of the Muslim Community v Bulgaria (2005) 41 EHRR 3; *Serif v Greece* (2001)
31 EHRR 20; *Hasan and Chaush v Bulgaria* (2002) 34 EHRR 55.

[103] *Supreme Holy Council of the Muslim Community v Bulgaria* (2005) 41 EHRR 3 [96].

4

EDUCATION

Introduction

Education is one of the essential foundations for individual fulfilment of potenti   **4.01**
al and participation in political, social and cultural affairs, and is critical for society as a whole.[1] It is of particular importance for minorities in society who may be
marginalized and economically disadvantaged.[2] Freedom of religion gives rise to
important issues in the context of education law, particularly given the religious
character of many schools in England and Wales and the fact that religious education and worship are requirements of the curriculum in state maintained schools.
The current system of state funded educational institutions allows a considerable
degree of flexibility to accommodate local circumstances, including respect for religious and cultural diversity for individuals and groups. But the practical challenges

---

[1] See *Bishop of Roman Catholic Diocese of Port Louis v Tengur* [2004] UKPC 9 in which the Privy
Council stated at [5]: 'In modern democratic states, the provision of an efficient and high-quality
educational system has come to be seen, for reasons too well known to require exposition, as one of
the prime functions of government.' See also *Phelps v London Borough of Hillingdon* [2001] 2 AC
619; *Adams v Bracknell Forest Borough Council* [2004] UKHL 29.

[2] See *The Parekh Report, The Future of Multi-Ethnic Britain* (The Runnymede Trust, 2002) 148;
H Ansari, *The Infidel Within: Muslims in Britain since 1800* (Hurst and Co, 2004) 298.

of adapting an education system to reflect a religiously and culturally plural society are enormous.[3]

4.02 This chapter first provides a brief overview of the statutory framework with reference to some of the important principles relating to the law of education. It then considers the impact of the Human Rights Act 1998 ('HRA 1998') and of Article 2 Protocol 1 of the European Convention on Human Rights ('ECHR') in particular on the law of education. Following this, specific issues are identified and examined in the light of the legal framework by reference to domestic and European case law.

Statutory Framework

Education Acts

4.03 The foundation of the state education system of England and Wales is now governed by the Education Act 1996 ('EdA 1996'). The EdA 1996 confers responsibility on the Secretary of State for securing provision for primary, secondary or further education.[4] The law is affected by more recent legislation including the School Standards and Framework Act 1998 ('SSFA 1998'), the Education Act 2002 ('EdA 2002'), and the Education Act 2005 ('EdA 2005') which have made substantial changes to the area. Further and higher education have been affected by the Teaching and Higher Education Act 1998 ('THEA 1998'), Learning and Skills Act 2000 ('LSA 2000') and the Higher Education Act 2004 ('HEA 2004').[5]

4.04 There are now broadly five different types of state maintained school in England: community schools, voluntary schools, foundation schools, academies (including city technology colleges) and pupil referral units. The system was significantly changed by the SSFA 1998 which abolished grant maintained schools with effect from 1 September 1999 and replaced them with foundation schools. In addition, under the SSFA 1998 county schools received community school status, and

---

[3] See *Swann Report: Education for All: The Report of the Committee of Inquiry into the Education of Children from Ethnic Minority Groups* (HMSO, 1985). See also R Jackson, *Rethinking Religious Education and Plurality* (RoutledgeFalmer, 2004); E Craig, 'Accommodation of Diversity in Education—A Human Rights Agenda?' (2003) 15(3) Child and Family Law Quarterly 279; and H Cullen, 'Education Rights or Minority Rights?' (1993) 7 International Journal of Law and the Family 143.

[4] EdA 1996, ss 10–11. For a detailed treatment of the area in general see J Ford, M Hughes, D Ruebain, *Education Law and Practice* (Jordans, 2005); O Hyams, *The Law of Education* (Jordans, 2004); J McManus, *Education and the Courts* (Jordans, 2004); P Leill, J Coleman, K Poole, *The Law of Education* (Butterworths, 1999).

[5] Further and higher education are beyond the scope of this book but note that they are affected by the provisions of the Employment Equality (Religion and Belief) Regulations 2003, SI 2003/1660 in so far as they relate to vocational training.

voluntary schools became voluntary-aided schools or voluntary-controlled schools.[6] There are also independent schools of various types. These may be managed by companies established under the Companies Acts, by registered charities, and by natural persons.[7]

The law relating to education is subject to three important general statutory **4.05** principles. First, it is the duty of a parent of a child of compulsory school age (between 5 and 16) to secure that the child receives 'efficient, full time education suitable to his age, ability and aptitude and to any special education needs he may have' by regular attendance at a school or otherwise.[8] Secondly, there is a principle that 'pupils are to be educated in accordance with the wishes of their parents, so far as that is compatible with the provision of efficient instruction and training and the avoidance of unreasonable public expenditure'.[9] Local education authorities ('LEAs'), other education providers and funders, and the Secretary of State must have regard to this general principle, but may also take into account other matters and may make exceptions to the general rule.[10] Thirdly, there is the principle that (subject to exceptions) LEAs (and other providers) must provide sufficient schools for their areas and provide all pupils with the opportunity of appropriate education.[11]

The statutory framework applies principally to maintained schools. However, inde- **4.06** pendent schools are not wholly outside the legislative framework and are subject to statutory registration, inspections, and to certain duties under the Children Act 1989.[12]

Race Relations Act 1976

The Race Relations Act 1976 ('RRA 1976') as amended by the Race Relations **4.07** (Amendment) Act 2000 and the Race Relations Act 1976 (Amendment) Regulations 2003[13] place a general statutory duty on local authorities in the education sector. Although religious groups are not expressly protected, some groups may be protected through indirect discrimination.[14] Alternatively, some religious groups will qualify as ethnic groups in accordance with the guidelines set down in

---

[6] SSFA 1998, s 20.

[7] See White Paper, *Higher Standards: Better Schools for All* (Cmd 6677, October 2005) for new proposals on local organization of state funded schools.

[8] EdA 1996, s 7.

[9] Ibid, s 9. See 4.26–4.27 below relating to the UK's reservation to Art 2 Protocol 1.

[10] *Watt v Kesteven County Council* [1955] 1 QB 408, 424 (per Denning LJ) and 429 (per Parker LJ); *Cumings v Birkenhead Corporation* [1972] Ch 12, 36.

[11] EdA 1996, s 14.

[12] An independent school is defined by s 463 EdA 1996 (as substituted by s 172 EdA 2002).

[13] SI 2003/1626.

[14] See 2.28 above.

Mandla v Dowell Lee.[15] Section 71 RRA 1976 provides that local authorities and governing bodies of (1) educational establishments maintained by LEAs; (2) institutions in the further education sector; and (3) institutions in the higher education sector, are under a general duty in carrying out their functions to have due regard to the need (a) to eliminate unlawful racial discrimination, and (b) to promote equality of opportunity and good relations between persons of different racial groups.[16]

4.08 By virtue of the Race Relations Act 1976 (Statutory Duties) Order 2001,[17] each LEA and governing body of the educational institutions referred to above is also required to (1) have a 'Race Equality Scheme' and review it every three years, (2) have a written statement of their policy for promoting race equality, (3) to assess the impact of their policies, including their race equality policy, on pupils, staff and parents of different racial groups including, in particular, the impact on attainment levels of such pupils, and (4) to monitor the operation of such policies.[18]

4.09 Section 35 RRA 1976 allows for preferential access to facilities or services to meet the special needs of persons of a particular racial group in regard to their education, training or welfare, or any ancillary benefits.

Equality Act 2006

4.10 The Equality Act 2006 ('EA 2006') provides an entirely new framework for the protection of religious discrimination. It makes discrimination on the grounds of religion or belief in the provision of education unlawful. Given the religious nature of many educational providers in England and Wales, a number of broad-reaching statutory exceptions to the general principle of non-discrimination have been enacted. Section 49 EA 2006 extends the prohibition against discrimination on the ground of religion or belief to (1) maintained schools; (2) independent schools (other than special schools); and (3) special schools (other than those maintained by an LEA).[19] The prohibition does not extend to educational institutions or establishments in the further or higher education sectors as these are covered by existing secondary legislation.[20]

---

[15] (1983) 2 AC 548 and see further 2.21–2.28 above.

[16] Note that the House of Lords held in *Wheeler v Leicester City Council* [1985] AC 1054, 1077 that the previous statutory provision had no application to the education functions of an LEA.

[17] SI 2001/3458.

[18] Ibid Arts 2–3. Note that the Commission for Racial Equality has published a Code of Practice to assist local authorities in meeting their duties under the RRA 1976 as amended. Guidance on race equality policies is also available on their website at <http://www.cre.gov.uk>. See also *R (Elias) v Secretary of State for Defence and Commission for Racial Equality* [2005] EWHC 1435 (Admin).

[19] A special school is defined in s 337(1) EdA 1996 as a school that is 'specially designed to make special educational provision for pupils with SEN'.

[20] See Employment Equality (Religion or Belief) Regulations 2003 and Chapter 5 below.

The section makes it unlawful for an educational institution to discriminate **4.11** against a person in respect of the terms on which it offers him admission as a pupil or by refusing to accept an application to admit him as a pupil. Where a person is already a pupil of the establishment it is unlawful to discriminate against him in the way the establishment affords him access to any benefit, facility or service or by refusing such access. It is also unlawful to exclude a pupil or subject him to any other detriment. A pupil of the establishment includes any person who receives education at the establishment.[21]

Section 50 provides for certain exemptions from the general requirement of non- **4.12** discrimination. Section 50(1) exempts maintained schools with a religious character from the prohibition on discrimination in s 49(1) (apart from the provisions making exclusion from a school unlawful, and prohibiting the subjection of a pupil to any other detriment). It also exempts to the same extent independent schools if such schools have a religious ethos, and schools conducted in the interest of a church or denominational body. The provision will therefore allow all such schools with a religious ethos to admit pupils or set admission terms for pupils based on the religious character or religious ethos of the school. It will also allow such schools to conduct themselves in a way which is compatible with their religious character or ethos.[22]

Section 50(2) provides that the discrimination provisions in s 49 that relate to **4.13** pupils' access to benefits, facilities and services will not apply to anything done in connection with the school curriculum or to acts of worship or other religious observance organized by or on behalf of an educational establishment. The exemption from the non-discrimination requirement also includes elements such as the provision of school library books, which are aimed at the delivery of a broad-based and balanced education to pupils. This particular exemption is aimed at avoiding any conflict with the existing legislative framework in respect of the content of the curriculum and religious worship.[23]

Section 51(1) specifically makes discrimination on grounds of religion or belief **4.14** by LEAs unlawful except in the areas listed in s 51(2). The prohibition contained in s 51(1) first creates an exception in relation to the obligation by the LEA to provide schools pursuant to s 14 EdA 1996. This effectively prevents an LEA from being bound to provide schools for pupils of different faiths or beliefs in the catchment area. Secondly, LEAs are granted an exception in relation to provision for transport for pupils of a particular school located outside the local area. LEAs,

---

[21] EA 2006, s 49(1).
[22] Ibid, s 50(1)(a), (b), (d), (e).
[23] Ibid, s 50(2).

therefore, do not have to provide subsidised transport for all children attending faith or non-faith schools. Thirdly, there is an exception for discrimination in the exercise of responsibilities under s 13 EdA 1996 (to contribute to the spiritual, moral, mental and physical development of the community through their provision of education to children). Section 51(2) allows discrimination in the exercise of these responsibilities in so far as they relate to the two previous points: provision of schools and transport.[24]

4.15 Section 52(1) prohibits discrimination on grounds of religion or belief in the exercise of the functions of all public authorities. Insofar as it is not excepted elsewhere, s 52(4)(k) excepts from the prohibition on discrimination, the exercise of any public functions in a number of areas that relate to faith and non-faith educational institutions. Those areas are (1) the curriculum; (2) collective worship; (3) transport; and (4) establishment, alteration or closure.[25] Section 52(4)(k) excepts further exercises of public functions from the prohibition on discrimination in this section, but only in respect of those schools which have a religious ethos. Those functions are (1) admissions and (2) the selection of members of governing bodies.[26]

4.16 Section 59 provides that it will not be unlawful under the provisions in Part 2 of the EA 2006 for schools with a religious ethos to restrict the provision of goods, facilities or services or to restrict the use or disposal of their premises, to ensure that the purpose for which the premises would be used does not conflict with the tenets of the school's faith (or faiths).[27] Section 61 provides an exception from Part 2 for anything done to meet the special needs of people of particular religions or beliefs in relation to their education, training or welfare, or the provision of ancillary benefits in connection with meeting such needs.[28]

Human Rights Act 1998

4.17 The HRA 1998 has had important implications for education law in general. It is not intended in this chapter to provide a detailed overview of this field but rather to focus on the provisions that relate specifically to freedom of religion, minorities and education.[29]

---

[24] Ibid, s 51(2)(a), (b), (c).
[25] Ibid, s 52(4) (k) (i), (iii), (v) and (vi).
[26] Ibid, s 52(4)(k) (ii) and (iv).
[27] Ibid, s 59(1).
[28] Ibid, s 61.
[29] See S Whitbourn, *Education and the Human Rights Act 1998* (NFER, 2003) and generally R Clayton & H Tomlinson, *The Law of Human Rights* (OUP, 2007) Ch 19; H Mountfield, *The Implications of the Human Rights Act 1998 for the Law of Education* (2000) 1 Education Law Journal 146.

Section 6 HRA 1998

Bodies such as LEAs and the Department for Education and Skills ('DfES') will **4.18**
clearly be considered public authorities within the meaning of s 6 HRA 1998.
The headteacher and governing body of a maintained school will also be considered as such.[30] The position of academies and of the self-governing Trust schools
envisaged in the Schools White Paper is less clear. Academies, although largely
publicly funded, are not maintained schools, are subject to the same regulatory
regime as independent schools, and operate under individual contracts with the
Secretary of State.[31] The government's position is that they should be considered
as public authorities and subject to judicial review.[32] However, the Joint Committee
on Human Rights expresses considerable doubt as to whether they will be treated
by the courts as being functional public authorities for the purposes of the HRA
1998.[33]

As regards independent schools that are privately funded, it seems highly unlikely **4.19**
that they are to be regarded as hybrid public authorities. The relationship between
parents and the governing body of an independent school is entirely different in
nature and is grounded in contract as opposed to public law.[34] That said, there are
a number of factors that would suggest that the provision of education is a function of a public nature and that private education providers might be considered
as public authorities. The state requires all children to receive education whether
in a state or privately funded school or at home in exceptional circumstances. It
also controls and monitors the provision of private education through registration
and inspection.[35]

The cases relating to judicial review are of some relevance and interest, although **4.20**
the test for judicial review is narrower than that relating to s 6 HRA 1998 and
the cases are, therefore, not decisive of the point. The courts have held that city
technology colleges (the predecessors to academies) are subject to judicial review.[36]
Further, in *R v Cobden Hall School, ex p S*[37] it was held that a pupil attending an

---

[30] See *Ali v Headteacher and Governors of Lord Grey School* [2006] UKHL 14; *R (Begum) v Headteacher and Governors of Denbigh High School* [2006] UKHL 26.

[31] See *P v Schools Adjudicator* [2006] EWHC 1934 (QB) [1]. Note that if the proposals in the White Paper (n 7 above) are adopted, the position as regards all state funded schools may be altered.

[32] *Hansard*, HL col WA46 (31 January 2006).

[33] See JCHR, Ninth Report of 2005–06, *Schools White Paper* (HL 113; HC 887).

[34] See *R v Muntham House School, ex p R* [2000] ELR 287 (decision of the governors of a non-maintainable fee-paying school did not have a sufficient public law character to make it amenable to judicial review). See also A Bradley, *Scope for Review: The Convention Right to Education and the Human Rights Act 1998* [1999] EHRLR 395.

[35] See 2.33–2.37 above for further discussion.

[36] See *R v Governor of Haberdashers' Aske's Hatcham College, ex p T* [1995] ELR 350 (judicial review available where a private school performed public functions as a city technology college); *R v Governors of Bacon's City Technology College, ex p W* [1998] ELR 488.

[37] [1998] ELR 389.

independent school on an assisted places scheme may judicially review a scheme to exclude him. But in *R v Fernhill Manor School, ex p A*[38] it was held that a pupil did not have rights in public law against a school merely because the school was subject to the registration regime under the EdA 2002.

4.21 In practice the distinction between state maintained and independent schools for the purposes of the application of ECHR rights may be less important than appears. It is clear from the House of Lords decision of *R (Williamson) v Secretary of State for Education and Employment*[39] that Article 9 and Article 2 Protocol 1 ECHR may be engaged in respect of pupils at independent schools as well as state schools. This position followed from the decision of the European Court of Human Rights ('ECtHR') in *Costello-Roberts v United Kingdom*[40] in which it was held that it was the state's responsibility under Article 1 ECHR to secure ECHR rights to everyone in its jurisdiction. In addition to this, all courts and tribunals are public authorities by virtue of s 6(3)(a) HRA 1998. This means that they have a positive obligation to give effect to the HRA 1998 and to interpret legislation so as to give effect to ECHR rights where possible.

4.22 However, the type of claim and the manner in which it is brought will differ depending on whether the school is a public authority or private. Local authorities and the governing bodies of state funded schools will be under a direct obligation to consider the ECHR rights of individuals as a result of the application of s 6 HRA 1998. A claim may be brought directly against a local authority or governing body of a state school under s 6. However, as regards independent schools, it will not be possible to rely on the direct application of ECHR rights. Rather it will be necessary to rely on their indirect application to a claim based upon a free-standing cause of action such as tort or breach of contract.

Section 13 HRA 1998

4.23 It is not clear whether the reference to a 'religious organization' in s 13 HRA 1998 includes state maintained schools with a religious character, privately financed religious schools or governing bodies made up of religious persons. There is in principle a difference between a state maintained school that has a religious character, and a religious school funded and administered entirely by a religious group, although the lines may not be so clearly drawn in a particular case. The Court of Appeal in *R (Williamson) v Secretary of State for Education and Employment*[41] expressed doubt that Parliament intended the concept of religious organizations to extend to schools, but did not need to decide the issue and therefore did not

---

[38] [1993] 1 FLR 620; [1994] ELR 67.
[39] [2005] UKHL 15.
[40] [1994] ELR 1.
[41] [2002] EWCA Civ 1926 [48] (per Buxton LJ), [181] (per Rix LJ).

consider it in any detail. The point was not developed in the decision of the House of Lords. In practice, the point may be academic as there is considerable doubt in any event as to the effect of s 13 overall.[42]

ECHR rights

In the field of education and freedom of religion, the most important ECHR **4.24** articles are likely to be Article 2 Protocol 1 and Articles 9 and 14. However, other substantive rights may also be relevant. A case involving discipline in schools may additionally engage Article 3; a request for time off school to celebrate a religious holiday may engage Article 8; while Article 10 may be engaged where teachers express their own religious views in a school setting. As regards respect for parental convictions, the ECtHR has expressly stated that the right contained in the second sentence of Article 2 Protocol 1 must be read together with Articles 8, 9 and 10 ECHR.[43] The scope of the rights contained in Articles 9 and 14 is considered in Chapter 2 above including detailed consideration of two House of Lords decisions relevant to Article 9, namely *R (Williamson) v Secretary of State for Education and Employment*[44] and *R (Begum) v Headteacher and Governors of Denbigh High School*.[45] Article 2 Protocol 1 is considered below.

Article 2 Protocol 1 provides: **4.25**

> No person shall be denied the right to education. In the exercise of any functions which it assumes in relation to education and teaching, the state shall respect the right of parents to ensure such education and teaching in conformity with their own religious and philosophical convictions.

The United Kingdom has entered a reservation with regard to Article 2 Protocol 1. **4.26** It provides:

> . . . in view of certain provisions of the Education Acts in force in the United Kingdom, the principle affirmed in the second sentence of Art 2 is accepted by the United Kingdom only so far as it is compatible with the provision of efficient instruction and training and the avoidance of unreasonable public expenditure.[46]

This reservation was entered to reflect the principle now contained in s 9 EdA **4.27** 1996 that provides a qualified respect for parental wishes in education. The effect is to qualify what is otherwise a right that is drafted without a qualifying subsection unlike other rights such as Articles 8–11 ECHR. The ECtHR will have

---

[42] See 2.38–2.39 above.

[43] *Kjeldsen, Busk Madsen and Pedersen v Denmark* (1976) 1 EHRR 711 [52]; *Valsamis v Greece* (1997) 24 EHRR 294 [25].

[44] [2005] UKHL 15.

[45] [2006] UKHL 26. See 2.73–2.74 above. See also 5.22–5.36 below for a discussion and comparison of the application of Art 9 in the context of employment.

[46] See HRA 1998, s 15(5) and Sch 2 Pt II.

regard to the United Kingdom's reservation when considering any case under Article 2 Protocol 1 but will not necessarily uphold the reservation in every case. It will depend upon the seriousness of the circumstances of the case and the importance of the right engaged.[47]

4.28   As regards the drafting of Article 2 Protocol 1, the issue of the right of parents to choose private education for their children was linked closely to freedom of religion. There was concern among the states about the use of education by totalitarian states that sought to exclude the wishes of parents about religious and philosophical education.[48] There was also concern about the funding of secular and religious education, and conversely the extent to which a parent's wishes could give rise to the 'ghettoization' of children according to moral and spiritual beliefs.[49] In the event these issues proved so controversial that this article could not be signed at the same time as the main body of the ECHR.[50]

4.29   Article 2 Protocol 1 provides primarily a right to education and secondarily a right to be educated in accordance with parental convictions. The two aspects of the right must be read together. There is therefore a potential tension within the right itself between a child's right to education and respect for parental beliefs. In addition a child and his parent both have a right to freedom of religion under Article 9. This may also involve a conflict between the respective interests in some cases.[51]

4.30   The ECtHR in *Kjeldsen, Busk Madsen and Pedersen v Denmark*,[52] a case involving the exemption of pupils from sex education, stated that parents are primarily responsible for the education and teaching of their children, and it is in the discharge of that 'natural duty' that the right of parents to require the state to respect their religious and philosophical convictions arises. It further stated that the aim of Article 2 Protocol 1 was to safeguard the possibility of pluralism in education, a possibility which it regarded as essential for the preservation of the democratic

---

[47] In *Angeleni v Sweden* (1988) 10 EHRR 123 Sweden's reservation under Art 2 Protocol 1 was upheld by the Commission in a case concerning exemption from religious instruction. But in *Campbell and Cosans v United Kingdom* (1982) 4 EHRR 293 the ECtHR dismissed an argument by the UK based upon the reservation and unreasonable expenditure in a case concerning corporal punishment in state schools. See also *SP v United Kingdom* (1997) 23 EHRR CD 139, a case concerning special needs education and Art 2 Protocol 1 where the Commission stated that the reservation may not withstand challenge under the ECHR although it did not have to decide the point as the case was inadmissible for other reasons.

[48] See *travaux préparatoires* 1, 128 in Council of Europe, *Collected Edition of the 'Travaux Préparatoires' of the European Convention on Human Rights*.

[49] See generally J Simor (ed), *Human Rights Practice* (Sweet & Maxwell, 2000–); R Clayton & H Tomlinson (n 29 above).

[50] Protocol 1 ECHR, 20 March 1952 entered into force on 18 May 1954.

[51] See 3.36–3.50 above for discussion of the conflict between rights of children and parents.

[52] (1976) 1 EHRR 711 [50]–[53]; see also *X v United Kingdom*, Application 8010/77 (1979) 16 DR 101.

society as conceived by the ECHR. It is therefore accepted at the European level, given the right of parents to choose an education for their children which accords with their religious principles, that the existence of faith schools in a state cannot be challenged as a matter of principle.[53]

The right to education was framed negatively to emphasize the limited obligation on the state to provide educational facilities. The primary obligation under Article 2 Protocol 1 is to secure access to existing educational institutions and the right to an effective education. In *Belgium Linguistic Case (No 2)*,[54] in a case about the right to education in the language of a national minority, the ECtHR stated:

> The negative formulation indicates . . . that the Contracting Parties do not recognise such a right to education as would require them to establish at their expense, or to subsidise, education of any particular type or at any particular level.

The right assumes that the state is primarily responsible for the planning and organization of an education system and that the individual has a right not to be excluded. In *Kjeldsen, Busk Madsen and Pedersen v Denmark*,[55] the ECtHR said that the setting and planning of the curriculum falls within the competence of the states and mainly involves questions of expediency on which it is not for the ECtHR to rule and that the curriculum may legitimately vary according to the country and era. A wide margin of appreciation is therefore likely to be granted in such a case by the ECtHR.

The state, in fulfilling the functions assumed by it in relation to education and teaching, must take care that it conveys information or knowledge in an objective, critical and pluralistic manner. It is forbidden from pursuing an aim of indoctrination that might be considered as not respecting parents' religious or philosophical convictions. But Article 2 Protocol 1 does not prevent states from imparting through education information of a directly religious or philosophical kind. It does not even prevent the integration of such teaching in the curriculum as in practice many subjects have some philosophical implications or complexion or religious aspect.[56] The obligation in Article 2 Protocol 1 extends to the administration of education, including the way in which discipline is enforced.[57]

The use of the word 'respect' in Article 2 Protocol 1 means more than simply acknowledge or take into account. It implies some positive obligation on the part

4.31

4.32

4.33

4.34

---

[53] This is linked to the recognition by the EU that individual states have differing church and state relationships. See 2.04 above.
[54] (1968) 1 EHRR 252, 280 [3].
[55] (1976) 1 EHRR 711 [53].
[56] Ibid.
[57] *Campbell and Cosans v United Kingdom* (1982) 4 EHRR 293 [33].

of the state.[58] The obligation extends to all schools—state and independently funded.[59] There has been considerable debate as to whether it applies to higher education. This will depend upon the availability and spread of higher education in the country concerned.[60] In the United Kingdom, where higher education is widely accessible, it has been accepted that Article 2 Protocol 1 will apply.[61]

4.35 In *Ali v Headteacher and Governors of Lord Grey School*,[62] a case concerning the application of Article 2 Protocol 1 in the context of school exclusions, Lord Bingham summarized the Strasbourg authorities on Article 2 Protocol 1 as follows:

> The underlying premise of the article was that all existing member states of the Council of Europe had, and all future member states would have, an established system of state education. It was intended to guarantee fair and non-discriminatory access to that system by those within the jurisdiction of the respective states. The fundamental importance of education in a modern democratic state was recognised to require no less. But the guarantee is, in comparison with most other Convention guarantees, a weak one, and deliberately so. There is no right to education of a particular kind or quality, other than that prevailing in the state. There is no Convention guarantee of compliance with domestic law. There is no Convention guarantee of education at or by a particular institution . . . . The test, as always under the Convention, is a highly pragmatic one, to be applied to the specific facts of the case: have the authorities of the state acted so as to deny to a pupil effective access to such educational facilities as the state provides for such pupils?

4.36 As regards the meaning of 'philosophical convictions' in Article 2 Protocol 1, the ECtHR has stated that this is more akin to the term 'beliefs' in Article 9 than to 'opinions' and 'ideas' in Article 10 and denotes views which attain a certain level of cogency, seriousness, cohesion and importance. In *Campbell and Cosans v United Kingdom*[63] the ECtHR stated that the term denotes such convictions as are worthy of respect in a democratic society and are not incompatible with human dignity, and which do not conflict with the fundamental right of the child to education. This should not be stretched so as to undermine the basis of human rights protection as a whole, which is to allow for pluralism, dissent and minority views in society.

---

58 Ibid [37]; *Valsamis v Greece* (1996) 24 EHRR 294 [27].
59 *Kjeldsen, Madsen and Pedersen v Denmark* (1970) 1 EHRR 74 [50], [51].
60 In *Belgium Linguistic Case (No 2)* (1968) 1 EHRR 252 [271] the ECtHR, in summarizing the argument of the Commission, stated that as Belgium was a highly developed country, the right to education included entry to nursery, primary, secondary and higher education. See also *Sulak v Turkey*, Application 24515/94 (1996) 84-A DR 98 (Art 2 Protocol 1 did not apply to higher education in Turkey).
61 See *Douglas v North Tyneside Metropolitan Borough Council* [2003] EWCA Civ 1847. See also *Patel v United Kingdom* (1982) 4 EHRR 256 [13]. Note in *X v United Kingdom* (1980) 23 DR 228 the Commission held that Art 2 Protocol 1 did not apply to vocational training.
62 [2006] UKHL 14 [24].
63 (1982) 4 EHRR 293 [36]; see also *Valsamis v Greece* (1996) 24 EHRR 294 [25].

This point was made by the House of Lords in *R (Williamson) v Secretary of State*   **4.37**
for Education and Employment[64] where a narrow definition of religious belief and
philosophical convictions was expressly rejected. Lord Walker stated:

> For the reasons already noted, the court is not equipped to weigh the cogency,
> seriousness and coherence of theological doctrines. Anyone who feels in any doubt
> about that might refer to the hundreds of pages of the law reports devoted to 16 years
> of litigation, in mid-Victorian times, as to the allegedly 'Romish' beliefs and devo-
> tions of the incumbent of St Alban's, Holborn . . . . Moreover, the requirement that
> an opinion should be 'worthy of respect in a "democratic society"' begs too many
> questions. As Mr Diamond (following Mr Dingemans) pointed out, in matters of
> human rights the courts should not show liberal tolerance only to tolerant liberals.[65]

Legal Issues

This section looks at various issues that have arisen in the context of freedom of   **4.38**
religion and education. In each case the relevant domestic statutory provision (if
any) is set out. The issue is then considered in the light of domestic decisions and
relevant ECtHR law. This is a developing area of the law that is likely to see a number of future cases argued under the provisions of the HRA 1998, the EA 2006
and the RRA 1976.

State provision for faith schools

The issue of state funding for new religious schools is a controversial one.[66]   **4.39**
England has a system of state maintained schools, a number of which have a religious character, which is unlikely to change in the near future given the proposals
in the Schools White Paper *Higher Standards: Better Education for All.*[67] There are
approximately 25,000 state funded schools in Britain. Of these in January 2004
there were almost 7,000 state maintained faith schools in England, making up
36 per cent of primary and 17 per cent of secondary schools. The overwhelming
majority of these faith schools (99 per cent) were Christian, ie all but 121. As at
2004 there were 32 Jewish; four Muslim; one Seventh Day Adventist; two Sikh;
one Greek Orthodox and a number of joint faith schools.[68]

---

[64] [2005] UKHL 15.

[65] Ibid [60] and [23] (per Lord Nicholls). See 2.57–2.62 above.

[66] See Commission for Racial Equality, *Schools of Faith* (CRE, 1990); J De Jong & G Snik, 'Why
Should States Fund Denominational Schools?' [2002] 36(4) Journal of Philosophy and Education
32–36; R Jackson, 'Should the State Fund Faith-Based Schools?' A Review of the Arguments [2003]
25(2) British Journal of Religious Education 89–102.

[67] See n 7 above.

[68] See National Office of Statistics: Schools: Annual Schools Census (DfES, January 2004). See
also JM Halstead, 'Faith and Diversity in Religious School Provision' in L Gearon (ed), *Education
in the United Kingdom: Structures and Organisation* (Fulton, 2002) 146–157.

4.40   In the 2001 White Paper *Schools Achieving Success*, the government committed itself in principle to an expansion of the number of state funded faith schools.[69] Since 1995 the government has given approval for a very small number of state Muslim and Sikh schools. But this has only come about after years of campaigning, in particular by Muslim groups. Since 1997 only five Muslim schools have been granted voluntary aided status.[70] There are also a significant number of privately funded faith schools, the vast majority of which are Catholic or Protestant.[71] The introduction of academies, a number of which have religious sponsors (mainly Christian), will also likely increase the number of schools with religious character.

4.41   There are two broad issues that relate to funding for schools and respect for religious beliefs. First, in England the state is not secular and has long provided funding to schools of a religious character—mostly Church of England or Roman Catholic. Increasingly adherents of other faiths, and in particular Muslims, not surprisingly wish to have state funding for schools founded on their own belief or value system. The question of funding may also involve loans, subsidies or other benefits that indirectly benefit persons of some religious groups more than others. Secondly, some religious groups, and many Muslim parents in particular, support single sex schooling for their daughters after puberty.

Domestic law

4.42   The obligation of the state to provide education is now governed primarily by s 14 EdA 1996. Section 14(1) provides that the local education authority shall secure that sufficient schools for providing primary and secondary education are available for the area. Section 14(2) requires the schools to be sufficient in number, character and equipment to provide for all pupils the opportunity of appropriate education. 'Appropriate education' is defined by s 14(3) as meaning education that 'offers such variety of instruction and training as may be desirable in view of (a) the pupils' different ages, abilities and aptitudes, and (b) the different periods for which they may be expected to remain at school including practical instruction and training appropriate to their different needs . . .'[72]

---

[69] Department for Education and Employment, *Schools Achieving Success* (Cmd 5230, 2001) para 5.30.

[70] Ibid 117–134; H Ansari, *Muslims in Britain* (Minority Rights Group International, 2002).

[71] Note also that although international law endorses the provision of separate schools for different religious groups, both the UN Committee on Rights of the Child and the Advisory Committee of the Framework Charter on the Protection of National Minorities have expressed support for integrated education in Northern Ireland for Catholics and Protestants. See Concluding Observations of the Committee on the Rights of the Child: UK, 15 February 1995, UN Doc CRC/C/15/Add 34 para 33; 9 October 2002, UN Doc CRC/C/15/Add 188 para 48; FCPNM Advisory Committee Opinion on the UK, 30 November 2001, para 36.

[72] Cf s 9 EdA 1996 which states that pupils are to be educated in accordance with the wishes of their parents although this is only a general principle and is qualified by compatibility with the provision of efficient instruction and avoidance of unreasonable public expenditure. See *R v Secretary*

The wording of s 14 EdA 1996 is broad enough to be read compatibly with Article 9 **4.43** and Article 2 Protocol 1. Neither Article 9 nor Article 2 Protocol 1 alone provides a challenge to the state funding arrangements as there is no direct obligation on the state to provide for education of a particular type. Further, there is an express exemption contained in the EA 2006 from the prohibition on discrimination on grounds of religion or belief where an LEA is exercising its functions under s 14 EdA 1996.[73]

State funding for faith schools   Even prior to the introduction of the relevant **4.44** provisions in the EA 2006, there was relatively little litigation in this area despite the fact that it is an issue of genuine and pressing concern for many minority religious groups. In *R v Secretary of State for Education and Science, ex p Yusuf Islam*,[74] a challenge against the Secretary of State's refusal to accord voluntary status to an independent Muslim primary school in a London borough was successful, although it was not argued on grounds of discrimination.[75]

On a slightly different point but of some interest in this area, the Court of Appeal **4.45** in *R (Douglas) v North Tyneside Metropolitan Borough Council*[76] considered whether a student loan scheme for higher education that had a cut-off age of 55 amounted to unjustified discrimination under Article 2 Protocol 1 and Article 14 ECHR against a 58 year old man. Having decided that Article 2 Protocol 1 applied to higher education, Scott Baker LJ went on to consider whether the differential treatment complained of under Article 14 was sufficiently linked to the exercise of the particular right. He held that the purpose of the funding arrangements was to encourage greater access to education for students and in turn to improve the skills and qualifications of the workforce. This was contrasted with the right in Article 2 Protocol 1 that was to participate in the education that existed at the time. He stated that the arrangements were not intended to prevent or hamper any individual from undertaking any course and noted that the right contained in Article 2 Protocol 1 was framed in a negative rather than a positive manner.[77]

---

of State for Education, ex p Talmud Torah Machzikei Hadass School Trust, The Times 12 April 1985 (education would be suitable if it primarily equipped a child for life within the community rather than the way of life of the whole country if it did not foreclose on a child's options to adopt some other way of life later). See also *R (R) v Leeds City Council Education* [2005] EWHC 2495 (Admin).

  [73] EA 2006, s 51(2)(a).
  [74] [1994] ELR 111.
  [75] Note that in *Waldman v Canada* Comm No 694/1996, 5 November 1999; (2000) 7 IHRR 368 the UN Human Rights Committee held that the provision of funding in Ontario whereby the only non-secular schools to receive full and direct funding were Roman Catholic, violated the right to equal and effective protection against discrimination under ICCPR Art 26 of a parent of a child who attended a private Jewish school.
  [76] [2003] EWCA Civ 1847.
  [77] At [59].

4.46   The decision may seem as a matter of principle to be too narrow a construction of the protection afforded by Article 14 and Article 2 Protocol 1. It is clear that direct funding of state education may engage ECHR rights. It is hard to see why this should not also apply to indirect funding arrangements such as school vouchers, subsidies and loans. The decision is perhaps best understood in its context. On the facts of the case the claimant completed his higher education without a loan. There were fall-back arrangements in place of fee waiver and hardship grant. In addition, age, unlike religion, is not one of the specified protected groups in Article 14 ECHR. Finally, the Court of Appeal, although it was not strictly necessary to do so, expressed its view that had Article 2 Protocol 1 been engaged, any limitations on the funding arrangement were justified. Importantly, as regards a future challenge to a funding arrangement that sought to discriminate on the grounds of religion, the Court of Appeal expressly considered that this would be a different matter and that the arrangements could be necessarily concerned with the right to education.

4.47   **State funding for single sex schools**   As regards the provision of funding for single sex education on the basis of a general preference, there have been a number of cases before the courts, prior to the enactment of the HRA 1998 and the EA 2006. The additional or separate issue of preference for sex education on religious grounds has not been tested as such and, with exemptions to the prohibition of discrimination provided for in the EA 2006, will limit claims.[78] It may be possible to formulate a claim on the basis of indirect race discrimination depending upon whether the relevant religious group would fall within the provisions of the RRA 1976.

4.48   There have been cases argued on the basis of the Sex Discrimination Act 1975 ('SDA 1975'). In *R v Birmingham City Council, ex p Equal Opportunities Commission*,[79] the House of Lords held that an LEA breached s 23 SDA 1975 if it knowingly maintained a system of education in its area under which girls had considerably fewer opportunities for selective education than boys. This was the case even if the LEA had no power to alter the situation because the schools were voluntarily aided. This meant that it could not in practice cease to maintain schools without the consent of the Secretary of State. Further, it could not change the status of the schools without the consent of the governing body and Secretary of State. Such consents were in the circumstances unlikely to be forthcoming.[80]

---

[78] EA 2006, s 51(2)(a).

[79] [1989] AC 1155.

[80] See also *R v Northamptonshire County Council, ex p K* [1994] ELR 397 (LEA in breach of SDA 1975 where it was under a duty to close a school because it could no longer provide adequate standards of education).

Following this decision, it was held in a number of other cases in the lower courts   **4.49**
that there was no breach of s 23 SDA 1975 on the facts. In *R v Birmingham City
Council, ex p Equal Opportunities Commission (No 2)*[81] it was held that the LEA
was not in breach of s 23 SDA 1975 where an imbalance occurred partly due to
existence of grant maintained schools. The relevant pool for consideration was
considered to be all the schools in the area rather than only the schools maintained
by the LEA.

ECHR law

The European cases themselves are highly fact and country specific and not   **4.50**
necessarily determinative of the outcome in domestic cases. However, the general
principles of non-discrimination and the need to justify any discrimination are
evident from the cases and should be adhered to. Primarily, the area of education
and discrimination will be a matter for the domestic authorities to consider and
adjudicate upon.

In the most recent case in this area, *Verein Gemeinsam Lernen v Austria*,[82] a challenge   **4.51**
was made to the state's unequal subsidy of private schools. The applicant association set up and ran a non-religious private school and complained that subsidies
were allocated to church schools on a more favourable basis contrary to Article 2
Protocol 1 together with Article 14. The Commission found that the different
treatment of church schools was justified in terms of Article 14 because the church
schools were so widespread. If the education services they provided fell to be met
by the state, there would be a considerable burden on the state as it would have to
make up the shortfall.[83]

In this context, the Commission and ECtHR have allowed a wide margin of appre-   **4.52**
ciation in considering any arguments on justification put forward by the state. In
practice the ECtHR is likely to give considerable weight to arguments put forward
by the United Kingdom on the grounds of financial constraints, the practicalities
of organizing and running a state education system, and the inherent difficulties
in trying to adopt measures to satisfy everyone.

School admissions

Parents with particular religious or philosophical convictions may prefer to send   **4.53**
their children to a school that reflects their beliefs. Correspondingly, faith schools,

---

[81] [1993] 1 FLR 338. See also *R v Secretary of State for Education, ex p Parveen Malik* [1994] ELR
121 (not unlawful to close school despite lack of single sex schools in the area); *R v Secretary of State
for Education, ex p Avon (No 2)* (1990) 88 LGR 737, (1990) *The Times* 15 June 1990.
[82] (1995) 20 EHRR CD 78.
[83] See also *W and KL v Sweden,* Application 10476/83 (1985) 45 DR 143 (no duty to subsidise
a Rudolf Steiner school); *X v United Kingdom*, Application 7782/77 (1978) 14 DR 179 (no violation
of Art 14 for unequal funding of denominational and non-denominational schools).

particularly those of minority religions, may wish to favour applications from pupils of the same religion or may have a quota establishing a fixed proportion of religious adherents.[84] There is flexibility in the system to allow for parental preference and conversely express provision in the EA 2006 for schools with religious character to maintain that character in their admission policy. There are two main issues to be considered here. First, although there is clear provision in the statutory framework for parents to express a choice and give reasons for that choice, it is not clear what weight religious convictions are to be given as opposed to other factors. Secondly, how a school itself determines religious preference may give rise to controversies over the relative religiosity of different parents and pupils.

Domestic law

4.54 The law on preference in admissions is now governed by s 86(1)–(3) SSFA 1998. Section 86(1) provides that an LEA shall enable parents to express a preference as to the school and give reasons for that preference. The LEA must comply with that preference unless any of the exceptions in s 86(3) and s 87 apply. Section 86(3) provides for exception on grounds of (a) prejudice to the provision of efficient education or the efficient use of resources; or (b) where preference would be incompatible with selection on the basis of ability or aptitude.[85]

4.55 As regards faith schools that wish to prefer on the basis of religious convictions, they may only do so if the school is oversubscribed. If the number of pupils to be admitted is lower than the number under s 89 SSFA 1998, then the LEA and the governing body have no power to refuse admission to a pupil whose parent expresses a preference under s 86(1) for that school.[86]

4.56 The School Admissions Code of Practice for England refers to policies that may be applied in the event of oversubscription to a school.[87] The Code in force at the date of writing expressly envisages that schools with a religious character will want

---

[84] Note that the government has rejected the idea of introducing quotas limiting the number of admissions from one particular cultural or religious group. See *Community Cohesion: A Report of the Independent Review Team, Chaired by Ted Cantle* (Home Office, 2001) paras 6.38–6.39.

[85] Note that SSFA 1998, ss 86(3)(b), (6) and 91 (special arrangement to preserve religious character of foundation or voluntary aided schools) were repealed by EdA 2002, Sch 4 para 3 and Sch 22 Pt 3.

[86] Faith schools cannot now agree 'special arrangements' with the LEA to keep places empty if they do not have sufficient applications from their pupils of the preferred religion: see EA 2002, s 49 (repealing SSFA 1998, s 91). Note that in *R v Stockton-on-Tees Borough Council, ex p W* [2000] ELR 93, the Court of Appeal decided that an LEA could refuse admission to a pupil even where it subsequently planned to admit further pupils to the school where parents moved into the catchment area. Hyams (n 4 above) at 329 fn 3 notes this appears to be contrary to s 85(6) SSFA 1998 and to the Schools Admissions Code of Practice for England (DfES/0031/2003) para 7.9.

[87] Note that at the date of writing, a new School Admission Code, School Admissions Appeals Code and Admissions Regulation were under consultation. The new codes came into force in February 2007, first affecting school admissions in 2008.

an admissions policy based on religious preference.[88] But it should not conflict with other legislation such as race relations legislation. However, it is not contrary to the RRA 1976 for a parent to express a preference on racial grounds and for this preference to be taken into consideration by the LEA.[89] The EA 2006 provides that schools with a religious ethos are exempted from the prohibition against discrimination on grounds of religion or belief in relation to admission of pupils.[90]

Parental preference on religious grounds The most common reason for not complying with parental preference is oversubscription to the particular school. This gives rise to the issue of the weighing up of various reasons given by parents for their choice and whether religion is simply one of a number of factors or whether it has any additional or overriding weight.[91]   **4.57**

In *R (O) v St James Roman Catholic Primary School Appeal Panel*[92] the High Court accepted without deciding the point that Article 8 ECHR can be engaged by an admissions decision to a state maintained religious school, where one sibling is already attending. It also accepted on the same basis that the right to respect for parents' convictions under Article 2 Protocol 1 may also be engaged.[93]   **4.58**

In *R (K) v London Borough of Newham*,[94] Collins J had to consider a challenge by a Muslim father who wished his daughter to attend a single sex school due to his religious convictions. The form for stating school preference did not enable a parent to state the reasons for choosing a single sex school and ultimately his daughter was rejected for admission. The court stated that due weight must be given to the religious convictions of a parent as a result of incorporation by the HRA 1998 of Article 2 Protocol 1 ECHR and that there was no question that this was an important consideration.[95] Collins J held that in the context of an admission case both the LEA and appeal panel must therefore give due weight to the fact that a parent's desire for single sex education stems from a real religious conviction.[96] This suggested that there should be a means of identifying religious conviction and that   **4.59**

---

[88] (DfES/0031/2003) para 3.9.

[89] See *R v Cleveland County Council, ex p Commission for Racial Equality* [1994] ELR 44.

[90] EA 2006, s 50(1).

[91] SSFA 1998, s 86(3)(a). See *R v Sheffield City Council, ex p M* [2000] ELR 85.

[92] [2001] ELR 469 [36].

[93] Note that in *T v Special Educational Needs Tribunal* [2002] ELR 704 the parents of an autistic child appealed against a decision that the child should be educated at a centre for autistic children based at a mainstream school. The parents wished him to be educated at home under the Lovaas programme. The court held that this preference did not amount to a philosophical conviction within the meaning of Art 2 Protocol 1. This decision appears to be based on the grounds that it relates to special needs education. It is difficult to reconcile with the approach in *R (Williamson) v Secretary of State for Education and Employment* [2005] UKHL 15; see also Clayton & Tomlinson (n 29 above) Ch 19.

[94] [2002] EWHC 405 (Admin).

[95] Ibid [29].

[96] Ibid [38].

---

attention could be drawn to this criteria on the relevant pamphlet or guidance note issued by the LEA.[97]

4.60 It is plainly important that due weight is given to the preference of the parent and that the rights of parent and child under Articles 9, 14 and Article 2 Protocol 1 are considered by the education authority in making a decision about admission. The approach taken by the courts to date would suggest that religion is simply one of a number of factors that will be taken into account, rather than there being an obligation to give it special weight.

4.61 The practical impossibility of avoiding discrimination was referred to by the Court of Appeal in *Schools Admissions Appeals Panel for the London Borough of Hounslow v London Borough of Hounslow*.[98] The appeal raised the general issue of the relationship between school admission appeals panels and local education authorities. It was held in the case that the School Admissions Appeal Panel's task under SSFA 1998, Sch 24 para 12 was not simply to rubber stamp the local education authority's decision, nor to take the original decision again. It could only uphold an appeal if it concluded that it was perverse in the light of the admission arrangements to refuse to admit the particular child. The Court of Appeal recognized that the panel and court were public authorities within s 6 HRA 1998 and that the court must take into account decisions of the ECtHR. It emphasized the importance of the requirement that discrimination has reasonable objective justification. In that case reference was made to proximity to the school and to children with elder siblings at the school, rather than to discrimination on religious grounds as a factor.

4.62 **Selective admissions policies in faith schools**   Even prior to the introduction of the relevant provisions in the EA 2006, the court upheld admissions policies based on religion in a number of cases involving state maintained schools with a religious character. In *R v Lancashire, ex p M*,[99] the High Court considered the legality of admissions criteria for non-denominational county schools that gave preference to those who had not attended Roman Catholic primary schools. It held that the school appeal committee was not acting unreasonably if it took religion into account. Similarly, in *R v Lancashire County Council, ex p F*,[100] the Divisional Court upheld a policy by a non-Roman Catholic school that rejected admissions from Roman Catholic pupils in favour of those who were non-Roman

---

[97] Ibid [39], [40]. But see *A v Special Educational Needs and Disability Tribunal and London Borough of Barnet* [2003] EWHC 3368 (Admin). See also in relation to special needs and religious belief: *R v Secretary of State for Education, ex p E* [1996] ELR 312; *G v London Borough of Barnet* [1998] ELR 480.

[98] [2002] EWCA Civ 900 [62].

[99] [1994] ELR 478.

[100] [1995] ELR 33.

Catholic in the event of oversubscription. Reference was made in the judgment to the fact that without such a policy those who were not Roman Catholics would not receive places.[101] Future challenges in this area are likely to be difficult, although the Privy Council in *Bishop of Roman Catholic Diocese of Port Louis v Tengur*[102] is of interest in this context. In that case a system for allocating places at a Roman Catholic secondary school whereby half the intake was Roman Catholic amounted to discrimination in the public domain and was therefore contrary to s 16 of the Constitution of Mauritius.[103]

A related issue that may continue to arise is as to the manner in which schools determine the relative religiosity of prospective pupils and parents. The Code states that admission criteria should be clearly defined and capable of being assessed objectively.[104] The requirement of objective assessment creates a particular problem in relation to religion.[105] The current Code expressly prohibits such interviews except for assessing the suitability of a child for a boarding place.[106] But it does allow for auditions to test aptitude for schools with specialism in a prescribed subject or discussion of subject choice for sixth form admissions.[107]

4.63

In *Governing Body of the London Oratory School v Schools Adjudicator*,[108] a challenge was made to the prohibition of interviews on a number of grounds including breach of ECHR rights. The complaint as regards Article 2 Protocol 1 was that written application forms were sometimes unreliable and that because the school was heavily oversubscribed, experience showed that interviews were an effective solution. The removal of interviewing affected both future and current pupils and would change the ethos of the schools as pupils were admitted with a lesser commitment to the Catholic faith. Jackson J, in rejecting this argument, held that although the claimant parents had a right to education in conformity with their

4.64

---

[101] At 40. See also *R v Governor of the Bishop Challenor Roman Catholic School, ex p Choudhury* [1992] AC 182 (Roman Catholic school can give priority to Christians where applications exceed available places).

[102] [2004] UKPC 9.

[103] See also *St Stephen's College v University of Delhi* (1992) AIR SC 1630; *TMA Pai Foundation v State of Karnataka* (2003) AIR SC 355.

[104] (DfES/0031/2003) para 3.6.

[105] In *R v Governors of La Sainte Union Convent School* [1996] ELR 98 leave for judicial review was granted on the basis that a baptism certificate was evidence that at least one parent was a practising Roman Catholic.

[106] Note *R (L) v Admissions Appeal Panel for Sacred Heart High School* (decision of Scott Baker J, 2 May 2001) decided under a previous version of the Code that allowed for admissions interviews, where a mother challenged the refusal to admit her daughter to a Catholic school following a written application and interviews. It shows the considerable difficulty in determining the relative commitment to faith of prospective pupils and parents.

[107] (DfES/0031/2003) para 3.16. Note that a new Admission Code came into force in February 2007 (see n 87 above).

[108] [2004] EWHC 3014 (Admin).

Catholic faith, this was not elevated to a right to be educated at the Oratory school. As regards the lesser commitment factor, he noted the potential effect but stated that the school would still remain a Catholic school and religious worship and Catholic activities would be an important part of school life such that it could not be said that the rights of existing pupils and parents under Article 2 Protocol 1 would be infringed by the removal of the interviewing process.[109]

4.65 The issue of how to establish religious convictions objectively is a hazardous one for local authorities. This is equally true for secular adjudicators, tribunals and courts that are ill-equipped for this exercise. The protection of subjective and individual beliefs contained in Article 9 and Article 2 Protocol 1 makes any objective assessment of religious beliefs by secular authorities problematic. This was expressly recognized by the House of Lords in *R (Williamson) v Secretary of State for Education and Employment*.[110] The focus by the court in these cases is likely to be in determining whether a fair procedure for making such a determination has been invoked.

4.66 One area which may be worth considering further is whether an admission policy into a faith school may be indirectly discriminatory under the RRA 1976 and/or Article 14. Many faith schools have, for example, oversubscription criteria based on attendance at certain churches for a specific number of years. Such policies have the potential to discriminate against recent immigrants who are less likely to have been in the country for long enough. Requirements to attend specific churches may also discriminate against recent immigrants who may prefer to attend churches with services in their language. There are no cases directly on point, although it is an area which may see future challenges to these policies as being unlawful.[111]

ECHR law

4.67 As referred to above, Article 2 Protocol 1 does not require a state to provide education of a particular type. It must also follow from this that it will not guarantee admission to a school of a particular type. But it is clear that the state has an obligation to safeguard ECHR rights and to ensure that admissions policy is carried out in accordance with Articles 9, 14 and Article 2 Protocol 1. As regards the right of access to education, in *Belgium Linguistic Case (No 2)* the ECtHR recognized that Article 2 Protocol 1 imposes an obligation on the state to ensure that no one is denied access to the educational institutions existing at a given time.[112] But it

---

[109] At [58]–[59]. Note that the Adjudicator's determination was quashed on other grounds and the school was permitted to interview candidates in the round of applications for September 2005 due to the lateness of the application. For future years should the governors wish to interview then any objection can be put before the Schools Adjudicator and the issues considered afresh: [64]–[65].

[110] [2005] UKHL 15.

[111] See eg factual scenario in *R v Bradford Metropolitan Borough Council, ex p Sikander Ali* [1994] ELR 299 which might have given rise to such a challenge.

[112] (1968) 1 EHRR 252 [4].

held that there was no right for individuals to be taught in a language of their own choice (or that of their parents). Nor was there a right of access to a particular school of choice.[113]

The curriculum

In England from the 1960s onwards there has been a development towards non-confessional religious education syllabuses, which emphasized the study of world religions and avoided advocating any particular religion.[114] However, the EdA 1988 required schools to offer a basic curriculum which included religious education and to reflect the fact that the religious traditions in Britain are in the main Christian whilst taking account of the teachings and practices of the other principal religions.[115] It reaffirmed the requirement of a daily act of worship and specified that this should be wholly or mainly of a broadly Christian character. **4.68**

The provision in the statutory framework for exemptions from religious education and religious worship in state maintained schools have alleviated the risk of potential grievances by parents. However, there are still a number of possible areas of controversy. First, minority religious groups may wish more than an exemption and may desire the state to provide for a form of religious instruction or worship in accordance with their beliefs. Secondly, there is an issue in relation to academies and independent schools and whether individual pupils may be exempt from religious instruction and worship. Thirdly, there is a question of whether individual pupils may be exempt from other subjects such as sex education or mixed sports lessons. **4.69**

Domestic law

It is the duty of the Secretary of State, LEA and governing body or headteacher of every maintained school to ensure that the curriculum at their school is balanced and broadly based and promotes the spiritual, moral, cultural, mental and physical development of the pupils at the school and of society.[116] They have a duty to secure that the National Curriculum is implemented in relation to the school.[117] Every maintained school is required to follow a basic curriculum that includes **4.70**

---

[113] See *Verein Gemeinsam Lernen v Austria* (1995) 20 EHRR CD 78; *X v United Kingdom*, Application 7782/77 (1978) 14 DR 179.

[114] See P Cumper, *School Worship: Praying for Guidance* [1998] 1 EHRLR 45 for a summary of arguments for and against worship as part of the school curriculum. See also C Hamilton & B Watt, *A Discriminating Education—Collective Worship in Schools* [1996] Child and Family Law Quarterly 28.

[115] Note that the UN Special Rapporteur on the Right to Education welcomed the continued presence of religious education on the curriculum in England as it added a spiritual dimension to education: Right to Education: Mission to the United Kingdom of Great Britain and Northern Ireland (England), 9 December 1999, UN Doc E/CN4/2000/6/Add 2 para 84.

[116] EdA 2002, s 78.

[117] Ibid, ss 88, 109.

provision for religious education for all pupils and sex education for pupils in secondary schools.[118] Under the EdA 1996 and the SSFA 1998 there is an 'agreed syllabus' of religious education. Section 375(3) EdA 1996 provides that 'every agreed syllabus shall reflect the fact that the religious traditions in Great Britain are in the main Christian whilst taking account of the teaching and practices of the other principal religions represented in Great Britain'.[119]

4.71   In a community school or a foundation or voluntary school without a religious character, the religious education should be in accordance with the agreed syllabus.[120] The education should not favour any particular religious denomination.[121] At a foundation or voluntary controlled school with a religious character, the religious education required by s 69(1) SSFA 1998 must be in accordance with an agreed syllabus adopted for the school.[122] The religious education to be given at a voluntary aided school with a religious character must be made in accordance with any provisions of the trust deed of the school or, if there is no provision in the deed, in accordance with the tenets of the religion or religious denomination specified in relation to the school.[123]

4.72   Each pupil in a maintained school must take part in an act of collective worship on each school day unless his parent requests that he be wholly or partly excused from such worship under s 71 SSFA 1998.[124] At a special occasion the governing body may decide that the worship should take place elsewhere than on the school premises.[125] The worship in a community school or a foundation school without a religious character must be 'wholly or mainly of a broadly Christian character'.[126] The education will be broadly of a Christian character if it 'reflects the broad traditions of Christian belief without being distinctive of any particular Christian tradition'.[127] Not every act of collective worship has to be of a Christian character as long as, taking the school term as a whole, most such acts within the school are of that character.[128] The character of the worship should be appropriate having regard to the family backgrounds of the pupils, their ages and aptitudes.[129]

---

118 Ibid, ss 80, 101.
119 EdA 1996, Sch 31 provides for the convening by an LEA of conferences for the purpose of reconsidering any agreed syllabus no later than five years from the date of the adoption of the syllabus or recommendation by a conference that the syllabus should continue.
120 SSFA 1998, s 69(1).
121 Ibid, Sch 19 para 2(5).
122 Ibid, Sch 19 para 3(2) and (3).
123 Ibid, Sch 19 para 3(4). In certain circumstances the religious education will be in accordance with an agreed syllabus adopted by the LEA: see Sch 19 para 4(2).
124 Ibid, s 70(1).
125 Ibid, Sch 20 para 2(6).
126 Ibid, Sch 20 paras 3(2) and (4).
127 Ibid, Sch 20 para 3(3).
128 Ibid, Sch 20 para 3(4).
129 Ibid, Sch 20 paras 3(5) and (6).

The exception to this provision for religious worship is where a standing advisory council on religious education has determined that this is not appropriate for the particular school.[130] The EA 2006 provides exemptions to the prohibition of discrimination on grounds of religion or belief to avoid any conflict with the existing legislative framework in respect of the content of the curriculum and religious worship.[131]

There are statutory exemptions from the provisions for religious education and worship in s 71 SSFA 1998. This permits the parent of a pupil at a maintained school (other than a special school) to request that the pupil be wholly or partly excused from receiving religious education or from attendance at religious worship. A pupil may also be withdrawn from a maintained school to allow him to receive religious education elsewhere but only where the LEA is satisfied that this will not interfere with the pupil's attendance at school except at the beginning or end of a school session.[132]   **4.73**

As regards sex education the Secretary of State must issue guidance to secure that when sex education is given to pupils in maintained schools, they are protected from teaching and materials that are inappropriate having regard to the age and religious and cultural background of the pupils.[133] On the request of a parent, a pupil at a maintained school may be wholly or partly excused from receiving all such sex education that is not comprised in the National Curriculum. No pupil can be required to attend or abstain from attending Sunday school or a place of religious worship as a condition of attending a maintained school.[134] The National Curriculum does not apply to academies or to independent schools although they may choose to follow it and in practice many do.   **4.74**

State maintained schools   There has been little litigation in this area, even before the EA 2006 came into force which creates exemptions for religious worship and the curriculum. This is despite of the fact that the current statutory framework is clearly based upon the teaching of one particular religious tradition, which seems out of kilter with the notion of the multi-cultural society and may not reflect the religious beliefs of the majority in any event.[135]   **4.75**

One exception is *R v Secretary of State for Education, ex p R and D*,[136] in which McCullough J had to consider whether the religious education at a school had   **4.76**

---

[130] EdA 1996, s 394 and in relation to the constitution of standing advisory councils on religious education see ss 390–3.

[131] EdA 2006, s 50(2).

[132] SSFA 1998, s 71(3).

[133] EdA 1996, s 403(1A) as inserted by LSA 2000, s 148.

[134] EdA 1996, s 398.

[135] See A Mawhinney, 'The Opt-Out Clause: Imperfect Protection for the Right to Freedom of Religion in Schools' [2006] ELJ 102.

[136] [1994] ELR 495, 499.

been integrated into the secular curriculum to the extent that it was not possible to withdraw solely from religious education. The argument was rejected on the facts but the judge also referred to the policy behind s 9 of the Education Reform Act 1988 as contemplating that pupils who did not come from Christian families should be able to take part in the daily act of collective worship even though those would, in the main, reflect the broader traditions of Christian belief.

4.77 **Academies and independent schools**   Independent schools are not bound by the National Curriculum although in practice many follow it. The question of whether exemptions may be requested from religious education and worship in independent schools is a slightly different one although it is clear that the ECHR rights may be engaged from the decision in *R (Williamson) v Secretary of State for Education and Employment*.[137] As regards interference with ECHR rights, it will depend very much on the manner and form of the religious teaching and worship. If, for example, one particular religion is taught by teachers who are themselves religious and it is taught as an absolute truth rather than from a more objective standpoint, then a pupil who is not of that religion may have good grounds for seeking an exemption. If, however, religious instruction takes a more historical or philosophical approach and covers major world religions as opposed to simply one religion then it may be more difficult for a pupil or parent to claim an interference with his ECHR rights. Similar issues will arise as regards worship although here it is more likely that an exemption would be justified. An interesting question is the role of freedom of choice and freedom of contract and the right to exit a particular school.[138]

4.78 **Sex education, sports and science**   There are a number of ways in which other subjects contained in a school curriculum may conflict with certain religious beliefs. Sex education is a highly contentious subject not only on religious grounds. Sports lessons may also conflict in some instances if they are not taught in a single sex environment. Another area of controversy, particularly relevant in the United States, is the teaching of theories about the origin of the species as part of biology lessons. In fact almost any subject within a curriculum could potentially impinge upon the belief system of a pupil or his parent. But it would plainly cause great difficulties for schools, teachers and pupils in general if certain pupils were able to obtain exemptions on religious grounds from subjects in which religion is incidental. In addition there may be compelling reasons as a matter of public policy and on the basis of best interests of the child for ensuring that information on certain subjects is provided to all pupils.

---

[137] [2005] UKHL 15.
[138] This point was relied upon in *R (Begum) v Headteacher and Governors of Denbigh High School* [2006] UKHL 26.

ECHR law

As regards the National Curriculum, the ECtHR has acknowledged that the **4.79** setting and planning of the curriculum are matters that fall, in principle, within the competence of the states.[139] In *Kjeldsen, Busk Madsen and Pedersen v Denmark*[140] the Danish education authorities had set out an integrated curriculum for schools which included the teaching of sexual education. The parents of several children complained that this offended their religious beliefs and argued that such teaching should be given in the home. The ECtHR noted in this case that the setting and planning of the curriculum mainly involved questions of expediency, on which it was not for the ECtHR to rule and whose solution may legitimately vary according to the country and the era. It also held that Article 2 Protocol 1 did not prevent states from imparting through teaching or education, information or knowledge of a directly or indirectly religious or philosophical kind and did not even permit parents to object to the integration of such teaching or education in the school curriculum. But it noted that the state must make sure that the context in which it is presented is objective, critical and pluralistic.[141]

In *Angeleni v Sweden*,[142] an atheist mother and daughter claimed a breach of **4.80** Articles 9, 14 and Article 2 Protocol 1 because the daughter was not given an exemption from religious instruction classes. The application under Article 2 Protocol 1 was dismissed as the Swedish government had entered a reservation stating that exemptions from teachings in Christianity could only be granted to 'children of another faith than the Swedish Church in respect of whom a satisfactory religious instruction has been arranged'. In rejecting the Article 9 claim, the

---

[139] Note that the UN monitoring bodies have taken a similar approach and have maintained that instruction in subjects such as the general history of religion and ethics is permissible if 'it is given in a neutral and objective way'. See eg ICCPR General Comment No 22, Art 18, 48th Session 1993, para 6; ICESCR General Comment No 13, Art 13, 21st Session 1999, para 28.

[140] (1976) 1 EHRR 711.

[141] See also *Alonso and Merino v Spain*, Application 51188/99 (25 May 2000) (admissibility decision) (complaint by parents about sex education classes taught as part of natural science curriculum held to be inadmissible following *Kjeldsen*). Note too that the UN Human Rights Committee has held that a course in the history of religion and ethics did not breach Art 18(4) ICCPR if it was 'given in a neutral and objective way and respects the belief of parents and guardians who do not believe in any religion': *Hartikainen v Finland*, Communication No 40/1978, Human Rights Committee, Selected Decisions under the Optional Protocol, 19 April 1981 (12th session). See also Art 5(1)(B) of the UNESCO Convention Against Discrimination in Education which expressly provides that 'no person or group of persons should be compelled to receive religious instruction inconsistent with his or their convictions'.

[142] (1988) 10 EHRR 123. Note too *Folgero v Norway*, Application 15472/02 (14 February 2006) (applicant parents' complaints of violations of Art 9 and Art 2 Protocol 1 where their children were refused exemption from religion, Christianity and philosophy teaching raised complex issues of fact and law and were declared admissible).

Commission noted that Article 9 essentially afforded protection against indoctrination of religion by the state. Article 14 was also rejected as the Commission noted that the aim of the Swedish policy of providing all children with sufficient factual religious knowledge was a legitimate aim for the purposes of Article 14. It further noted that she had in fact been exempted from most religious instruction and that the Swedish government aimed at teaching about religion and not in religion.[143]

4.81   As regards worship in the school, there have not been any cases at the European level of actual forced worship. But in *Valsamis v Greece*,[144] the applicants, who were Jehovah's Witnesses, complained of the penalty of one day's suspension imposed on their daughter for refusing to take part in a school parade and cited Article 2 Protocol 1 and Articles 3, 9, and 13. They claimed that participation by their daughter in a National Day parade violated their deeply held commitment to pacifism, which forbade any conduct or practice associated with war or violence. As regards Article 2 Protocol 1, the majority of the ECtHR expressed surprise that the state curriculum required a pupil to parade on a national holiday but stated that it could not discern anything, either in the purpose of the parade or in the arrangements made for it, that could offend the applicants' pacifist convictions. As regards Article 9 the ECtHR noted at the outset that the applicant was exempted from religious education and the Orthodox mass on the grounds of her own religious beliefs. Having already held that the obligation to take part in the parade was not such as to offend her parents' religious conviction, it rejected the claim under Article 9.[145]

4.82   The position of the ECtHR is that the state is primarily responsible for matters of organization of a curriculum. The underlying concern is to protect against indoctrination and forced worship but not to prevent a state from setting up an integrated curriculum that teaches religion in a neutral manner. Overall the ECtHR and Commission have been highly deferential to the needs of the state

---

[143]   See also *CJ, JJ and EJ v Poland*, Application 23380/94 (1996) 84-A DR 46 (no discrimination or breach of Art 9 in a case where children were exempt from religious instruction but effectively required to reveal that fact in their class certificates); *Bernard v Luxembourg*, Application 17187/90 (1993) 75 DR 57 (admissibility decision). See also concern of the UN Committee on the Rights of the Child that it should not entail students having to reveal their religious beliefs: Concluding Observations of the Committee on the Rights of the Child: Greece, 1 February 2002, UN Doc CRC/C/15/Add 170 para 44; Norway, 25 April 1994, UN Doc CRC/C/15/Add 23 para 9.

[144]   (1997) 24 EHRR 294.

[145]   Note that two judges of the ECtHR in a joint dissenting opinion found that there had been a violation of both Art 2 Protocol 1 and Art 9. In their view the parents' perception of the parade had to be accepted by the ECtHR unless obviously unfounded and unreasonable. The majority decision should also be compared to the decision in *Darby v Sweden* (1991) 13 EHRR 774 in which the Commission held that being forced to pay taxes to a church to which one did not belong had serious implications for the *forum internum*. See also US Supreme Court in *West Virginia State Board of Education v Barnette* 319 US 624 (1943) (court upheld exemptions from flag saluting for Jehovah's Witness children).

and the historical role of established churches in Europe in questions of worship and religious teaching.

Religious symbols in schools

The United Kingdom has not sought to legislate directly on the issue of religious symbols including clothing in state maintained schools. The resulting situation is one of considerable plurality—some schools have uniform policies, while others do not. Some schools have prescribed alternative uniforms to take into account the religious and cultural traditions of their pupils. There are good arguments for having a uniform policy during the years of compulsory education and a DfES survey has found that a majority of parents were in favour of a uniform policy.[146] Equally the degree of diversity that exists across England would suggest that a certain amount of accommodation is possible even with a uniform policy. The key issue in this area is whether in schools that prescribe a uniform policy there should be exemptions made to that policy to accommodate religious needs. An issue that has not been contentious to date in England is the existence of religious symbols in schools such as crosses on classroom walls.[147] **4.83**

Domestic law

School uniform policy is principally a matter for school governing bodies. There is no specific provision in the legislative framework relating to accommodation of religious traditions and cultural needs as regards clothing and symbols in the school. There is guidance issued by the DfES on school uniform including clothing required for physical education.[148] It states that governing bodies should consult parents for their views and concerns before deciding on the introduction of a new uniform policy or amending an existing one.[149] It advises that schools must be sensitive to needs of different cultures, races and religions and refers to the expectation that schools should accommodate those needs within a general uniform policy. For example Muslim girls should be allowed to wear appropriate dress and Sikh boys to wear traditional headdress.[150] The uniform policy should not discriminate on the grounds of gender.[151] Importantly the DfES does not consider it appropriate that any pupil should be disciplined for non-compliance with **4.84**

---

146 DfES Survey published 9 May 2003.

147 See generally R McManus, 'School Uniform and the European Convention on Human Rights' [2006] ELJ 87; S Knights, 'Religious Symbols in Schools: Freedom of Religion and Education' [2005] EHRLR 499; D McGoldrick, *Human Rights and Religion—The Islamic Headscarf Debate in Europe* (Hart, 2006).

148 DfES Circular 1264/2002.

149 Ibid, para 4.

150 Ibid, para 10.

151 Ibid, para 12.

a school uniform policy which results from them having to adhere to a particular cultural, race or religious code.[152]

4.85 **Accommodation in uniform policy** This issue was considered most recently by the House of Lords in *R (Begum) v Headteacher and Governors of Denbigh High School*.[153] In that case a female Muslim pupil challenged the decision of the school not to permit her to wear a jilbab (full length gown) to school by an application for judicial review with reference to Article 9 and Article 2 Protocol 1. The school had a majority of Muslim pupils. In consultation with representatives of the local Muslim community it had designated an alternative uniform based on the shalwar khameez which permitted the wearing of a hijab specifically to accommodate local religious and cultural needs. This was not satisfactory for the appellant whose own religious beliefs required her to wear a more covered form of dress to school. A majority of the Lords held that there had been no interference with her rights given that she had a choice of two alternative schools where she would have been permitted to wear her jilbab.[154] The minority argued that there was likely an interference on the facts but that it was justified in the circumstances.[155]

4.86 The House of Lords in *Begum* cited the decision of the Grand Chamber in *Sahin v Turkey*[156] as recognizing the high importance of Article 9, the value of religious harmony and tolerance between opposing or competing groups, and of pluralism and broadmindedness, the need for compromise and balance, the role of the state in deciding what is necessary to protect the rights and freedoms of others, the variation of practice and tradition among member states, and the permissibility in some contexts of restricting the wearing of religious dress.[157] Lord Bingham formed the view that in the situation whereby the school had taken advice, and had been told that its policy conformed with the requirements of mainstream Muslim opinion, the school was fully justified in acting as it did. He noted that the school had enjoyed a period of harmony and success to which the uniform policy was thought to contribute and that it was feared that acceding to the request to wear the jilbab would or might have significant adverse repercussions. In those circumstances it would be 'irresponsible of any court, lacking the experience, background and detailed knowledge of the headteacher, staff and governors, to overrule their judgment on a matter as sensitive as this'.[158]

---

152 Ibid, para 11.
153 [2006] UKHL 15.
154 At [24] (per Lord Bingham).
155 At [92] (per Baroness Hale). See 2.73–2.74 above.
156 (2005) 41 EHRR 8.
157 Ibid [32].
158 Ibid [34].

Lord Nicholls also referred to *Sahin* which emphasized the margin of appreciation **4.87** accorded to national authorities. He acknowledged that the doctrine as such had no application in a domestic setting but noted that, in the United Kingdom, Parliament had considered it right to delegate to individual schools the power to decide whether to impose requirements about school uniforms. It followed therefore that a domestic court should accept the decision of Parliament to allow individual schools to make their own decisions about uniforms and that the decision did not have to be made at a national level, and that national differences between Turkey and the United Kingdom were irrelevant.[159]

Baroness Hale adopted a more nuanced approach to the question of proportion- **4.88** ality, recognizing at the outset that the question was more difficult in the case of a young girl than in the case of an adult who wished to manifest his religion in a particular form of dress.[160] However, she also acknowledged the task of schools as being to educate the young from many and diverse families and communities and to 'promote the ability of people of diverse races, religions and cultures to live together in harmony'. To that end a school uniform could play an important role in easing ethnic, religious and social divisions. She also recognized a point that might have been taken in the case, namely that the school was a good school which explained why Shabina Begum wanted to stay there. In that sense her choice may have been arguably constricted.[161] Ultimately she was of the opinion that the school was trying to achieve a balance between conflicting views and accommodate religious and cultural diversity in allowing girls to wear the shalwar khameez and the hijab.[162]

Displays of religious symbols in schools   This issue has not apparently given **4.89** rise to controversy or litigation in England but has been a highly contentious issue in other jurisdictions such as the United States and Germany. There is no specific legislation or DfES guidance relating to this subject in England. The United Kingdom is not a secular state and religious education and worship is a requirement in state maintained schools. As such the existence of religious symbols in schools per se is permissible. However, ECHR rights might be engaged where a school displays religious symbols relating to one religion but not other religions where those are strongly represented among the pupils. For example, displaying a crèche with the nativity scene at Christmas time but not a Menorah (if there are a

---

[159] Ibid [59]–[64]. See also [83] (per Lord Scott): '...[T]he direction to Shabina to attend school wearing the proper school uniform can only be attacked as an unlawful direction under domestic law if the school uniform rules that she was being required to obey were themselves so unreasonable as to be unlawful, or if the decision to insist upon Shabina observing the school uniform rules was similarly unreasonable. I regard both contentions as being virtually unarguable.'
[160] Ibid [94].
[161] Ibid [97].
[162] Ibid [98].

number of Jewish pupils) or a cross on a school wall may discriminate against non-Christian pupils and parents who wish to have their religions represented. Different considerations will apply to a school with a religious ethos as opposed to a school without one.[163]

4.90 The issue of religious clothing and symbols in academies and independent schools may also indirectly engage ECHR rights under Articles 9, 14 and Article 2 Protocol 1.[164] Similar issues to those referred to above in relation to the National Curriculum will arise involving the manner in which the claim is brought, the character of the school and the question of freedom of contract and choice to leave the school.[165]

ECHR law

4.91 At the European level there have been three cases argued on the issue of religious clothing in educational institutions. It should be noted at the onset that they relate to Turkey and Switzerland, countries that maintain a national policy of secular education in their state schools. In *Karaduman v Turkey*,[166] a Muslim female student was denied the right of graduating from her university because she refused to have her identity photograph taken without a headscarf. The university rules prohibited the wearing of headscarves in state institutions as a breach of the principle of secularity and the requirement of no headscarves in photographs was also for the purposes of proper identification. As regards Article 9 the Commission stated (1) that the applicant, having chosen to do her studies in a state secular university, had to comply with the university regulations; (2) that in a country where the majority of the population are of one religion, the manifestation of rituals and symbols may pressurize those who do not practise that religion or are of a different religion; and (3) that secular universities may legitimately ensure that certain currents of fundamental beliefs do not impinge upon public order.

4.92 In *Dahlab v Switzerland*,[167] the ECtHR considered under Articles 9 and 14 a prohibition on teachers wearing headscarves in the classroom of state schools in Switzerland. The state required strict denominational neutrality and a clear separation between church and state. The ECtHR held that the restriction was

---

[163] In Germany, the Federal Constitutional Court considered a claim by parents who were theosophists who objected on ideological grounds to the placing of a crucifix in every classroom as a legal requirement in Bavarian *Volksschule*, BVerfGE 93, 1. A majority of the Court (5:3) declared the Bavarian Law invalid as a violation of Art 4(1) of the Basic Law which guarantees freedom of faith and conscience.

[164] Note that *Mandla v Dowell Lee* [1983] 2 AC 548 concerned the right of Sikh pupils to wear a turban in an independent school based on the RRA 1976. See 2.21–2.22 above.

[165] See 4.75–4.77 above.

[166] Application 16278/90 (1993) 74 DR 93.

[167] Application 42393/98 (15 February 2001).

prescribed by law and pursued a legitimate aim, namely the protection of the rights and freedoms of others, public safety and public order. It further stated that it was difficult to assess the impact on pupils but that it could not be denied that the scarf might have some proselytizing effect and that it was difficult to reconcile the wearing of the headscarf with a message of tolerance, respect and above all equality which teachers were required to convey. As regards sex discrimination, the restriction was aimed at preserving neutrality and not directed against her as a woman and could have been applied to a man in a different context.

4.93 In *Sahin v Turkey*[168] the vice-chancellor of Istanbul University issued a circular which banned religious attire and in particular students wearing the Islamic headscarf and beard from access to lectures, courses and tutorials. A female Muslim claimed that the circular infringed Article 9 and Articles 8, 10 and 14 together with Article 9 and Article 2 Protocol 1. She argued that she had been entitled to wear the headscarf for four years at the University of Bursa which had not caused any disruption, disturbance or threat to public disorder; that the headscarf was not incompatible with principles of secularism; and that it was not applied, apparently, to Jewish skull caps or Christian crucifixes and therefore discriminated against Muslims. The government argued that the principle of secularism was a prerequisite for a liberal democracy and noted that the ban only affected Muslims in the state education system and that the ban on veils and beards was a direct response to previous confrontations between radical groups at the university.

4.94 The Grand Chamber (upholding the earlier decision of the ECtHR) stated that the principle of secularism was fundamental to Turkish society and that a margin of appreciation was particularly appropriate when it comes to the regulation by the state of the wearing of religious symbols in teaching institutions, since rules on the subject vary from one country to another depending on national traditions and there is no uniform European conception of the requirements of 'the protection of the rights of others' and of 'public order'. In dismissing the applicant's claim, the ECtHR stated that the interference was based on two principles—secularism and gender equality.[169]

4.95 A contrast may be drawn between a secular state such as Turkey and the United Kingdom, which is not secular and in which religion has a central position in the public sphere. But overall the ECtHR grants a wide margin of appreciation in this area, acknowledging the relative position of church and state in the different countries.

---

[168] (2005) 41 EHRR 8.
[169] See also J Marshall, 'Freedom of Expression and Gender Equality' (2006) 69 MLR 452; N Lerner, 'Religious Symbols How Wide the Margin of Appreciation? The Turkish Headscarf Case, the Strasbourg Court, and Secularist Tolerance' (2006) 13 Williamette J Int'l L & Dispute Resolution 65–85.

Discipline and time off

4.96 Education and freedom of religion have raised a number of additional issues and will continue to do so. The very nature of education requires engagement with a way of life both in terms of the curriculum requirements in a school and the provision made for non-academic activities. In most instances the inherent flexibility built into the system that allows for parents to request an exemption from a number of activities will provide respect for religious beliefs. However, it is always important to consider that the system may reflect in all sorts of subtle ways the religious and cultural traditions of the majority or ruling elite. From the choice of school trips, extra-curricular activities and provision for school food and drink, to time-tabling, regard should be had to the pupils in the school as a whole and to the need to respect the various religions and traditions within the pupil population.

Discipline in schools

4.97 Most of the controversy in this area initially related to parents who wanted to prevent schools from using corporal punishment to discipline pupils in schools. The law in England has now been changed. Section 548(1) EdA 1996 bans corporal punishment in all schools.[170]

4.98 In *R (Williamson) v Secretary of State for Education and Employment*,[171] the House of Lords considered Article 9 and Article 2 Protocol 1 ECHR in connection with parents who challenged the ban on corporal punishment in schools contained in s 548 EdA 1996 which they argued conflicted with their religious beliefs. The House of Lords held that there was an interference with the parents' beliefs for the purposes of Article 9, but they held that this was prescribed by law and was for the legitimate aim of protecting children and that the means chosen were not disproportionate and therefore it was justified in accordance with Article 9(2).[172]

4.99 At the European level, there are two decisions relating to corporal punishment as it then applied under the law in the United Kingdom. In *Campbell and Cosans v United Kingdom*,[173] the ECtHR upheld a complaint under Article 2 Protocol 1 by two mothers who objected to their children being subjected to corporal punishment in state schools.[174] In *Costello-Roberts v United Kingdom*,[175] the ECtHR rejected a claim based on Articles 3 and 8 ECHR by parents of a child in an independent

---

[170] Corporal punishment means punishment which, justification apart, constitutes battery: s 548(4) EdA 1996.

[171] [2005] UKHL 15.

[172] [2005] UKHL 15 [81]–[86] (per Baroness Hale).

[173] (1982) 4 EHRR 293.

[174] See also *Christian Education v Minister of Education* (2000) 4 SA 757 cited in *Williamson* [67]–[68] (per Lord Walker).

[175] (1993) 19 EHRR 112.

school about the use of corporal punishment. The punishment in that case fell short of the protection provided by Article 3 and the court considered that it did not entail adverse effects for the boy's physical or moral integrity to bring it within Article 8. It thereby confirmed that not every act of corporal punishment will violate these rights.

Reference was not made in either case to Article 9 but it is clear from the decision in *R (Williamson) v Secretary of State for Education and Employment*[176] that both this and Article 2 Protocol 1 will be engaged in a case relating to corporal punishment. **4.100**

Absence for religious holidays, festivals and pilgrimages

The taking off of the occasional day is unlikely to provoke any issue in relation to education and is envisaged in the statutory framework. However, a regular commitment that involves a pupil's absence on a regular basis or a considerable amount of time taken out of the school calendar will create an issue as regards the school timetable and statutory requirements on parents to ensure their child receives full education. **4.101**

If a parent fails to perform his duty under s 7 EdA 1996 to ensure that his child receives efficient full time education, the LEA may commence a process leading to a school attendance order.[177] It is a criminal offence to fail to comply with such an order.[178] It is also a criminal offence for a child who is registered at a school to fail to attend regularly.[179] Section 444(3)(c) provides a defence for the parent where the child is absent 'on any day exclusively set apart for religious observance by the religious body to which his parent belongs'.[180] This provision will not assist a child whose religious beliefs are different to his parent's. It also does not envisage a scenario where a parent wishes their child to travel abroad to a holy site that may involve a number of days of travel but which are not necessarily exclusively set apart for that purpose. **4.102**

There appear to have been no cases at the domestic level in England relating to this issue. On the issue of taking time off school for religious days or pilgrimages, the ECtHR in *Casimiro and Ferreira v Luxembourg*[181] considered the admissibility of a complaint by parents and a pupil who were Seventh Day Adventists that requiring the pupil to attend school on a Saturday was an interference with his requirement of strict Sabbath observance. The relevant domestic legislation allowed **4.103**

---

[176] [2005] UKHL 15 [27] (per Lord Nicholls).
[177] EdA 1996, s 437.
[178] Ibid, s 443.
[179] Ibid, s 444.
[180] See *Marshall v Graham* [1907] 2 KB 112 in which it was held that it was not necessary for Church of England pupils to take the whole day off for religious observance.
[181] Application 44888/98 (27 April 1999).

pupils to be exempt from school for a period of between 8 and 30 days for the celebration of religious rituals applicable to their particular beliefs. The ECtHR contrasted this with the taking off of one day every week which had repercussions on the normal school timetable and amounted to a substantial proportion of school time. It also took into account the government's submission as to the disruption this would cause to education of other pupils. In conclusion the ECtHR declared the complaint inadmissible on the grounds that although there was an interference with freedom of religion it was justified with regards to the principle of respecting the right to education. The restriction was accordingly proportionate to its aim.

4.104 There are a number of employment cases about taking time off for worship. Previously, these might not have been considered to be of assistance or relevant in the area of education that is compulsory while employment is treated more as a voluntary and consensual submission to terms of contract. However, the House of Lords considered the Strasbourg employment cases in *R (Begum) v Headteacher and Governors of Denbigh High School* in the context of a case about education.[182] The House of Lords therefore in that case effectively elided the Strasbourg decisions relating to education with those relating to employment and professional situations, and considered both from the perspective of the free choice of the applicant. This may arguably represent a more principled approach, but it does not sit easily with the reality of a state funded education system where parents may as a matter of fact have little choice. What the decision does make clear is that it will be necessary for an applicant or claimant to deal expressly with the issue of choice and explain how it impacts in the particular case. Reference should be made to the employment decisions in this area referred to in Chapter 5 below.[183]

Transport

4.105 The question of in what circumstances an LEA must fund transportation for a pupil to attend a school as a result of a religious preference is linked as a policy issue to the question of state funding for schools with a religious character. The issue of chief concern is whether the state is obliged to fund transportation so that a pupil can attend a school of religious character in accordance with the religious beliefs of his parents and himself in circumstances where there is a nearer available school for that child to attend.

4.106 The provisions for an LEA relating to transportation are contained primarily in s 509 EdA 1996. Under s 509(1) and (1A) an LEA is under a duty to make such

---

182 [2006] UKHL 26. See Chapter 5 below.
183 See 5.60–5.67.

arrangements for the provision of transport and otherwise as it considers necessary, or as the Secretary of State may direct, for the purpose of facilitating the
attendance of persons receiving education. The EA 2006 expressly provides
exemption from the prohibition of discrimination on the grounds of religion or
belief in the LEA's provision of transport for schools.[184]

When considering whether or not the LEA is required to provide free transport **4.107**
under s 509(1) EdA 1996, the LEA must have regard (among other matters) to the
age of the person and the nature of the route, or alternative routes, which he could
reasonably be expected to take. An LEA must also have regard under s 509(4)(b)
to any wish of the child's parent for the child to be provided with education or
training at a school in which the education provided is that of the religion of the
denomination to which the parent adheres.

The religious factor is not given any priority in the legislation among all the **4.108**
factors that must be considered and therefore a judge has a considerable discretion
in determining the outcome of the case. In *R (R) v Leeds City Council*,[185] the
claimants applied for judicial review of the decision of the authority not to provide free school transport for a pupil to attend Jewish schools in Manchester. The
authority decided that it was inappropriate to provide free transport given the
distances involved, the cost, and the fact that there was a school in Leeds that
offered Hebrew studies adapted to the demands of the Jewish community and
other suitable Leeds schools. It was held that the decision was neither irrational
nor *Wednesbury* unreasonable. As regards Article 9 it was held that there was no
infringement given that the pupil was attending the schools even though the
authority had declined to fund the transport.

In *R (T) v Leeds City Council*,[186] a challenge was brought where a policy provided **4.109**
for a discretionary payment for attendance at certain Christian schools, but not
for other religious schools. The application for judicial review failed on the basis
that there was not an Orthodox Jewish school within a comparable distance to the
Christian schools for which funding was provided. In that case Turner J held that
the statute did not impose a duty to comply with a parent's wishes concerning
religious education.[187]

---

[184] EA 2006, s 51(2).
[185] [2005] EWHC Admin 2495.
[186] [2002] ELR 91, 97. See also *R v Rochdale Metropolitan Borough Council, ex p Schemet* [1994] 1 ELR 89.
[187] In *R v Kent County Council, ex p C* [1998] ELR 108, 114 McCullough J stated that in considering a challenge to a refusal to provide free transport where the refusal is based upon the view that
there was a nearer suitable school, the function of the court is to examine whether the view was lawfully reached, which in most cases will require no more than a consideration of the rationality of its
conclusion. Note that this case was decided prior to enactment of the HRA 1998 and that ECHR
rights were not considered.

5

EMPLOYMENT

Introduction

Access to employment and legal protection during the course of employment is **5.01** of fundamental importance to the individual concerned. There is no right to work in English law, but it is the means by which many essential aspects of life may be effectively realized.[1] It provides the means to sustain private and family life through the provision of wages in consideration for labour and services. It also plays a more general role in the fulfilment and development of the individual and is of key importance for society as a whole.[2]

As with education, it is an area that is of considerable significance for minorities **5.02** including religious minorities. Whether the employer is the state or a private person, the practices and policies in the workplace are likely to reflect the traditions and

---

[1] Note that the UK signed the European Social Charter in 1961 which came into force in 1965 (and was revised in 1996). It makes provision for a number of social and economic rights including the right to work (Art 1) and to just conditions of work (Art 2). These have not been incorporated into English law.

[2] See *Foley v Interactive Data* [1988] Cal Rptr 211 cited with approval by Lightman J in *BCCI v Ali* [1999] IRLR 508 [1].

127

customs of the majority of the workforce. This means that some employees may be at a disadvantage, for example, as regards the hours of work and choice of days off. Related to this, there has been some recognition of the economic marginalization of ethnic and religious minorities in employment.[3] In this context the results of the 2001 Census show a striking disparity in the statistics on employment where individuals are grouped by religious beliefs.[4]

5.03 Employment law in England is rooted in the common law and the contract of employment. It is, therefore, based upon the concept of freedom of contract, freedom in the labour market, and the ability to choose employer and employee. But it is an area where there is complex and ever increasing statutory intervention that has sought to regulate and affect the common law principles. In relation to the application of freedom of religion in employment, the enactment of the Human Rights Act 1998 ('HRA 1998') was an important step, although the more recent implementation of the Employment Equality (Religion or Belief) Regulations 2003 ('Employment Regulations 2003') is likely to be of greater significance in this area. Overall, the impact of freedom of religion in the workplace is likely to be the subject of future litigation. In *Copsey v WWB Devon Clays Ltd*,[5] in the context of a dispute about a Christian employee who wished to observe Sunday as a day of rest, the Court of Appeal acknowledged the potentially far reaching effects of the right.

5.04 This chapter first provides a brief overview of the relevant statutory framework with reference to the key statutes and statutory instruments including the Employment Regulations 2003. It then considers the impact of the HRA 1998 on the law. Following this, general and then specific issues are identified and examined in the light of the legal framework by reference to domestic and European case law.

Statutory Framework

Employment Acts

5.05 Employment law was initially based almost entirely on common law and the contract of employment. Significant inroads were made into this field by statutory intervention beginning with the Contracts of Employment Act 1963. The law relating to employment was substantially consolidated eventually in the Employment Rights Act 1996 ('ERA 1996') and that relating to employment tribunals and the Employment Appeal Tribunal ('EAT') in the Employment Tribunals Act 1996.

---

3 See *Ethnic Minorities and the Labour Market*, Prime Minister's Strategy Unit (Cabinet Office, 2003); *The Parekh Report, The Future of Multi-Ethnic Britain* (The Runnymede Trust, 2002) 192–204; *Muslims in the UK: Policies for Engaged Citizens* (Open Society Institute, 2005) 196–251.
4 UK Census 2001.
5 [2005] EWCA Civ 932 [3].

More recently there have been a number of other statutory enactments including the Employment Rights (Dispute Resolution) Act 1998, the National Minimum Wage Act 1998, the Employment Relations Act 1999, and the Employment Act 2002. At the same time EC law has had a considerable impact on the area and in particular in relation to discrimination law, maternity and paternity leave and working time. This has led to provisions in the Equal Pay Act 1970, the Sex Discrimination Act 1975, the Race Relations Act 1976, the Disability Discrimination Act 1995 and the Working Time Regulations 1998.[6] However, until the coming into force of the Employment Regulations 2003 (implementing Equal Treatment Directive 2000/78/EC) there was no specific protection against religious discrimination in employment in English law.[7]

Race Relations Act 1976

In some circumstances the Race Relations Act 1976 ('RRA 1976') may provide protection for individuals who are discriminated against in employment. It protects both private and public sector employees. Although religious groups are not expressly protected, some groups may be protected through indirect discrimination.[8] Alternatively, some religious groups will qualify as ethnic groups in accordance with the guidelines set down in *Mandla v Dowell Lee*.[9] On 6 April 2006 the Commission for Racial Equality's new statutory Code of Practice on racial equality in employment came into effect. It contains a set of recommendations and guidance on how to avoid unlawful racial discrimination and harassment in employment.[10]   **5.06**

Equality Act 2006

The Equality Act 2006 ('EA 2006') prohibits discrimination on grounds of religion or belief in the exercise of the functions of all public authorities.[11] To that extent it would in principle apply to a public authority acting as an employer. However, there is an exception to this where the actions are provided for by the provisions in   **5.07**

---

[6] SI 1998/1833. See I Smith, G Thomas & D Mead, *Industrial Law* (LexisNexis UK, 2003) for an introduction to employment legislation. See generally *Harvey's on Employment Law* (Butterworths) for a practitioner guide in this area.

[7] Council Directive (EC) 2000/78 establishing a general framework for equal treatment in employment and occupation [2000] OJ L303/16. Note too the Employment Equality (Sexual Orientation) Regulations 2003, SI 2003/1661, which came into force on 1 December 2003; and the Employment Equality (Age) Regulations 2006, SI 2006/1031, which came into force on 1 October 2006.

[8] See 2.28 above.

[9] (1983) 2 AC 548 and see further 2.21–2.28 above.

[10] See further <http://www.cre.gov.uk>.

[11] EA 2006, s 52(1).

the Employment Regulations 2003 (as to which see below).[12] This means that in practice the Employment Regulations 2003 will govern the case where the issue relates to employment.

Employment Equality (Religion or Belief) Regulations 2003

5.08 The Employment Regulations 2003 came into force on 2 December 2003.[13] They make it unlawful to discriminate on grounds of religion or belief in employment and vocational training, and prohibit direct and indirect discrimination, victimisation and harassment. The general pattern of the Employment Regulations 2003 follows the Sex Discrimination Act 1975 ('SDA 1975') and RRA 1976 and they are very similar in their definition of discrimination to the Employment Equality (Sexual Orientation) Regulations 2003.[14]

5.09 Religion or belief is defined in reg 2 as any religion, religious belief, or philosophical belief.[15] This is likely to be given a broad interpretation in line with the interpretation of Article 9 of the European Convention on Human Rights ('ECHR'), although it will be necessary to draw a distinction between political opinions and philosophical and religious beliefs.[16] The decision of the House of Lords in *R (Williamson) v Secretary of State for Education and Employment*[17] makes it clear that it is not appropriate for public authorities and the courts to adjudicate upon the seriousness, cogency and coherence of religious beliefs. On this point Lord Walker cited with approval Richards J in *R (Amicus) v Secretary of State for Trade and Industry*,[18] a decision concerning the Employment Equality (Sexual Orientation) Regulations 2003.[19]

5.10 Direct discrimination, defined in reg 3(1)(a), occurs where a person is treated less favourably than another on grounds of religion or belief.[20] Indirect discrimination, defined in reg 3(1)(b), occurs where a provision, criterion or practice, which is applied generally, puts persons of a particular religion or belief at a disadvantage and cannot be shown to be a proportionate means of achieving a legitimate aim. The comparison between the person of a particular religion or belief and others must be such that the relevant circumstances in the case are the same or not materially different.[21]

---

[12] Ibid, s 52(4)(m).

[13] SI 2003/1660. Note there are a number of amendments to these regulations to date.

[14] See also N de Marco, *Blackstone's Guide to the Employment Equality Regulations 2003* (OUP, 2004).

[15] As amended by EA 2006, s 77(1). Note that it includes a lack of religion or belief.

[16] See 2.57–2.62 above. See also *Kosteki v Macedonia*, Application 55170/00 (13 April 2006) (when employee seeks to rely on a particular exemption in law it is not oppressive nor in conflict with Art 9 to require some level of substantiation).

[17] [2005] UKHL 15.

[18] [2004] EWHC 860 (Admin) [36]–[40].

[19] [2005] UKHL 15 [57], [22] (per Lord Nicholls).

[20] As amended by EA 2006, s 77(2).

[21] See *Wong v Igen (EOC Intervening)* [2005] EWCA Civ 142 (on interpretation and application of provisions as to the shifting of the burden of proof in discrimination legislation contained in SDA 1975 and RRA 1976).

Victimization, within the meaning of reg 4, occurs where a person receives less **5.11**
favourable treatment than others by reason of the fact that he has brought (or given
evidence or information in) proceedings, made an allegation or otherwise done
anything under or by reference to the Employment Regulations 2003. Harassment,
under reg 5, occurs where a person is subjected to unwanted conduct on grounds
of religion or belief with the purpose or effect of violating his dignity, or creating an
intimidating, hostile, degrading, humiliating or offensive environment for him.

Regulations 6 to 21 prohibit discrimination, victimization and harassment in employ- **5.12**
ment and vocational training. Regulation 6 protects employees against discrimination
in relation to the offering of employment, the terms of employment and opportunities for promotion, transfer, training and receiving any benefits. In addition to
employees, the Employment Regulations 2003 also protect contract workers (reg 8),
office-holders (reg 10), police (reg 11), barristers' and advocates' pupils (regs 12 and
13), and partners in firms (reg 14). The Regulations apply also to prohibit discrimination by trade organizations (reg 15), bodies conferring professional and trade qualifications (reg 16), providers of vocational training (reg 17), employment agencies
(reg 18), and further and higher education institutions (reg 20). Discrimination,
victimization or harassment occurring after the relevant relationship has ended is
unlawful if it arises out of, and is closely connected to, the relationship (reg 21).

There are a number of exceptions that are provided for by the Employment **5.13**
Regulations 2003. Regulation 7 provides an exception to discrimination on
grounds of religion or belief where being of a particular religion or belief is a genuine and determining occupational requirement and it is proportionate in the circumstances to apply that requirement. It also provides an exception for employers
with an ethos based on religion or belief where being of a particular religion or
belief is a genuine occupational requirement for a post and it is proportionate to
apply the requirement in the particular case.

Three other categories of general exceptions apply. An exception to discrimina- **5.14**
tion, victimization, and harassment applies where an act is done for the purpose of
safeguarding national security (reg 24). There is an exception where an act is done
for the purpose of affording persons of a particular religion or belief access to facilities for training that would fit them for particular work where the act compensates
for disadvantages linked to religion or belief suffered by those persons (reg 25).
Sikhs are the subject of a specific exception relating to requirements as to the wearing
of safety helmets on a construction site (reg 26).

Human Rights Act 1998

At the time of enactment of the HRA 1998, it seemed likely that it would have a **5.15**
significant impact in the field of employment law, although it was unclear how

this would develop in relation to the horizontal application of ECHR rights to employees of private businesses. The impact is still being worked out and the recent decision of the Court of Appeal in *Copsey v WWB Devon Clays Ltd*[22] leaves this issue unresolved. In this regard there is an interesting comparison to be drawn between education and employment law. As regards the former it is far more readily accepted by Strasbourg that ECHR rights are engaged, whereas in a number of decisions relating to employment, it has been held that there is no interference with a right on the basis of freedom of contract. Additionally, in relation to the application to private organizations, the direct application of ECHR rights has not been conceded.

5.16 Brooke LJ in the Court of Appeal in *R (Begum) v Headteacher and Governors of Denbigh High School*[23] distinguished the employment cases from Strasbourg as being particular to that field and did not think they had application in relation to education. However, on appeal the House of Lords rejected this approach and considered the employment cases were relevant in an education context, looking at both from the perspective of freedom of choice.[24] If there is considered to be no interference in the context of education (because a pupil could choose another school in the area) it will likely be difficult in many employment cases to argue against freedom of contract. Notwithstanding the approach of the majority of the House of Lords, a distinction may be drawn between education and employment based upon the fact that the state has an obligation to guarantee a right to education within the framework of the existing system of schools and institutions. The state can secure the right both through state funded institutions or privately funded ones. This contrasts with the lack of protection in the ECHR for the right to work, although the right to earn a livelihood has been regarded as important in Strasbourg.[25] A distinction may also be drawn on the basis of the deemed voluntary nature of employment as opposed to the compulsory nature of education. However, neither European nor domestic case law to date has dealt with these issues in any depth.

Section 6 HRA 1998

5.17 It may seem anomalous that an employee of a public authority such as a local governmental organization is better protected than the employee of a private business in respect of ECHR rights. But the primary focus of the ECHR is to protect the individual against the state. It was not intended to affect private businesses

---

[22] [2005] EWCA Civ 932.
[23] [2005] EWCA Civ 199 [62] (per Brooke LJ).
[24] [2006] UKHL 15 [23]–[25] (per Lord Bingham).
[25] *Young, James and Webster v United Kingdom* (1982) 4 EHRR 38. Note too that the Social Charter provides a right to work as do other international instruments, although these are not part of English law and cannot be relied upon directly, though they may be referred to in situations of ambiguity.

directly although it is clear that the HRA 1998 may have an indirect impact on them either through the development of general principles of trust and confidence, reasonableness, and fairness, or through the application of ss 3 and 6 HRA 1998 by the courts and tribunals. In *Copsey v WWB Devon Clays Ltd*[26] the Court of Appeal made reference to Article 1 ECHR and to the obligation on member states to secure to everyone within their jurisdiction the rights and freedoms defined in Section I ECHR. In that case it was accepted that Article 9 may be engaged although no concessions were made about its horizontal effect.[27]

In the area of religion and employment the distinction between public and private **5.18** employers may also be important for a further reason. As regards the ECHR, the state itself cannot claim to be a victim and rely on ECHR rights. However, private religious organizations may be able to claim ECHR rights on behalf of individuals. If all employers were to be treated as emanations of the state, it would be difficult to square this with the fact of religious employers being able to rely on the ECHR rights.

There are three categories that an employer may fall into for the purposes of the **5.19** ECHR. There are those that are public authorities such as local authorities, governmental departments or state run companies. There are those that are private entities. In between there are employers that may be part state owned and part private and those that are essentially privately owned but are carrying out public functions within the meaning of s 6(3). It is the hybrid category that is most difficult to define for these purposes and will have to be worked out on a case by case basis.[28]

In summary, the divide between state and private employer is still an important **5.20** one in employment law and it will affect the way in which a claim may be brought relating to the HRA 1998. If the employer is considered to be a public authority within the meaning of s 6, a claim may be brought in the High Court (but not the tribunal) directly against the employer. If, however, the employer is not a public authority then an employee will have to base his claim upon another cause of action—such as unfair dismissal or equal pay—but may then also rely on the HRA 1998.[29]

Section 13 HRA 1998

As regards employment law, s 13 might be invoked by a religious organization **5.21** in the position of employer that wished to employ workers of a particular faith.

---

[26] [2005] EWCA Civ 932 [4] (per Mummery LJ).

[27] Ibid [5]. Note the position as regards the right to education and the ECtHR's reference in *Kjeldsen, Busk Madsen and Pedersen v Denmark* (1976) 1 EHRR 711 to Art 1.

[28] See further 2.33–2.37 above.

[29] *Copsey v WWB Devon Clays Ltd* [2005] EWCA Civ 932 [5]. See also *X v Y* [2004] EWCA Civ 662 (ERA 1996 so far as possible to be read in a way compatible with Arts 8 and 14 ECHR).

This area is, however, governed by the Employment Regulations 2003 which prescribe in some detail the circumstances in which religious organizations may discriminate in employment.[30] Where there are specific statutory provisions regulating a particular issue, it seems unlikely that s 13 would be interpreted in such a way so as to be determinative of a case. As referred to in Chapter 2 above, it is very unclear in any event whether s 13 has any additional impact on the balance to be drawn between competing rights or between competing groups.[31] In *R (Amicus) v Secretary of State for Trade and Industry*,[32] it was conceded by all parties that s 13 added nothing.

Article 9 ECHR

Employment cases

5.22 There have been a number of employment cases brought to Strasbourg under Article 9. For this reason and because the nature of application of Article 9 to a private employer is still unclear, it is worth examining some of them in more detail before considering their impact in relation to specific issues that arise in employment law. In what follows below, the cases on Article 9 are considered as well as some of the relevant cases on Articles 8, 10 and 11 which also involve broadly the concept of conscience and view points.

5.23 In *Copsey v WWB Devon Clays Ltd*,[33] the Court of Appeal were divided in their analysis of the European cases. Overall the three judges had different views as to the correct approach, with one regarding the court as bound by the 'clear line' of authorities from the Commission leaving it to the House of Lords or to Parliament to draw the distinction, one holding that the European cases were not consistent, and a third looking at the case from the perspective of domestic employment law without regard to Article 9. The House of Lords in *R (Begum) v Headteacher and Governors of Denbigh High School* disagreed and stated that there was 'a coherent and remarkably consistent body of authority which our domestic courts must take into account and which shows that interference is not easily established'.[34] However, when the recent decisions of the European Court of Human Rights ('ECtHR') are looked at as a whole, including the decisions relating to trade unions, it is not entirely apparent that there is such a clear line of authority in this area.

5.24 In *Ahmad v United Kingdom*,[35] the Commission considered whether Article 9 was engaged in the context of a devout Muslim who claimed unfair dismissal when the

---

[30] See also the Employment Equality (Sexual Orientation) Regulations 2003 and *R (Amicus) v Secretary of State for Trade and Industry* [2004] EWHC 860 (Admin).

[31] See 2.38–2.39 above.

[32] [2004] EWHC 860 (Admin) [41].

[33] [2005] EWCA Civ 932.

[34] [2006] UKHL 15 [24] (per Lord Bingham).

[35] (1981) 4 EHRR 126.

state school where he was employed as a teacher refused to employ him on a full time basis in circumstances where he would be absent for some time on Friday afternoon to attend the mosque. Previously he had been employed at a school that was too far from the mosque, but when he was transferred to a nearer school he considered that his religious duty required attendance at Friday prayer. The Commission noted that he had originally freely accepted teaching obligations which proved incompatible with attendance at the mosque. It noted that his first school had been able to accommodate his absence for a short period on Friday but difficulties arose at subsequent schools as a result of his unauthorized absence. The Commission held that it could not be said that the school failed to consider his right to freedom of religion and concluded that there had been no interference under Article 9(1).

In *Kontinnen v Finland*,[36] the applicant worked for the state railways and five years after his engagement had joined the Seventh Day Adventist Church. From then he wished to observe the Sabbath on Saturdays, commencing at sunset on Friday. He only needed to leave early on about five Fridays in the winter when sunset came early and offered to make up the missed hours. He was dismissed after he started to leave work early on Fridays. The Commission said that he was dismissed for refusing to respect his working hours and even if it were motivated by his religious convictions these could not be considered as protected by Article 9(1). It noted that he was free to resign his post and regarded this as the ultimate guarantee of his right to freedom of religion. The complaint was held to be manifestly ill-founded.   **5.25**

In *Stedman v United Kingdom*,[37] the applicant was a Christian who did not wish to work on Sundays for her private sector employer. At some stage after she had been engaged she was asked to work on Sundays within the terms of her contract and was dismissed when she refused to do so. Relying on *Kontinnen v Finland*,[38] the Commission said that had the applicant been employed by the state and dismissed in similar circumstances, such dismissal would not have amounted to an interference with her rights under Article 9(1). A fortiori an employee cannot expect such protection in the private sector.   **5.26**

In *Kalaç v Turkey*,[39] the ECtHR considered whether the dismissal of a Muslim judge advocate employed by the Turkish air force, due to his 'unlawful fundamentalist opinion', violated Article 9. It held that in exercising his right under Article 9, an individual may need to take his specific situation into account. In choosing to pursue a military career, Mr Kalaç was freely accepting a system of military discipline   **5.27**

---

[36] (1996) 87 DR 68.
[37] (1997) 23 EHRR CD 168.
[38] (1996) 87 DR 68.
[39] (1997) 27 EHRR 552.

that by its very nature implied the possibility of limiting certain rights and freedoms that would not be relevant to civilians. He was permitted to fulfil the obligations of normal Muslim practice such as praying five times a day, keeping the fast of Ramadan and attending Friday prayers at the mosque. The order was not based upon his religious opinions or beliefs but on his conduct and attitude, which according to the Turkish authorities breached military discipline and infringed the principle of secularism. Accordingly, the compulsory retirement did not amount to an interference with the right guaranteed by Article 9 as it was not prompted by the way the applicant manifested his religion.[40]

5.28 In *Pichon and Sajous v France*,[41] the ECtHR ruled inadmissible a claim by two French pharmacists, who had been convicted under the consumer code for failing to fill prescriptions for contraceptive pills, that their rights under Article 9 had been violated. The ECtHR noted that while the sale of contraceptives was legal and prescriptions could not be filled other than in pharmacies, the applicants could not give precedence to their religious beliefs and impose them on others. It noted specifically that the applicants were free to manifest their beliefs outside the professional sphere and that Article 9 did not always guarantee the right to behave in a manner governed by belief.[42]

Relevant non-Article 9 cases

5.29 The approach of the Commission and ECtHR in the decisions above relating to Article 9 can be contrasted with the approach of the ECtHR in other cases involving employment situations where ECHR rights have been invoked. In *Vogt v Germany*,[43] the ECtHR considered the dismissal from a state school of a teacher on grounds that she was a member of the German communist party. The ECtHR considered that there was an interference with Articles 10 and 11 and then went on to consider whether it was justified. Finding a violation of both articles, it noted the effect of dismissal on the reputation of the person and the loss of livelihood and the reality of finding alternative employment. It further carried out a balancing exercise between the right of the individual to express political views and competing interests such as national security, the rights of pupils and others not to be indoctrinated.

5.30 A similar analytical approach was adopted in *Smith and Grady v United Kingdom*,[44] where the ECtHR considered a complaint by two members of the armed forces

---

[40] Ibid [28]–[31]. Note that the Commission below had given the opinion that there was a violation of Art 9 on the ground that the interference was not prescribed by law and that the relevant provisions did not afford adequate protection against arbitrary decisions.

[41] Application 49853/99 (2 October 2001).

[42] Note generally the recent admissibility decision in *Ivanova v Bulgaria*, Application 52435/99 (14 February 2006) (applicant complained that she had been dismissed from her employment as a result of her religious beliefs).

[43] (1996) 21 EHRR 205.

[44] (1999) 29 EHRR 493.

who had been discharged when it was discovered that they were homosexual. They complained of a violation of their rights under Articles 8 and 14. In that case, the United Kingdom conceded that there had been an interference with Article 8 but that it was justified under Article 8(2). It was not argued that they had waived their rights under Article 8 when they initially joined the forces and no argument was made that they were free to resign from the forces and seek alternative employment. The ECtHR held without reasoning that in the circumstances of the case the investigations into their sexuality and the subsequent discharges amounted to an interference with Article 8. The court then considered in a lengthy judgment whether the interference was justified. In finding the interference unjustified, it noted among other matters the unique nature of the military and the difficulty with transferring military skills and qualifications to civilian life, that would reflect the seniority and status that they had achieved in the airforce. It also noted that the judgment in *Kalaç v Turkey*[45] was to be distinguished on the basis that Mr Kalaç was dismissed on grounds of his conduct while the applicants were discharged on grounds of their innate personal characteristics.[46]

In *Young, James and Webster v United Kingdom*,[47] the ECtHR considered an agreement between British Rail and three railway unions under which British Rail could fairly dismiss any employee who refused to join a union unless the employee's religious beliefs prevented him from joining such a union. The majority of the ECtHR held that there had been a violation of Article 11 as compulsory membership was introduced after the workers were already in employment and the consequence of not joining was harsh. It also took into account that applicants had a limited number of unions to choose from and could not form their own union.[48]   **5.31**

In *Sibson v United Kingdom*,[49] the ECtHR considered a case where an employee had resigned from the TGWU and joined another union following allegations of mishandling of union funds. The employer claimed it was contractually entitled to move the employee to another depot. The employee claimed constructive dismissal. The ECtHR distinguished *Young, James and Webster v United Kingdom*[50] on the basis that the employee did not object to rejoining the TGWU because of   **5.32**

---

[45] (1997) 27 EHRR 552.

[46] Ibid [92]–[93]. Note too *Van der Musselle v Belgium* (1984) 6 EHRR 163 (voluntary entry into legal profession did not prevent potential breach of the ECHR if individual could only enter on terms that might interfere with a right).

[47] [1981] IRLR 408.

[48] See also *Sigurjonsson v Iceland* (1993) 16 EHRR 462 in which the ECtHR held that a requirement that a taxi licence holder be a member of an association of taxi drivers violated Art 11 ECHR. The ECtHR was concerned by the fact that the applicant could not earn a living as a taxi driver if he were not a member of the association.

[49] (1994) 17 EHRR 193.

[50] [1981] IRLR 408.

personal objections to trade union membership and was not faced with the prospect of a dismissal. As a result he was not subjected to a form of treatment striking at the very substance of freedom of association guaranteed by Article 11.

5.33   In *Sorensen and Rasmussen v Denmark*,[51] the ECtHR considered applications by two employees in the private sector who complained of a violation of Article 11 on the grounds of closed shop agreements that required them to join a particular trade union. In one case the employee joined the union as required despite the fact that he disagreed with its political views, in the other he was dismissed when he failed to pay membership fees of the union. The Danish government argued (1) that there could be no interference in a situation where an employee was aware of the requirement of union membership prior to employment; and (2) any interference would be justified under Article 11(2) on the grounds of protection of the rights and freedoms of others.

5.34   The majority of the Grand Chamber, in finding a violation of Article 11, noted that regard must be had to the fact that the protection of personal opinions guaranteed by Articles 9 and 10 is one of the purposes of the guarantee of freedom of association, and that such protection can only be effectively secured through the guarantee of both a positive and a negative right to freedom of association.[52] As regards engagement in the private sector, the ECtHR noted, in the context of Article 11, that although the essential object is to protect the individual against arbitrary interference by public authorities with the exercise of the rights protected, the national authorities may in certain circumstances be obliged to intervene in the relationship between private individuals by taking reasonable and appropriate measures to secure the effective enjoyment of those rights.[53] Further, on the facts of the case, the ECtHR rejected the notion of freedom of contract and the choice of the employee to leave and find alternative employment, stating that individuals applying for employment often find themselves in a vulnerable situation and are only too eager to comply with the terms of employment offered.[54]

5.35   In comparing the approaches taken in the above cases a number of points are worth making. First, it is not easy to reconcile the approach taken in the Article 9 decisions with those relating to Articles 10 and 11. In cases involving Articles 10 and 11 Strasbourg appears far more willing to find that there has been an interference with the right, and focuses on whether the restriction on the right is justified. It also recognizes the positive obligation imposed on the state that effectively requires it to ensure ECHR rights are respected by private employers. This can be contrasted with the very narrow approach taken in Article 9 cases. Secondly, while

---

[51] Applications 52562/99 and 52620/99 (11 January 2006).
[52] Ibid [54].
[53] Ibid [57].
[54] Ibid [59]–[64].

it is plain that certain professions, such as pharmacists, doctors and the military, may require religious beliefs to be subjugated to the needs of the job, rather than trying to carve these out by way of a list as Strasbourg appears to have done in Article 9 cases, it would be preferable to recognize the interference and deal with it on the basis of justification.

Further, the issue of consent and freedom of contract in employment cases needs **5.36** to be looked at carefully and treated in a systematic way. There may well be cases in which an employee can be said to have freely consented to terms of employment, but if the ECHR is to have meaning as a living instrument and is to be an effective means of protection, the reality and practicality of the employment situation should be taken into account. In *Sorensen and Rasmussen v Denmark*,[55] the Grand Chamber considered the realities of the labour markets in the relevant employment sectors in the case. There is no reason as a matter of principle why this approach should be confined merely to Article 11 cases.[56] It is clear, however, that it will be important for applicants to raise expressly the issue of a lack of free choice in domestic cases if they wish to make this point.

General Legal Issues

There are three aspects of employment law that need to be considered further **5.37** as they have a bearing on the way in which ECHR rights are applied in this area. First, is the extent to which implied terms of contract of trust and confidence, and reasonableness include respect for freedom of religion. Secondly, in the context of dismissals the concept of fairness and the extent to which this includes consideration of religious issues must be examined. Thirdly, the nature of the contractual relationship between employee and employer should be looked at. In this respect it is necessary to understand how far the doctrine of freedom of contract applies and whether an employee can contract out of his ECHR rights, for example, or waive his right to freedom of religion. To some extent the Employment Regulations 2003 have circumvented these issues in the context of discrimination.[57] However, in a situation where there is no issue of discrimination they are still important considerations.

Implied terms

An important question in this context is the impact of ECHR rights on the con- **5.38** tract of employment between private parties. Broadly there are three possibilities: (1) that they have no impact as it was never intended that the rights were to affect

---

[55] Ibid.
[56] See also D O'Dempsey, A Allen, S Belgrave & J Brown, *Employment Law and the Human Rights Act 1998* (Jordans, 2001) 159.
[57] See 5.08–5.14 above.

the contractual bargaining position of parties; (2) that the common law will be developed so as to be consistent with ECHR rights; and (3) the courts would develop the common law by creating new causes of action.[58] This issue is far from resolved and is likely to be the subject of future litigation. Focusing on the second of these possibilities, there are two main ways in which ECHR rights may influence the construction of the contract of employment—through development of the implied terms of 'trust and confidence' and the use of 'reasonableness' in cases of ambiguity.

Trust and confidence

5.39 There is a term implied into every contract of employment that the employer shall not:

> Without reasonable and proper cause, conduct itself in a manner calculated [or] likely to destroy or seriously damage the relationship of trust and confidence between employer and employee.[59]

This was concerned initially with prohibiting forms of behaviour by the employer that would render working for that employer intolerable.[60] It is inherently flexible as a concept and has been developed by the courts to include not acting in a manner that would stigmatize an employee once he has left that workplace.[61] It has not been expressly acknowledged by the courts to date that the obligation to maintain trust and confidence is broad enough to include a duty not to do anything that is likely to interfere with the employee's ECHR rights. Any express statement of this nature would appear to require a private employer to consider an employee's ECHR rights and as regards employers in the private sector this would go further than what was originally intended by the HRA 1998. However, the judgment of Neuberger LJ in the Court of Appeal decision in *Copsey v WWB Devon Clays Ltd*[62] is of interest in this context. Although he was considering the concept of 'fairness' as including consideration of an employee's religious rights, it could equally well be applied to the implied term of 'trust and confidence' and 'reasonableness'.

5.40 Considered under the rubric of trust and confidence, an employer would be able to justify any act in circumstances where he can show that the act was (a) done in furtherance of a legitimate business aim and, (b) was reasonably proportionate to

---

[58] See L Mulcahy (ed), *Civil Law and the Human Rights Act* (Butterworths, 2002) para 5.15.
[59] *Woods v WM Car Services (Peterborough) Ltd* [1981] IRLR 347 [17], EAT, affd [1982] IRLR 413.
[60] Ibid.
[61] See eg *Malik v Bank of Credit and Commerce International SA* [1997] ICR 606; *TSB plc v Harris* [2000] IRLR 197, EAT.
[62] [2005] EWCA Civ 932 [82]–[84].

the achievement of that legitimate aim. This form of justification is somewhat different (textually at least) to the qualifications as set out in Article 9(2) and likely to be more appropriate in the context of a private employer. This would mean of course that the public authority employer may be subjected to a different test of justification, namely the Article 9(2) qualification.[63]

Reasonableness

The concept of 'reasonableness' of the conduct of the employer has been separate   **5.41** to some extent from the issue of the implied term of trust and confidence. In other words, whether the employer acted reasonably or not has been treated as irrelevant to the question of whether the employer acted in breach of its obligations to maintain trust and confidence.[64] But this has not invariably been the case and, in other decisions, the courts have been more willing to consider reasonableness as a factor.[65] Given that the test for implying a term of trust and confidence outlined above refers to 'without reasonable or proper cause', it would seem too fine a distinction to state that reasonableness may not be a bench mark against which conduct may be judged.

As the concept of reasonableness is flexible and must be judged according to all the   **5.42** circumstances of the case and to the standards of the age, it would be appropriate for this to include taking into account an employee's religious or philosophical beliefs.

Fairness

In the context of unfair dismissal protected by s 98 ERA 1996, the concept of fair-   **5.43** ness is central to the court's consideration of the issues. It involves both procedural and substantive fairness. In most cases concerning freedom of religion, the issue at stake will be substantive fairness. When assessing fairness of a decision to dismiss, the tribunal is required to take into account the reasonableness or otherwise of the decision in light of all the circumstances of the case.

It has been suggested by the Court of Appeal in *Copsey v WWB Devon Clays Ltd*,[66] that fairness was broad enough to include consideration of the employee's religious convictions. To that extent, Neuburger LJ considered that Article 9 ECHR did not take matters any further, and he analysed the competing interests of the

---

[63] See further discussion in Mulcahy (n 58 above) paras 13.23–13.27.
[64] *Western Excavating v Sharp* [1978] QB 761; *White v Reflecting Road Studs* [1991] IRLR 331, EAT.
[65] *Woods v WM Car Services (Peterborough) Ltd* [1981] IRLR 347 [17], EAT, affd [1982] IRLR 413.
[66] [2005] EWCA Civ 932 [82]–[84].

parties in accordance with the provisions of the ERA 1996 rather than the HRA 1998.[67] While the approach to the question of fairness appears to be sound, it leaves entirely unanswered the question of the scope and application of Article 9.

Contracting out of ECHR rights

5.44 There are compelling arguments that can be made on both sides as to whether employer and employee should be able to contract out of the rights contained in the ECHR. There may be different considerations according to whether the employer is a public authority or not. As regards private employers at least, the arguments for permitting contracting out of ECHR rights relate to freedom of contract, certainty in terms of employment and the fact that private businesses are not bound by the HRA 1998 unless they are performing public functions. On the other hand there is an air of unreality about the reliance on freedom of contract in the relationship between employer and employee.[68] This in itself is evident from the considerable statutory inroads into such freedom. As regards public authority employers, contracting out of rights would appear to be incompatible with their duty to consider the rights of individuals.

5.45 Leaving aside the question of whether an employer is a public authority or private individual, all the circumstances of the case need to be looked at. The situation may be one where the employee realistically has a number of alternatives open to him, is in a position of relative power in bargaining, and freely consents to a restriction of his right to take time off for religious holidays. Or it may be a requirement of the employment, made clear before engagement, that an employee acts in such a way that may interfere with his own beliefs, for example a pharmacist dispensing birth control pills or a doctor in examining women. In these scenarios, there does not seem to be, as a matter of principle, a reason not to uphold the bargain on the basis that there is free consent or a justification for any restriction. This can be contrasted with the case where an employee has little bargaining power, there is a situation of mass unemployment in the sector he works in, and where he consents reluctantly, having raised the issue with a prospective employer.[69]

---

67 Ibid [89]–[91]. See also *Liddiard v Post Office* [2001] EWCA Civ 940 (HRA 1998 added nothing to applicant's claim for unfair dismissal).

68 See G Morris, *The European Convention on Human Rights and Employment: To Which Acts Does It Apply* [1999] EHRLR 496; P Elias & J Coppel, 'Freedom of Expression and Freedom of Religion: Some Thoughts on the Glen Hoddle Case' in J Beatson & Y Cripps (eds), *Freedom of Expression and Freedom of Information: Essays in Honour of Sir David Williams* (OUP, 2000).

69 See Lindsay J (2001) 30 ILJ 1, 10 who extra-judicially has suggested that the answer may depend upon the relative bargaining positions of the parties. See also discussion in Smith, Thomas & Mead, *Industrial Law* (LexisNexis UK, 2003) 53–4.

Specific Legal Issues

Engagement and dismissal

The engagement and dismissal of employees is an area in which both ECHR **5.46** rights and the Employment Regulations 2003 will have an impact. Employers that are considered public authorities within the meaning of s 6 HRA 1998 will have to consider the rights of prospective and current employees under Articles 9 and 14. Both public authority and private employers will be affected by the Employment Regulations 2003. In addition both public and private employers will have to ensure that their conduct does not breach implied terms of trust and confidence such that an employee might regard himself as constructively dismissed, and that any dismissal is fair in the circumstances.

The compatibility of working terms with the manifestation of religious and philo- **5.47** sophical beliefs is a difficult area. There are at least four possible scenarios: (a) the prospective employee informs the employer that he has a particular religious belief that may conflict with the terms of employment and freely accepts the terms anyway; (b) the prospective employee informs the employer that he has a particular religious belief and reluctantly accepts the terms of employment because he feels that he has little choice; (c) the prospective employee fails to tell his employer of his religious belief in accepting terms of employment but there is a subsequent conflict, for example when working hours are changed in accordance with the terms of the contract; and (d) the prospective employee has no beliefs that conflict with the terms of employment at the date of his engagement but later adopts a religious belief that does conflict.

As regards Article 9 and 14, the law could take an approach based upon waiver of **5.48** ECHR rights and freedom of contract or alternatively regard Article 9 as being potentially engaged and look at the question in terms of justification. There are some employment situations where self evidently the nature of the employment requires some restriction upon individual's rights, for example military service or medicine. These situations might be singled out as being special cases. However, as suggested above, this involves drawing an arbitrary line between different types of employment. It may be more principled to regard Article 9 as being engaged and look at the issue as a matter of justified interference. This would bring the Article 9 employment cases from Strasbourg in line with employment cases involving other ECHR rights.

Domestic law

The statutory law relating to engagement and dismissal does not refer specifically **5.49** to freedom of religion. However, it is flexible enough to be construed compatibly with Articles 9 and 14 ECHR. How this will be applied in relation to both public authority and private employers by the courts is likely to be the subject of future litigation.

5.50 In *Copsey v WWB Devon Clays Ltd*,[70] the Court of Appeal had to consider what impact Article 9 had on an unfair dismissal claim brought by an employee against a private sector employer. Mr Copsey was a Christian employee who sought to manifest his religious beliefs by observing Sunday as a day of rest. The reason for his dismissal was a refusal to agree to a contractual variation in his working hours so as to provide that he should work a seven day shift including a Sunday, if needed. The tribunal found that the employer had sought to offer Mr Copsey several alternative positions although all included a requirement to work on Sundays. The employer had also taken soundings from his colleagues who would be disadvantaged if a special case were made for him. The tribunal, whose decision was upheld by the EAT, found he was dismissed because he refused to accept a change to the seven day shift pattern and the dismissal was not in any way connected to his religious beliefs. It was for a sound business reason and an economic necessity for the employer and the decision to dismiss fell within the band of reasonable responses an employer could adopt and was fair.

5.51 Mummery LJ in the Court of Appeal considered that the real issue was whether the link between his dismissal and his wish to manifest his belief was sufficiently material to bring the circumstances of the dismissal within the ambit of Article 9. But for the 'clear line of decisions' by the Commission to the effect that Article 9 is not engaged where an employee asserts Article 9 rights in relation to his hours, he would have thought it was and would have then considered the justification arguments under Article 9(2). These cases referred to the employee as being free to resign in order to manifest his religious beliefs. Mummery LJ made a number of critical comments relating to the three decisions cited but did not believe it was the function of the Court of Appeal to question the non-interference approach, leaving it to the House of Lords or Strasbourg to take a different approach.[71]

5.52 Rix LJ in his judgment sought to draw a distinction between cases in which the employee tried to change his contract of employment and those where the employer chose to change the contract of employment. On that basis he found the decision in *Stedman v United Kingdom*,[72] where the employer sought to alter the terms of contract, but which followed *Kontinnen v Finland*[73] in which the employee chose to alter the contract, incomprehensible. In that sense he did not think that the courts were required to follow *Stedman v United Kingdom*. He reasoned that

---

[70] [2005] EWCA Civ 932.
[71] Ibid [39].
[72] (1997) 23 EHRR CD 168.
[73] (1996) 87 DR 68.

where an employer seeks to change the working hours and terms of his contract of employment with his employee in such a way as to interfere materially with the employee's right to manifest his religion, then Article 9(1) ECHR is potentially engaged. One solution was to find a reasonable accommodation with the employee. If this were found then there would be no material interference. If a reasonable solution were offered to the employee, but not accepted by him, then it remained possible to say that there is no material interference; alternatively, one could speak of justification under Article 9(2).[74]

A third approach to the case was outlined by Neuberger LJ in his judgment. **5.53** He preferred to regard the case as one of interpretation of the statutory provisions relating to unfair dismissal in the ERA 1996. He considered that dismissing an employee because he is not prepared to work on a certain day of the week on the grounds of a genuinely held religious belief could, depending on the facts, amount to unfair dismissal. He drew a distinction between a case where an employee is specifically engaged to work on a Sunday and subsequently comes to believe in a religion which does not permit him to work on a Sunday, and a case where an employee is engaged on the basis that he does not have to work on a Sunday and then is required to do so. In the first case, he suggested that it might be unfair for the employer not to consider whether he could accommodate the employee, although it would require pretty exceptional additional facts to amount to a case of unfair dismissal. In the second case, he stated that it would be hard to see how the employer could challenge his dismissal of the employee as unfair, even if the terms of the contract permitted a variation. But it was important to emphasize that the ERA 1996 should not be invoked so as to impose unreasonable stringency or impractical constraint on the way in which an employer runs his business. Having reached that conclusion, he did not see how Article 9 takes matters any further than the ERA 1996.[75]

The decision in *Copsey v WWB Devon Clays Ltd* must now be read in the light of **5.54** the House of Lords judgment in *R (Begum) v Headteacher and Governors of Denbigh High School*.[76] Although the House of Lords were considering a case involving education, they considered the authorities relating to both education and employment. Lord Bingham expressly referred to the judgment in *Copsey* and held that there was a 'coherent and remarkably consistent body of authority' from Strasbourg which had to be taken into account.[77] As regards future cases where an employee may wish to raise Article 9 in relation to engagement or dismissal, it will be critical to adduce evidence of the effective lack of free choice if this issue is to be run.

---

[74] [2005] EWCA Civ 932 [71]–[72].
[75] Ibid [82]–[84], [89]–[90].
[76] [2006] UKHL 15.
[77] Ibid [24]. See also [51] (per Lord Hoffmann) and 5.23 above.

Given the decision of the House of Lords in *Begum*, it appears that the doctrine of free choice and freedom of contract will prevail in the absence of specific facts suggesting otherwise.[78]

5.55 The decision of the European Court of Justice ('ECJ') in *Prais v Council*[79] should also be noted in the context of engagement and freedom of religion. In that case a Jewish woman relied on Article 9 ECHR in her complaint that she was unable to sit an examination to qualify for a EC job because it took place on Saturday. The ECJ dismissed her complaint on the facts because she had not notified the board sufficiently early, but it suggested that had she raised the issue at the outset the employer would have been under a duty to consider her request for examinations on a different day.

5.56 It should be noted that in *Copsey v WWB Devon Clays Ltd*[80] there was no issue as to discrimination and the events in any event occurred before the enactment of the Employment Regulations 2003 such that there was no consideration of either Article 14 ECHR or the provisions of the Regulations. However, in many cases involving engagement and dismissal for reasons related to the manifestation of religious beliefs, there may well be a claim based upon discrimination.

ECHR law

5.57 The Strasbourg cases referred to above at 5.24–5.34 arguably reflect a number of different approaches to cases involving dismissals and ECHR rights. In some cases, the decision appears to turn on a specific category of employment in which restrictions on individual rights will be inevitable by virtue of the nature of the employment. Examples of this type of employer are the military or hospitals or pharmacies, for example *Kalaç v Turkey*[81] and *Pichon and Sajous v France*.[82] In these cases the Commission has simply stated that there is no interference with freedom of religion.

5.58 A second strand in the case law is the concept of freedom of contract as in *Ahmad v United Kingdom*,[83] *Kontinnen v Finland*[84] and *Stedman v United Kingdom*.[85] In these cases the Commission and ECtHR have essentially upheld the bargain between the parties and decided that in the circumstances there can be no interference. A more consistent approach with other case law may be to consider that there is an interference but to examine whether or not it is justified. In essence the European courts are unwilling to involve themselves in a balancing exercise

---

[78] See 2.73–2.74 above for further consideration of *Begum*.
[79] [1976] ECR 1589, [1976] 2 CMLR 708.
[80] [2005] EWCA Civ 932.
[81] (1997) 27 EHRR 552.
[82] Application 49853/99 (2 October 2001).
[83] (1981) 4 EHRR 126.
[84] (1996) 87 DR 68.
[85] (1997) 23 EHRR CD 168.

between employee and employer, but the difficulty with their approach is that it suggests that the domestic courts do not need to consider that balance either. If the reference to the 'rights of others' is construed as meaning the rights of all members of a democratic society including those of the employer then this will allow the proper balancing exercise to take place. As a result of these decisions, it will in any event be particularly important for any applicant to adduce clear evidence of the lack of choice so as to amount to an interference with Article 9 rights.

A third strand in the case law is the decisions where the European courts have con- **5.59** sidered that there is an interference and have then gone on to consider whether it is justified. These cases have involved dismissals in the context of other Articles, for example Articles 8, 10 and 11 ECHR such as in *Smith and Grady v United Kingdom*,[86] *Vogt v Germany*[87] and *Jensen and Rasmussen v Denmark*.[88] In these cases the ECtHR has not taken the simple approach that there can be no interference because of freedom of contract. The approach here has been more nuanced, recognizing that the concept of freedom of contract does not provide an answer in cases where an individual's skills may not be readily transferable or where an individual's options in the job market may be limited following a dismissal.

Working hours and time off

Many of the cases involving complaints about failure to respect religious beliefs **5.60** where they conflict with an employer's schedule have culminated in the employee taking time off anyway and being dismissed as a result. These cases have been considered above under engagement and dismissal. In this section, the position relating to time off work for prayer and for religious festivals is considered generally. There are basically two types of scenario where these issues are relevant. An employee may require time off on a regular basis in order to perform a religious requirement such as prayer or to observe the Sabbath. Alternatively, an employee may wish to take time off on a more ad hoc basis either to coincide with a yearly religious festival or holiday or for a one off pilgrimage. In both scenarios, the way in which work and time-tabling is structured by the employer is likely to reflect the traditions of the majority religion. This must be taken into account when considering requests by minorities.[89]

Domestic law

Until relatively recently there were no government controls expressly relating to **5.61** hours worked.[90] That changed with the compliance with the EC Working Time

---

86 (1999) 29 EHRR 493.
87 (1996) 21 EHRR 205.
88 Applications 52562/99 and 52620/99 (11 January 2006).
89 See provisions of the Employment Regulations 2003 in this regard and 5.08–5.14 above.
90 Note that there was some protection of minorities through indirect discrimination provision: see *JH Walker v Hussain* [1997] ICR 291 and 2.28 above.

Directive[91] although it did not seek to determine the actual hours worked. These are still a matter of agreement and contract between employer and employee.

5.62 **Working Time Regulations 1998** The Working Time Regulations 1998 ('1998 Regulations') came into force on 1 October 1998.[92] They apply entitlements in four areas—a 48 hour working week, night working, rest breaks and paid annual holiday. Although there is considerable flexibility in the Regulations, none of the provisions specifically envisage that workers may need to take time off for religious reasons.

5.63 A worker may give notice to the employer of the dates he wishes to take his holidays, subject to the employer requiring the worker to take his holiday on particular dates. The worker must give twice the number of days notice as the days' leave he requests. The employer can prevent the worker from taking leave on a particular day by giving notice equivalent to the same number of days as the length of leave the employee wishes to take. These notice provisions can be overridden by contractual provisions that may provide for different periods of notice.[93] There are all manner of exceptions and permitted contracting out of the Working Time Regulations.[94] There are specific sectors that are excluded such as sea fishing, the activities of doctors in training, and services such as the armed forces and police.[95] Importantly, the Regulations do not apply at all to a worker who has agreed in writing with his employer that they should not apply.[96]

5.64 **Sunday trading** The Sunday Trading Act 1994 was enacted to reform the law relating to Sunday trading and to give certain protections to shop workers who did not wish to work on Sundays. This is a classic example of legislation that is tacitly based upon the religious customs and traditions of the majority although it is framed in general and religiously neutral language. The relevant provisions for opting out of Sunday trading are now contained in ss 36–43 ERA 1996 but relate only to shop workers or betting workers.[97]

5.65 A 'protected shop worker' or an 'opted out shop worker' may refuse to work on Sundays. Any provision in contract that provides for him to work on that day will be unenforceable. A dismissal because an employee refuses to do Sunday work will be automatically unfair. Further, an employer cannot subject an employee to any form of detriment because he is a protected or opted out shop worker, although he

---

[91] Council Directive (EC) 93/104 concerning certain aspects of the organization of working time [1993] OJ L307/18.
[92] Enacting Directive (EC) 93/104 and certain provisions of Council Directive 94/93 (EC) on the protection of young people at work [1994] OJ L216/12.
[93] 1998 Regulations, reg 15.
[94] Ibid, regs 18–27.
[95] Ibid, reg 18.
[96] Ibid, reg 23.
[97] Derived from Sunday Trading Act 1994 and Shops Act 1950.

may offer financial and other inducements to such a worker if he is prepared to work on Sundays. Similar provisions apply to betting workers.[98] It should be noted that the Sunday trading provisions contained in the ERA 1996 do not protect applicants for employment. However, employees (prospective or existing) will now be protected by the Employment Regulations 2003.

This Sunday trading legislation is of interest in that it specifically creates an exception which protects adherents of the majority religion. The need for this exception, however, partly reflects the extent to which Christianity has become secularized and the commercial power of consumerism. It may also be seen as a concession to the leaders of the established religion. In that respect it differs in character from other legal exceptions such as the exemption for Sikhs from wearing motor cycle helmets. These exemptions are created on the basis that the majority has been able to enact legislation through the normal democratic procedure, whereas the minority is not able to do this. In addition in many of the cases of exemption, they do not confer an advantage on a particular group that is desired or required by the majority, for example exemption from meat slaughter regulations or the right to carry a religious dagger. The Sunday trading legislation is open to challenge. First, it creates an exception only for certain categories of worker in limited sectors. Secondly, it puts adherents of the majority religion in a better position than those of minority religions which have an alternative day of rest or celebration.[99] **5.66**

ECHR law

See consideration of the case law above at 5.24–5.26 and 5.57–5.59. **5.67**

Clothing and religious symbols

The issue of clothing and religious symbols in the workplace has already led to some significant cases. Some people regard it as a religious duty to wear certain garments such as the turban, the yarmulke and the hijab. It raises some interesting questions that are framed slightly differently to those in an educational context. Some employers have prescribed uniforms or a dress code, although these may be capable of adaption to suit individual requirements. Difficulties arise when employers justify restrictions on the grounds of hygiene, health or safety. Another area of contention may be where the employer offers a service to the public and perceives that restrictions are required in order to promote the business, for example on the basis that the public would prefer employees dressed in a particular manner. **5.68**

---

[98] See *Williams v ASDA Stores Ltd* (EAT/306/96) in which the EAT held that an employee had not shown that he had been dismissed for asserting his statutory right under the Sunday trading provisions.

[99] See also O'Dempsey et al (n 56 above) 178–9.

Domestic law

5.69　There are no specific laws, policies or codes stating what an employee should wear at work in many types of employment. There are obvious exceptions to this for certain industries such as medicine, construction, the military and the police. These restrictions may have a number of different rationales such as health and safety, worker solidarity, and promoting a particular work ethic among the employees as a whole. Some exemptions have been carved out on religious grounds. Most notably, Sikhs working in the construction industry are exempt from the requirement of wearing hard hats while they are wearing turbans.[100]

5.70　A number of cases were brought prior to the enactment of the HRA 1998 and the Employment Regulations 2003. These have been argued either as dismissal cases or brought under the RRA 1976. Although the legal framework and cultural climate have changed, they are worth considering in relation to the justifications claimed by the employer and the treatment by the courts. Under Article 9 ECHR an employer will have to show that any interference is justified. An important factor in discriminating under the Employment Regulations 2003 will be for the employer to show that there is a 'genuine occupational requirement' that necessitates a restriction. Some of the more important pre-HRA 1998 cases are considered below.[101] Recently, in *Mohammed v West Coast Trains Ltd*,[102] the EAT handed down its first decision regarding religious discrimination under the Employment Regulations 2003.

5.71　In *Mohammed v West Coast Trains Ltd*[103] the EAT considered a claim under the RRA 1976 and the Employment Regulations 2003 by Mr Mohammed whose religious beliefs required him to have a beard of minimum length. His employers, on the other hand, required beards to be neatly trimmed. He was asked to trim his beard and refused and was dismissed as a result. His claim was dismissed by the tribunal on the grounds that he had not shown a discriminatory act after the Regulations came into force and because he had not demonstrated that he had a prima facie case of either conscious or unconscious discrimination. Mr Mohammed appealed primarily on the ground that the tribunal had taken insufficient account of the delay in dealing with his statutory questionnaire. He also alleged the tribunal's findings were perverse. The EAT held that it was open to the tribunal to

---

[100]　See Employment Act 1989, s 11.

[101]　See also *Schmidt v Austicks Bookshops Ltd* [1977] IRLR 360, EAT (SDA claim—employer imposed rule of no trousers for women at work—EAT held no discrimination because there were rules for both sexes); *Burrett v West Birmingham Health Authority* [1994] IRLR 7, EAT (female nurse required to wear cap not less favourably treated than male employees because uniform requirement applied to both); *Smith v Safeway plc* [1996] IRLR 456, CA (restriction on long hair for men upheld because there were rules for both sexes).

[102]　UKEAT/0682/05/DA.

[103]　Ibid.

find that the claim of discrimination had not been substantiated. The issue of his beard was not raised after September 2003 and therefore only raised before the Regulations came into effect, and another employee had kept his beard tidy but untrimmed in compliance with the company's policy. His appeal was dismissed.

In *Singh v Lyons Maid Ltd*,[104] a case decided before the RRA 1976, a Sikh produc- **5.72** tion worker at an ice-cream factory agreed to a requirement of no beards when he was engaged. During his employment the employee underwent a spiritual revival and decided to adhere to the requirements of his religion regarding uncut hair. He was dismissed and claimed unfair dismissal. The company argued that the rule was designed on the grounds of hygiene and avoiding bacteriological infection of its product. The tribunal dismissed his claim, holding that the rule was not unreasonable and that it was a term that the employers regarded as fundamental. They could see nothing unreasonable in a dismissal based on a refusal by the employee to comply with a term of his contract.

In *Panesar v Nestle Co Ltd*,[105] the Court of Appeal rejected an application for leave **5.73** to appeal in a case involving a Sikh who alleged indirect discrimination on the basis that it was a requirement in the chocolate factories where he wished to work that men be clean shaven. Denning LJ noted that the company had presented experts in food hygiene in support of the no beard rule. He ruled that the finding of the tribunal was essentially one of fact against which there was no appeal except on a point of law. He also referred to Article 9 ECHR, stating that it was not the law in England although much regard was given to it, but that there would be no breach because the rule was for the protection of public health.[106]

In *Kuldip Singh v British Rail Engineering Ltd*,[107] the EAT considered a claim by **5.74** a Sikh of indirect discrimination under the RRA 1976. A new production controller declared an area where Sikhs worked as a 'hard hat area' and an employee complained on religious grounds when he was obliged to take less well paid work with loss of promotional prospects. The issue in the case was whether this was justified and in particular (a) the effect on others of making an exemption for one person and (b) the possibility of ensuing liability on the employers if the applicant did not wear protective headgear. The EAT stated that it was not wrong for the tribunal to take these matters into account, and rejected arguments based on the significant exemptions granted to Sikhs historically during the war, and statutory exemptions for motor cyclists, and upheld the restriction.

---

[104] [1975] IRLR 328.
[105] [1980] ICR 144.
[106] Ibid, 147. See also *Singh v Rowntree Mackintosh Ltd* [1979] ICR 554 (employer with a no beards rule could not be said to have acted unreasonably if he adopted a standard supported by medical evidence and with the approval of a local food and drugs officer).
[107] [1986] ICR 22, EAT.

5.75 In *Kingston and Richmond Area Health Authority v Kaur (Tajwinder)*,[108] the EAT considered an appeal by the Health Authority against the decision of the tribunal that a refusal to allow a trainee Sikh nurse to wear trousers beneath her uniform dress amounted to unlawful race discrimination contrary to ss 1(1)(b) and 4(1) RRA 1976. The EAT overturned the decision of the tribunal on the basis that the Health Authority was bound by the Enrolled Nurses Rules, Approval Instrument 1969.[109]

5.76 Other religious groups that were not considered to be racial or ethnic groups for the purposes of the RRA 1976 were not protected against discrimination prior to the HRA 1998 and the Employment Regulations 2003.[110] In *Dawkins v Crown Suppliers (PSA) Ltd*,[111] the Court of Appeal rejected the appeal of a Rastafarian who was not considered for a job as a van driver while wearing dreadlocks tucked under a hat. The public authority employer expected its employees to have short hair. On the basis that Rastafarians were held not to be an ethnic group the Court of Appeal did not consider the case further. No reference was made in the case to Article 9 ECHR.

ECHR law

5.77 To date the only case decided in Strasbourg relating directly to the question of religious clothing and employment is that of *Dahlab v Switzerland*.[112] This case is dealt with above at 4.92. It relates specifically to the situation of a teacher in a state school and justifications for the restriction on wearing a hijab refer directly to her position as a state employee and the influence she had over her pupils. It is not therefore likely to be of much assistance in determining cases outside the sphere of education and the specific context.

5.78 Of interest in this area is the decision in *X v United Kingdom*,[113] in which the Commission considered the case of a Sikh who had been convicted 20 times for failing to wear a crash helmet. The Commission found that the alleged requirement imposed by statute was justified on the grounds of public safety and that there was no violation of Article 9 ECHR. Although the decision in this case does not relate to an employment situation, it is likely that the ECtHR would show considerable deference to a finding by a domestic court based on public health or safety.

5.79 In an employment context the Report of the Human Rights Committee in *Singh Binder v Canada*[114] is relevant. Mr Binder, a Canadian Sikh, claimed discrimination

---

[108] [1981] ICR 631.

[109] Note the comment of Browne-Wilkinson J presiding at 636: 'We find it regrettable that the requirements as to uniform are so inflexible, and so inflexibly operated, that they do not permit of any variation to meet the genuine and deeply felt convictions as to dress of minority groups; whether those groups are to be treated as racial or religious groups.'

[110] Save in respect of indirect discrimination in certain cases: see *JH Walker v Hussain* [1996] ICR 291.

[111] *The Times* 4 February 1993.

[112] Application 42393/98 (15 February 2001).

[113] (1978) 14 DR 234.

[114] 208/1986, HRC Report 1990, Vol IIA/45/40 IX F.

on the grounds of his religion and ethnicity after his employment as a maintenance electrician with the Canadian Railway Company was terminated for his
refusal to wear safety headgear at work in place of his turban. He based his claim
on Article 18 of the International Covenant on Civil and Political Right 1966.
The Committee found that his claim to wear a turban was a manifestation of his
religious beliefs which was subject to restrictions on grounds of public safety or
health and that the interference with his religious rights was accordingly justified
in the interest of public safety under Article 18(3).

Religious employers

So far the consideration has been focused on the employee as the religious adherent.   **5.80**
It is also necessary to consider what issues arise when the employer is a religious
organization or church or when they impose a requirement that employees are of
a certain religious character. This raises many controversial issues relating to the
church and state divide, to the concept of the liberal state, and discrimination law.
There are cases where it is self-evident that the person holding an office within a
religious group will be of that religion, such as the vicar of a parish church or the
imam of a mosque. Issues may then arise as to the relative religiosity of individual
candidates for the post. There are equally many positions within religious organizations where an individual's private religious or philosophical beliefs cannot
necessarily be said to be essential to carrying out that job, such as gardeners, clean-
ers or kitchen staff.

Domestic law

There are two general exceptions contained in the Employment Regulations 2003   **5.81**
to the prohibition on discrimination on the grounds of religion or belief. The first
is where a particular religious belief is a 'genuine and determining occupational
requirement' for the job, having regard to the nature of the work, and it can be
shown that it is proportionate to apply that requirement in the particular case.[115]
The second exception applies to employers who hold 'an ethos based on religion
or belief' and it can be shown that a particular religion or belief is a genuine
occupational requirement which is a determining factor and is proportionate.[116]

This leads to the question of whether a relationship of employment exists between   **5.82**
the individual and the religious organization. This is partly a question of fact and
partly of law. There are situations in which such a relationship will be likely, for
example where a religious organization employs gardeners, cooks or administrative
staff. This will have consequences also for whether an individual is able for rely on

---

[115] Employment Regulations 2003, reg 7(2). See also EA 2006, s 52(4)(m) and 5.07 above.
[116] Ibid, reg 7(3).

the unfair dismissal legislation. For the purposes of dismissal it will be necessary to show that a contract of service exists between employer and employee.

5.83   The nature of the relationship between a religious organization and its appointed religious leader and other people working within the organization has been considered in a number of cases. The early cases concern questions of dismissal and therefore of whether a contract of service existed. In *Re Employment of Church of England Curates*,[117] Parker J held that a curate in the Church of England was not employed under a 'contract of service' within Part I (a) of the First Schedule to the National Insurance Act 1911. He stated that the position of a curate is the position of a person who holds an ecclesiastical office, rather than the position of a person whose rights and duties are defined by contract.[118]

5.84   In *President of the Methodist Conference v Parfitt*,[119] the Court of Appeal considered an unfair dismissal claim brought by a Methodist minister. The issue was whether the parties had entered into a contract of service. The court held that having regard to all the circumstances it was impossible to conclude that any contract, let alone a contract of service, came into being between a newly ordained minister and the Methodist Church when the minister was received into full connection.

5.85   In *Davies v Presbyterian Church of Wales*,[120] the House of Lords considered an unfair dismissal claim by a minister of the Presbyterian Church of Wales who had been inducted pastor of a united pastorate in Wales. Lord Templeman held that the claimant could not point to any contract between himself and the church. The book of rules did not contain terms of employment capable of being offered and accepted in the course of a religious ceremony.

5.86   A similar issue arose in *Diocese of Southwark v Coker*,[121] in the context of an unfair dismissal claim by an assistant curate of the Church of England. Again the claimant failed. Mummery LJ in the Court of Appeal analyzed the reason underlying the absence of a contract between a church and a minister of religion in these cases as lack of intention to create a contractual relationship. He stated that special features surrounding the appointment and removal of a Church of England priest as an assistant curate, and surrounding the source and scope of his duties, preclude the creation of a contract 'unless a clear intention to the contrary is expressed'.[122]

---

[117] [1912] 2 Ch 563, 568–9.
[118] See also *Scottish Insurance Commissioners v Church of Scotland* [1914] SC 16 in which the Court of Session, applying the 'control' test, reached the same conclusion regarding assistants to ministers of the Church of Scotland.
[119] [1984] ICR 176.
[120] [1986] ICR 280.
[121] [1998] ICR 140.
[122] See also *Barthope v Exeter Diocesan Board of Finance* [1979] ICR 900, EAT (in the context of an unfair dismissal claim, a stipendiary lay reader was not employed under a contract of service); *Santokh Singh v Guru Nanak Gurdwara* [1990] ICR 309 (Granthi (priest) at a Sikh temple not an employee); *Birmingham Mosque Trust Ltd v Alavi* [1992] ICR 435.

More recently the House of Lords in *Percy v Church of Scotland Board of National*   **5.87**
Mission[123] considered a sex discrimination claim brought against the Church of
Scotland by a former minister of the church. The claim raised the issue of whether
Ms Percy's relationship with the church constituted 'employment' as defined in
s 82(1) SDA 1975. The House of Lords considered the earlier case law relating to
this issue in some detail. They noted that the earlier cases concerned dismissals and
whether a contract of service existed, whereas the test for the purposes of s 82 was
wider and included a contract for services. In that contest the earlier dismissal cases
had to be treated with caution and Lord Nicholls observed that holding an office,
even an ecclesiastical office, and the existence of a contract to provide services were
not necessarily mutually exclusive. He further stated that it was time to recognize
that employment arrangements between a church and its ministers should not
lightly be taken as intended to have no legal effect and, in consequence, its ministers
denied this protection of employment legislation. On the facts the documents
showed that Ms Percy entered into a contract with the Board to provide services to
the church on agreed terms and conditions. Her rights and duties were defined by
contract rather than by the office to which she was appointed.[124]

In addition to the exceptions in the Employment Regulations 2003,[125] there are   **5.88**
exceptions to the Employment Equality (Sexual Orientation) Regulations 2003
which otherwise protect job applicants, persons in employment including employees, workers, and self-employed persons against discrimination on the grounds of
their sexual orientation. There are two key genuine occupational qualifications:
(1) where being of a particular sexual orientation is a genuine requirement; and
(2) for organized religions where there is a requirement as to sexual orientation in
order to comply with the doctrine of the religion or to avoid conflicting with the
religious convictions of a significant number of the religion's followers.[126] There are
also some offices that only members of the Church of England may hold. These
include the monarchy.[127]

Generally, however, where the employer discriminates on the basis of religion, it   **5.89**
will be necessary for him to demonstrate that there is a 'genuine occupational
requirement' in the selection of workers on religious grounds. As yet there is little
precedent in English law as to how this will be interpreted. In Northern Ireland,
which has had protection against religious discrimination in employment
since the Fair Employment Act 1976 came into force, the current provisions in the

---

[123] [2005] UKHL 73.
[124] See also *The New Testament Church of God v Stewart* UKEAT/0293/06/DA (27 October 2006).
[125] Employment Regulations 2003, reg 7.
[126] See *R (Amicus) v Secretary of State for Trade and Industry* [2004] EWHC 860 (Admin).
[127] See Act of Settlement 1700, s 2; Lord Chancellor (Tenure of Office and Discharge of
Ecclesiastical Functions) Act 1974.

Fair Employment and Treatment (Northern Ireland) Order 1998 have a test of 'the essential nature of the job requires it to be done by a person holding, or not holding a particular religious belief'.[128]

ECHR law

5.90 There are no cases at the Strasbourg level which have dealt with these issues directly although it seems that it is an area where future litigation is likely. It is clear that a religious organization can possess an Article 9 right as a representative of its members.[129] As regards the question of discrimination, given the existing case law on discrimination from Strasbourg and the fact that respect will be given in principle to the relationship between church and state in a particular member state, it is likely that a wide margin of appreciation will be granted in such cases.

---

[128] SI 1998/3162 (NI 21), art 70(3).
[129] See 2.56 above.

6

IMMIGRATION AND ASYLUM

Introduction

There are a number of ways in which religious freedom may be relevant in the **6.01** context of immigration and asylum law. In many parts of the world, freedom to express religious views, to change one's religion, or to establish and preach a non-state religion is not respected. This may give rise to claims by individuals who arrive in the United Kingdom and make a claim for refugee status. The protections contained in the Human Rights Act 1998 ('HRA 1998'), the Equality Act 2006 ('EA 2006'), and the Race Relations Act 1976 ('RRA 1976') will also be relevant to any case involving a decision taken by the Home Office whether involving the removal or the entry clearance of an individual.

Although the protection afforded by the 1951 Refugee Convention is different to **6.02** that under Article 9 of the European Convention on Human Rights ('ECHR'), the refugee law cases on religious persecution are considered in this chapter as relating to the issue of freedom of religion generally. In addition, there are a number of decisions relating to the conscientious objection to military service abroad which have arisen in the immigration context. Religious issues have also been at the forefront of a number of family law cases involving issues such as polygamy, child marriage, divorce, and custody under the Immigration Rules. Article 9 may not necessarily be directly engaged in all of these cases but they are of considerable

157

interest in understanding the way in which religious questions are dealt with by the courts here. Finally, the provisions in the Immigration Rules relating to entry clearance for religious leaders and workers are referred to.

Statutory Framework

Refugee Convention

6.03 The statutory framework relating to asylum and immigration is highly complex. It is notable for the flurry of primary legislation in this area, particularly in the last ten years. Refugee law is part of international humanitarian law, rather than immigration law. This is governed by the 1951 Convention Relating to the Status of Refugees and its Protocol of 1967 (collectively the 'Refugee Convention'). Although the definition of a refugee and the principle of non-refoulement are matters of international law, the application of the Refugee Convention is affected by primary and secondary legislation in the United Kingdom dealing with a whole raft of related matters including the procedural aspects of bringing an application, rights of appeal, detention of individuals, welfare support, and health care. The most litigated substantive issue as regards refugee law relates to the definition of Article 1A(2) of the Refugee Convention.[1]

Immigration and Asylum Acts

6.04 As regards immigration law, the Immigration Act 1971 ('IA 1971') is the cornerstone of the law and provides the structure of the system of entry control for the United Kingdom. It has been supplemented, amended and replaced in part by a raft of Acts: the Immigration Act 1988, the Asylum and Immigration Appeals Act 1993, the Asylum and Immigration Act 1996, the Special Immigration Appeals Commission Act 1997, the Immigration and Asylum Act 1999, the Nationality, Immigration and Asylum Act 2002, the Asylum and Immigration (Treatment of Claimants etc) Act 2004, the Asylum, Immigration and Nationality Act 2006 ('AINA 2006').[2]

---

[1] See generally E Feller, V Turk & F Nicholson, *Refugee Protection in International Law: UNHCR's Global Consultations on International Protection* (Cambridge University Press, 2003); G Goodwin-Gill, *The Refugee in International Law* (OUP, 2007); J Hathaway, *The Rights of Refugees under International Law* (OUP, 2005). For effective domestic incorporation of the Refugee Convention see *R (European Roma Rights Centre) v Immigration Officer at Prague Airport* [2004] UKHL [40–42] (per Lord Steyn) and 6.28 below.

[2] The AINA 2006 obtained royal assent on 30 March 2006. Some but not all of its provisions are in force. See generally *Macdonald's Immigration Law & Practice* (6th edn, Butterworths, 2005); M Symes & P Jorro, *Asylum Law & Practice* (Butterworths, 2003); N Blake & R Husain, *Immigration, Asylum & Human Rights* (OUP, 2003).

Immigration Rules and Home Office policies

The Immigration Rules[3] are made by the Secretary of State for the Home Department **6.05**
in accordance with ss 1(4) and 3(2) of the IA 1971. There has been considerable
debate as to the legal status of the Rules and whether they are legally binding or not.
The Court of Appeal referred to them in an early case as being rules of practice laid
down for the guidance of those entrusted with the administration of the IA 1971,
and although not delegated legislation or rules of law, they had the force of law for
those hearing immigration appeals.[4] The intersection of the Immigration Rules
and the ECHR is considered below.

In addition to the Rules, there are various policies such as the Home Office policy **6.06**
to grant humanitarian protection. Most of these policies are now incorporated into
the Immigration Directorate Instructions ('IDIs'), Asylum Policy Instructions,
Nationality Instructions, and the Operational Enforcement Manual.[5] The instructions are important guidance, not only for the policies which operate outside of the
Rules, but also for the latest Home Office practice in the interpretation of the Rules.[6]

Race Relations Act 1976

All immigration laws are inherently discriminatory on grounds of nationality, **6.07**
since they must distinguish between nationals of the legislating state and non-
nationals. Although on the face of it, immigration laws in the United Kingdom do
not purport to discriminate on racial or religious grounds, their effect has been to
discriminate indirectly against certain groups.[7] A 1985 report produced by the
Commission for Racial Equality showed that, for example, visitors from the New
Commonwealth or Pakistan were 30 times more likely to be refused than visitors
from the Old Commonwealth.[8] The RRA 1976 (as amended by the Race
Relations (Amendment) Act 2000) allows a minister and immigration officials to
discriminate on the grounds of nationality or ethnic or national origin (but not
race or colour) in the administration of immigration, asylum and nationality law.[9]

As the report by the Immigration Law Practitioners' Association notes, while the **6.08**
exemption concerning decisions on the grounds of nationality is reasonable enough
in immigration law, to be able to discriminate on grounds of nationality in the

---

[3] The current version of the Rules is contained in HC 395 (as amended).
[4] *Pearson v Immigration Appeal Tribunal* [1978] Imm AR 212.
[5] These are all to be found on the Immigration and Nationality Directorate website at
<http://www.ind.homeoffice.gov.uk>.
[6] For a detailed treatment see *Macdonald's*, Symes & Jorro, Blake & Husain (n 2 above).
[7] See 1.07–1.09 above.
[8] *Immigration Control Procedures: A General Investigation* (CRE, 1985).
[9] RRA 1976, s 19D.

treatment of asylum seekers, for example when taking decisions on detention, or exceptional leave to remain, rather than on the basis of an individual's claim of persecution, is questionable.[10] The provisions in the RRA 1976 as amended which relate to immigration and asylum make the distinction between 'race' and 'colour' on the one hand, and 'national' or 'ethnic' origins on the other, critical. To date, as is explained elsewhere, the case law on this is highly problematic and impacts on religious groups in different ways.[11] It is likely that future challenges will be made to this problematic legislation.

6.09   Section 71 RRA 1976 imposes a duty on public authorities to have due regard to the need to eliminate unlawful discrimination and to promote equality of opportunity and good relations between persons of different racial groups. The requirement of promotion of good race relations between persons of different racial groups applies to the Home Office and immigration officials when carrying out their functions relating to immigration and asylum administration and decision making.[12]

Equality Act 2006

6.10   The EA 2006 contains a prohibition on all public authorities in the carrying out of their functions from discriminating on the grounds of religion or belief.[13] This will include all immigration officials and other emanations of the Home Office who are involved in administration and decision making in the area of immigration and asylum.[14]

6.11   This general prohibition is subject to an exception for a decision to prevent someone entering the country, or to deport someone from the country, where this decision is made on the grounds that it is conducive to the public good, or that it is undesirable to permit the person to remain in the United Kingdom.[15] There is a further exception to this created for the purposes of people entering the country to provide services in connection with a religion or belief, such as a minister or clergyman.[16] There is also a general exception on grounds of national security,

---

[10] A Dummett, 'Ministerial Statements—the Immigration Exception in the Race Relations (Amendment) Act 2000' (ILPA, April 2001). Note that in *R (Tamil Information Centre) v Secretary of State for the Home Department* [2002] EWHC 2155 the court held ultra vires a ministerial authorization which allowed immigration officers to discriminate when examining passengers on the basis of statistics or intelligence. See further *Macdonald's* (n 2 above) para 1.30.

[11] See 2.21–2.30 above.

[12] RRA 1976, s 71A as amended by Nationality, Immigration and Asylum Act 2002, s 6.

[13] EA 2006, s 52. See 2.42–2.44 above.

[14] See 6.11 below.

[15] EA 2006, s 52(4)(f).

[16] Ibid, s 52(4)(g).

provided that the national security requirement justifies the action in question, which may be relevant in the area of immigration law.[17]

EC law

Domestic immigration law is affected by the EC law on free movement rights.[18] It is also affected by EU migration law generally.[19]

6.12

Human Rights Act 1998

Section 6 HRA 1998

Refugee and immigration law involve public officials in a large number of guises. There are entry clearance officers working abroad determining applications for entry clearance to the United Kingdom, immigration officers working at the various ports of entry into the country, housing officers, asylum support officers, benefit officers, and various Home Office officials, all of whom have the power to take decisions affecting the individual seeking entry or a variation or extension of their leave to remain. In addition prison officials and custody officers have control over individuals subject to detention. These officials and the judges, tribunal members and (previously adjudicators) are all public authorities within the meaning of s 6.[20]

6.13

ECHR rights

General comments

In most public law areas such as education, the statutory framework is to be interpreted compatibly with the HRA 1998. The way in which the rights contained in the ECHR interrelate with the immigration and asylum statutory framework is slightly different in that it is envisaged that persons may make free-standing representations on human rights grounds.

6.14

There are broadly three types of case where the rights contained in the ECHR may be relevant. First, there are cases involving persons claiming protection on the basis of a fear of ill-treatment that will be inflicted on them were they to be returned to

6.15

---

[17] Ibid, s 63. See *A(FC) and X(FC) v Secretary of State for the Home Department* [2004] UKHL 56 (power to detain foreign nationals only on grounds that they posed a risk to national security breached Art 14). See also *R (Al-Rawi) v Secretary of State for Foreign and Commonwealth Affairs and Secretary of State for the Home Department* [2006] EWCA Civ 1279 in relation to nationality discrimination generally.

[18] See generally N Rogers & R Scannell, *Free Movement of Persons in the Enlarged European Union* (Sweet & Maxwell, 2005).

[19] See T Spijkerboer, *European Migration Law* (Ashgate, 2006).

[20] See Blake & Husain (n 2 above) para 1.4.

their country of nationality or habitual residence. These are cases where the person will most likely have made a claim for recognition as a refugee. There are some cases, however, where a claim will not succeed under the Refugee Convention, but where a person may still rely on ECHR rights. Secondly, there are cases where persons are claiming that they cannot return to their country of origin because of some physical, mental or other detrimental effect emanating from their own particular circumstances that would result from such a return. These cases have frequently invoked Articles 3 and 8, although as a matter of principle may also invoke Article 9. In some of the cases, a person may also have brought a claim under the Refugee Convention. Thirdly, people have argued that refusing to admit them to the United Kingdom is a breach of their ECHR rights. In this context Article 8 is most frequently invoked.

6.16 The rights contained in the ECHR are not confined to those who are lawfully in the United Kingdom.[21] Article 1 ECHR requires the states to 'secure to everyone within their jurisdiction the rights and freedoms' in the ECHR. However, the immigration status of an individual may be highly relevant to the question of whether there is a violation of the right.[22] Further, public authorities are under a duty to comply with s 6 HRA 1998 whether they are located within the territory of the United Kingdom or outside.[23] However, the United Kingdom is not to be held indirectly responsible by a decision taken to expel a person, for all the acts of other states which may violate the ECHR which that person may in fact experience as a result of the expulsion.

6.17 A distinction has been drawn by the courts in immigration and asylum cases involving ECHR rights between so-called (i) 'domestic' and (ii) 'foreign' cases. The distinction was explained by the House of Lords in *R (Ullah) v Special Adjudicator*.[24] In that case it was stated that domestic cases involve an application of an ECHR right within the territory of the contracting state itself. This was contrasted with foreign cases, which involve an application of the ECHR outside the territory of the contracting state where the right is engaged by virtue of a decision taken by the contracting state itself which will have direct consequences outside that state that engage the right, for example a decision by the Home Office to remove a person under immigration laws which may then place that person in a situation abroad in violation of the rights contained in Article 9. In reality, the distinction is far less black and white (as Lord Bingham himself acknowledged) as the application of the ECHR itself derives from the fact that a decision is taken within the territory of the contracting state and ultimately relates to where the substance of the breach occurs.[25]

---

[21] *D v United Kingdom* (1997) 24 EHRR 423.
[22] *Berrehab v Netherlands* (1988) 11 EHRR 322.
[23] *Loizidou v Turkey* (1995) 20 EHRR 90.
[24] [2004] UKHL 26 [9].
[25] Ibid.

The issue before the House of Lords in *R (Ullah) v Special Adjudicator* was whether **6.18** and in what circumstances a decision by a contracting state to remove a person under immigration powers from the territory could engage ECHR rights other than Article 3 where the substance of the breach occurs abroad. Lord Bingham summarized the existing Strasbourg case law on the extra-territorial effects of the right and concluded that reliance could be placed on other ECHR rights in a 'foreign' case where the applicant can show that removal will seriously interfere with his rights under the ECHR such that there is a flagrant breach.[26]

This leads to the question of what will amount to a flagrant violation, which will have **6.19** to be worked out on a case by case basis. The House of Lords in *R (Ullah) v Special Adjudicator* did not attempt to lay down any parameters in this respect although Lord Carswell referred to the role of the court in delineating the scope as follows:

> The concept of a flagrant breach or violation may not always be easy for domestic courts to apply—one is put in mind of the difficulties which they have had in applying that of gross negligence—but it seems to me that it was well expressed by the Immigration Appeal Tribunal in *Devaseelan v Secretary of State for the Home Dept . . . .* when it applied the criterion that the right in question would be completely denied or nullified in the destination country. This would harmonise with the concept of a fundamental breach, with which courts in this jurisdiction are familiar.[27]

As regards the issue of proportionality, Lord Bingham in the linked appeal in **6.20** *R (Razgar) v Secretary of State for the Home Department*[28] suggested that in the great majority of cases the decision taken pursuant to the lawful operation of immigration control would be found to be proportionate.[29]

Article 9

There have been relatively few Article 9 cases in the immigration context at the **6.21** High Court level or above. This is no doubt related to the fact that immigration decisions may impact more immediately on a person's family and private life (Article 8) and may place a person in a situation of bodily harm (Article 3). The courts have effectively narrowed the scope of other articles in the immigration and asylum context. The application of Article 8 has been restricted by the assumption that for the vast majority of cases the Immigration Rules themselves have already struck the balance between the public interest and the private right.[30]

---

[26] Ibid [24].

[27] Ibid [69].

[28] [2004] UKHL 27 [20].

[29] See also *Huang v Secretary of State for the Home Department* [2005] EWCA Civ 105 [59] in the context of an Art 8 claim where the Court of Appeal held that a claim would only succeed where it was so 'exceptional on its particular facts that the imperative of proportionality demands an outcome in the appellant's favour notwithstanding that he cannot succeed under the Rules'. *Huang* will be heard by the House of Lords in February 2007.

[30] See 6.20 above.

However, the same cannot be assumed for Article 9. First, the Immigration Rules themselves in most part are not primarily concerned with religious freedom. Secondly, the courts have to date not had an opportunity to test this in relation to Article 9. Thirdly, the decision in *Huang v Secretary of State for the Home Department*[31] is the subject of considerable criticism on this point.[32]

6.22 The House of Lords in *R (Ullah) v Special Adjudicator*[33] held that interference with religious freedom in a receiving state will engage Article 9. However, Lord Bingham expressly stated in that context:

> I find it hard to think that a person could successfully resist expulsion in reliance on article 9 without being entitled either to asylum on the ground of a well-founded fear of being persecuted for reasons of religion or personal opinion or to resist expulsion in reliance on article 3. But I would not rule out such a possibility in principle unless the ECtHR has clearly done so, and I am not sure it has.[34]

6.23 Article 9 may also be engaged in relation to immigration decisions which affect the location of a person within the United Kingdom.[35] Article 9 has arisen in a number of other cases involving immigration decisions and conscientious objection to military service (see 6.57–6.65 below). The current climate of increasing controls on Muslims in the United Kingdom in relation to anti-terrorism measures, including the deportation of persons not considered to be conducive to the public good, may also invoke religious discrimination issues.[36] However, the express exemptions enacted in the EA 2006 in this area and in relation to national security will inevitably make challenges difficult.[37]

Article 14

6.24 There have been numerous justified complaints from religious minorities over the last few decades about various aspects of immigration law which indirectly discriminated against certain groups. The notorious primary purpose rule, which required a couple to show that the spouse entering the United Kingdom was not doing so for the primary purpose of gaining entry to the United Kingdom, was abolished in 1997. This had led to numerous unjust refusals which impacted

---

[31] [2005] EWCA Civ 105.
[32] See eg *Macdonald's* (n 2 above) para 8.22. Note that *Huang v Secretary of State for the Home Department* is pending appeal to the House of Lords.
[33] [2004] UKHL 26 [21].
[34] Ibid.
[35] *R (Kazema) v Secretary of State for the Home Department* [2002] EWHC Admin 2157 (dispersal to an area where no religious services were conducted in the appellant's language did not violate Art 9 as her English was improving).
[36] See 2.17 above.
[37] See 6.11 above.

particularly on couples with a South Asian background.[38] Virginity tests carried out by immigration officials at Heathrow airports on South Asian brides were also abolished amidst a media scandal.[39]

A recent case involving Articles 12 and 14 concerned the provisions relating to **6.25** sham marriages in s 19 of the Asylum and Immigration (Treatment of Claimants etc) Act 2004. The issue in *R (Baiai) v Secretary of State for the Home Department (No 1)*[40] was the compatibility of the new regime (by which a person who is subject to immigration control and who wishes to enter into a civil marriage in the United Kingdom—ie a marriage other than according to the rites of the Church of England—has to apply to the Secretary of State for a certificate of approval to marry) with Articles 12 and 14 ECHR. It was held in relation to discrimination that the s 19 regime constituted direct discrimination on the grounds of religion and nationality which was not justified in the interests of immigration control. That discrimination was not justified because there was no evidence that those who married in non-Anglican religious ceremonies were more likely to engage in sham marriages than those who married in Anglican religious ceremonies. Accordingly, the s 19 regime violated Article 14.[41]

Legal Issues

Fear of persecution on religious grounds

For centuries, persons have been granted asylum in the United Kingdom on the **6.26** basis of religious persecution within their own countries. But one of the ironies of the medieval period was that England was welcoming certain groups such as Huguenots escaping from ill-treatment because of their religious affiliation, while at the same time persecuting other religious groups living in the country.[42] Jewish refugees escaped from Russia in the late nineteenth century, Armenian Christians from Turkey following the 1905 genocide, while there was a mass migration of Jewish people from Germany and central Europe as a result of Nazi atrocities. More recently Jehovah's Witnesses have been targeted in a number of places, Baha'is in

---

[38] See S Sachdeva, *The Primary Purpose Rule in British Immigration Law* (Trentham Books, 2003).
[39] See S Juss, *Discretion and Deviation in the Administration of Immigration Control* (Sweet & Maxwell, 1997) 109.
[40] [2006] EWHC 823 (Admin).
[41] At [146]. The case is pending appeal. See also *A(FC) and X(FC) v Secretary of State for the Home Department* [2004] UKHL 56 (power to detain foreign nationals only on grounds that they posed a risk to national security breached Art 14).
[42] See 1.05–1.06 above.

Iran, non-Muslims or Muslim converts in Muslim countries. Some contemporary forms of persecution of religious groups are recognized internationally.[43]

6.27 The twentieth century saw the massacre of Jews at the hands of the Nazis, and the failure of the international community to protect the refugees fleeing from persecution during World War II led to the current refugee protection regime. It is clear from policies and atrocities that take place the world over that religious persecution is ever alive and will continue to be an important basis for refugee protection. The break-up of the Soviet Union dissolved a state that was on its face ideologically opposed to religion, but in its place permitted the rise of different forms of nationalism and fundamentalism that in turn have proved to be intolerant of certain forms of religion in various ways.[44]

Definitions and scope of protection

6.28 The Refugee Convention protects against persons fleeing from religious persecution. Although the Refugee Convention is not formally incorporated into UK law it is given primacy over the Immigration Rules and thereby is effectively incorporated.[45]

6.29 The refugee definition contained in the Refugee Convention is as follows:

> Any person who owing to well-founded fear of being persecuted for reasons of race, religion, nationality, membership of a particular social group or political opinion, is outside the country of his nationality and is unable or, owing to such fear, is unwilling to avail himself of the protection of that country; or who, not having a nationality and being outside the country of his former habitual residence, is unable or, owing to such fear, is unwilling to return to it.[46]

6.30 The UNHCR *Handbook on Procedures and Criteria for Determining Refugee Status*[47] contains only three paragraphs addressing religious persecution.[48] The *travaux préparatoires* to the Refugee Convention show that religion-based persecution formed an integral part of the refugee definition but that there was no attempt to

---

[43] See eg UN Sub-Commission on Prevention of Discrimination and Protection of Minorities res. 1985/21, UN doc E/CN 4/1986/5.

[44] See <http://www.forum18.org> for up-to-date information on religious freedom worldwide. Note that the US State Department produces an annual report on international religious freedom with separate country reports including the UK pursuant to s 102(b) of the International Religious Freedom Act of 1998.

[45] Asylum and Immigration Appeals Act 1993, s 2; *R v Secretary of State for the Home Department, ex p Sivakumaran* [1988] AC 958; *R v Uxbridge Magistrates' Court, ex p Adimi* (2001) QB 667; *R (European Roma Rights Centre) v Immigration Officer at Prague Airport* [2004] UKHL 55.

[46] Art 1A(2) of the 1951 Convention as amended by Art 1(2) of the 1967 Protocol.

[47] UNHCR, *Handbook on Procedures and Criteria for Determining Refugee Status under the 1951 Convention and the 1967 Protocol relating to the Status of Refugees*: UN doc HCR/IP/4/Eng/REV.1, re-ed (Geneva, January 1992). This is instructive as evidence of state practice: see Art 31 Vienna Convention of the Law of Treaties 1969.

[48] Ibid, paras 71–73.

define the terms as such.[49] There has overall been relatively little interpretative guidance on religion-based claims.[50]

The UNHCR has issued *Guidelines on International Protection: Religion Based* **6.31**
Refugee Claims (the 'Guidelines').[51] It notes that claims to refugee status based on religion can be among the most complex and that decision makers have not always taken a consistent approach.[52] It further notes that when determining such claims, it is useful to draw on Article 18 of the Universal Declaration of Human Rights ('UDHR'), and Articles 18 and 27 of the International Covenant on Civil and Political Rights ('ICCPR'). Relevant regional instruments include Article 9 ECHR, Article 12 of the American Convention on Human Rights 1969, and Article 8 of the African Charter of Human and Peoples' Rights 1981. International instruments will therefore inform the interpretation of the term 'religion'.[53]

Definition of religion   The Guidelines note specifically that establishing the **6.32**
sincerity of belief, identity, and/or a certain way of life may not necessarily be relevant in every case.[54] Where for example the persecutor imputes or attributes a religion to an individual or has identified him as belonging to a particular group, the individual may be persecuted on the basis of religion, even if he adamantly denies being of the religion.[55] The Guidelines must be interpreted in accordance with international law instruments including Article 9 ECHR, which would suggest that the religion should be given a wide interpretation.[56] Further as the UN Human Rights Committee notes, religion is 'not limited . . . to traditional religions or to religions and beliefs with institutional characteristics or practices analogous to those of traditional religions'.[57]

---

[49] Records of the 1951 Conference of Plenipotentiaries on the Status of Refugees and Stateless Persons available at <http://www.unhcr.org>.

[50] See K Musalo, 'Claims for Protection Based on Religion or Belief' (2004) 16 IJRL 165.

[51] UNHCR, *Guidelines on International Protection No 6: Religion Based Refugee Claims under Article 1A(2) of the 1951 Convention and/or the 1967 Protocol Relating to the Status of Refugees*, HCR/Gip/04/06, 28 April 2004 reproduced in (2004) 16 IJRL 500.

[52] Ibid, para 1.

[53] Ibid, para 2.

[54] Ibid, para 9.

[55] Note that in *L (China) v Secretary of State for the Home Department* [2004] EWCA Civ 1441 a Falun Gong supporter was found by the adjudicator to have made a case on the basis of membership of a particular social group rather than on the grounds of religion. It was not appealed on the issue of religion and the Court of Appeal was unwilling to consider this point. On appeal on the issue of membership of a social group it was held that the fact that members of Falun Gong were persecuted could not itself qualify them as members of a particular social group because they did not share characteristics which it was beyond their power to change or which were so fundamental to their identity or conscience that they ought not to be required to change. See *K and Fornah v Secretary of State for the Home Department* [2006] UKHL 46 for a recent consideration of a particular social group in a case involving female genital mutilation.

[56] UNHCR, *Guidelines on International Protection No 6*, paras 3–10. See 2.57–2.62 above.

[57] Human Rights Committee, General Comment No 22, 20 July 1993, UN doc CCPR/C/21/Rev.1/ADD.4, 27 September 1993, para 2. See *Kinuthia v Secretary of State for the Home Department* [2001] EWCA Civ 2100 [9]: 'In considering whether there is persecution on Convention grounds,

6.33 **Well-founded fear of persecution**   'Persecution' for the purposes of the Refugee Convention is not defined either in the Convention itself or elsewhere in international law.[58] Notwithstanding the lack of legal definition regard should be had to interpretation of the Convention as a 'living instrument', particularly bearing in mind the subject matter. The UNHCR paper on interpretation of Article 1 notes:

> The on-going development of international human rights law subsequent to the adoption of the 1951 Convention has helped to advance the understanding, expressed in the UNHCR Handbook, that persecution comprises human rights abuses or other serious harm, often but not always with a systematic or repetitive element. While it is generally agreed that 'mere' discrimination may not, in the normal course, amount to persecution in and of itself (though particularly egregious forms undoubtedly will be so considered), a persistent pattern of consistent discrimination will usually, on cumulative grounds, amount to persecution and warrant international protection.[59]

6.34 The Guidelines note that persecution for reasons of religion may take various forms, for example prohibition of membership of a religious community, of worship in community with others in public or in private, of religious instruction, of discriminatory measures imposed on individuals on the basis of their beliefs or practices, or because they have changed their faith. They specifically refer to discrimination in communities where there is a dominant religion or where there is a close relationship between the state and religious institutions. Although mere membership of a religious community is not usually sufficient to substantiate a claim to refugee status, special circumstances may prevail taking into account the overall political and religious situation in the country of origin.[60]

6.35 **Limitations on the exercise of religious freedom**   The Guidelines note that Article 18(3) ICCPR permits restrictions on the 'freedom to manifest one's religion or belief' where the limits are 'prescribed by law and are necessary to protect public safety, order, health, or morals, or the fundamental rights and freedoms of others'.[61] Limitations must be directly related and proportionate to the specific need on which they are predicated. Permissible restrictions may include measures to prevent criminal activities (for example, ritual killings), or harmful traditional practices or practices that harm the best interests of a child as judged by international law standards. The case law on Article 9(2) will assist in considering whether the restrictions are justified.[62] The criminalization of hate speech, including where

---

it does not appear to me relevant in the present case to consider the attitude of the adopted religion to other religions or what the international community may think of it.'

[58] Note that it is defined for the purposes of international criminal law in the 1998 Statute of the International Criminal Court.

[59] UNHCR, *Interpreting Article 1 of the 1951 Convention Relating to the Status of Refugees*, April 2001, para 17.

[60] UNHCR Handbook (n 47 above) para 71. See Guidelines, paras 11–14.

[61] Guidelines (n 51 above) paras 15–16.

[62] See 2.77–2.91 above.

it is done in the name of religion, is specifically mentioned as a legitimate restriction.[63] The fact that a restriction on the exercise of religious freedom is supported by the majority of the public in the country of origin is not decisive.[64]

In determining whether restrictions or limitations rise to the level of persecution the Guidelines state: **6.36**

> [T]he decision-maker must not only take into account international human rights standards, including lawful limitations on the exercise of religious freedom, but also evaluate the breadth of the restriction and the severity of any punishment for non-compliance. The importance or centrality of the practice within the religion and/or to the individual personally is also relevant. The decision-maker should proceed cautiously with such inquiries, taking into account the fact that what may seem trivial to an outsider may be central to the claimant's beliefs. Where the restricted practice is not important to the individual, but important to the religion, then it is unlikely to rise to the level of persecution without additional factors. By contrast, the restricted religious practice may not be so significant to the religion, but may be particularly important to the individual, and could therefore still constitute persecution on the basis of his or her conscience or belief.[65]

Discrimination   The Guidelines note that religion-based claims often involve discrimination. Despite the fact that discrimination is prohibited under international law, it must reach a certain level for the purposes of refugee status. A distinction is to be drawn between discrimination resulting in preferential treatment, and that which amounts to persecution because it seriously restricts the claimant's enjoyment of fundamental human rights. Examples of discrimination that would amount to persecution include serious restrictions on the right to earn a livelihood, to access education, and/or health services. The existence of discriminatory laws or laws protecting freedom of religion is not in itself determinative—it is necessary to make an assessment of the implementation of such laws and their effect. However, guidance may be sought from the case law under Article 14 ECHR in determining what amounts to discrimination.[66] **6.37**

Forced conversion or compliance to religion   The Guidelines state that forced conversion to a religion is a serious violation of the fundamental right to freedom of thought, conscience and religion, and would often satisfy to the objective component of persecution. In addition the claimant must demonstrate a subjective appreciation that the conversion would be persecutory to him personally.[67] Forced compliance may take the form of coerced religious education that is incompatible **6.38**

---

[63] See 2.16 above.
[64] See 2.05 above.
[65] Guidelines (n 51 above) para 16.
[66] Ibid, paras 17–19. See 2.94–2.116 above.
[67] Ibid, para 20.

with an individual's own religious convictions, an obligation to attend religious ceremonies or swear an oath of allegiance to a particular religious symbol, or the imposition of a particular religious legal code based on religious doctrine (for example, death for adultery).[68]

6.39   In determining whether there is persecution, the policies or acts with which the individual must comply, the extent of interference with his beliefs, identity and way of life, and the punishment for non-compliance must be examined. Forced compliance could rise to the level of persecution if it becomes an intolerable interference with the individual's own religious belief and/or if non-compliance would result in disproportionate punishment. Reference may be had to the analysis of what amounts to an interference for the purposes of Article 9 ECHR.[69]

6.40   **Gender**   The Guidelines expressly state that particular attention should be paid to the impact of gender on religion-based refugee claims, as men and women may fear or suffer persecution for reasons of religion in different ways to each other. Examples are given of young girls who are pledged in the name of religion to perform slave duties or sexual services, forced into underage marriage, punished for honour crimes, or subjected to forced genital mutilation. Where state actors are unwilling or unable to protect the claimant from such treatment, it should not be mistaken as a private conflict, but should be considered as a valid basis for refugee status.[70]

6.41   **Exclusions to application of the Refugee Convention**   There are various exclusions to the application of the Refugee Convention. In particular Article 1F states that its provisions shall not apply to:

> [A]ny person with respect to whom there are serious reasons for considering that:
>
> (a) he has committed a crime against peace, a war crime, or a crime against humanity, as defined by the international instruments drawn up to make provision in respect of such crimes;
>
> (b) he has committed a serious non-political crime outside the country of his refuge prior to his admission to that country as a refugee;
>
> (c) he has been guilty of acts contrary to the purposes and principles of the United Nations.

6.42   This is subject to the principle of non-refoulement as recognized in customary international law and enshrined in various treaties including the Refugee Convention.[71]

---

[68] Ibid, paras 21–23.

[69] Ibid, para 21. See 2.71–2.76 above.

[70] Ibid, para 24.

[71] Refugee Convention, Art 33. For other international law examples of the principle see eg Art 13 ICCPR; Convention Against Torture and Other Cruel, Inhuman or Degrading Treatment or Punishment, Art 3(1); Organization of African Unity Convention Governing the Specific Aspects of Refugee Problems in Africa, Art 2(3).

The principle applies to any act of refoulement that would have the effect of exposing a refugee or asylum seeker to (i) a threat of persecution; (ii) a real risk of torture, or cruel, inhuman or degrading treatment or punishment; or (iii) a threat to life, physical integrity, or liberty. It prohibits refoulement to any territory where the refugee or asylum seeker would be at risk including a territory where he may be indirectly at risk, for example where there is a risk that he might subsequently be removed to a territory where he would be at risk. It is subject only to the overriding reason of national security and public safety in circumstances where the threat does not equate to danger of torture or cruel, inhuman or degrading treatment or punishment and would not come within the scope of other non-derogable customary principles of human rights.

Procedural matters

The *Guidelines* set out a number of general points of particular relevance to examining religion-based refugee claims. These can be summarized as follows: (1) religious practices, traditions or beliefs may be complex and may vary from one branch of a religion to another and there is therefore a need for reliable, accurate, up-to-date, country specific information; (2) determinations can benefit from the assistance of independent experts or the use of evidence from other adherents of the same faith; (3) decision makers need to be objective and not arrive at conclusions based on their own experiences, even where they may belong to the same religion as the claimant; (4) decision makers need to appreciate the interplay between religion and gender, race, ethnicity, cultural norms, identity, way of life and other factors; (5) in selecting interviewers and interpreters there should be sensitivity regarding cultural, religious or gender aspects that could hinder open communication; (6) interviewers should be aware of the potential for hostile biases by interpreters against or towards claimants.[72] **6.43**

Credibility is a central concern in all refugee claims but, due to the complex nature of religious beliefs, traditions and practices, it may cause a particular issue in religion-based claims. The Guidelines refer to the importance of open-ended questioning that it designed to elicit the individual's own beliefs rather than view them through the kaleidoscope of the interviewer. It is important to note that individuals may be persecuted on the basis of their religion despite the fact that they have little or no substantive knowledge of a religion's tenets or practices. There may well be good reasons for a lack of knowledge about particular beliefs and these need to be explored. Greater knowledge may be expected from someone who claims to be a religious leader or who has undergone religious instruction, than someone who is not. Credibility may raise particular difficulties where there is a conversion post **6.44**

---

[72] Guidelines (n 51 above) paras 27–34.

departure, and a rigorous and in depth examination of the circumstances and genuineness of the conversion will be necessary. However, the test remains the same, namely whether the individual would have a well-founded fear of persecution on return.[73]

Domestic law

6.45 **Persecution** In line with academic opinion, there has been a tendency in the courts to consider ill-treatment and persecution on grounds of religion in accordance with the internationally recognized framework of human rights.[74] For this reason it is necessary to have a firm understanding of the protections afforded to freedom of religion within Article 9 ECHR. It is clear for example that both aspects of the right, ie the internal and external manifestation of belief, are protected under Article 1A of the Refugee Convention.[75] Despite the fact that the wording of the Refugee Convention refers only to religion and not to thought, conscience and belief it should not be taken as leading to a more exclusive interpretation than under Article 9.[76]

6.46 As is the case generally with freedom of religion, the courts should avoid focusing unduly on the particular nature of an individual's beliefs. The more important issue in any given case is likely to be how such beliefs are viewed by the agent of harm. Someone may have a well founded fear of persecution if they are perceived to be of a particular religion, notwithstanding that they do not in fact subscribe to any of its beliefs.[77] Equally persecution may result not because of the religion of the asylum seeker but due to the particular beliefs of the persecutors.[78] However, the definition of what amounts to religion is not without difficulties.[79]

6.47 What amounts to persecution will plainly be a question of fact taking into account all the circumstances of an individual case. In *Ahmad v Secretary of State*

---

[73] Ibid, paras 28–33. See also API, October 2006, Assessing the Asylum Claim, para 8.5.1.

[74] *Ravichandran v Secretary of State for the Home Department* [1996] Imm AR 97; *Lazarevic and Radivojevic v Secretary of State for the Home Department* [1997] Imm AR 251; *Gashi v Nikshiqi* [1997] INLR 96.

[75] See *Wang v Minister for Immigration and Multicultural Affairs* [2000] FCA 1599; *Farajvand v Minister for Immigration and Multicultural Affairs* [2001] FCA 795.

[76] See 2.57–2.62 above.

[77] *Bastanipour v INS* 980 F 2d 1129 (7th Cir, US Court of Appeals, 1992).

[78] *SCAT v Minister for Immigration and Multicultural and Indigenous Affairs* [2002] FCA 962. Note the importance of substantiating evidence: see *Z and T v United Kingdom*, Application 27034/05 (28 February 2006) (application declared inadmissible due in part to unsubstantiated claims of risk of attack).

[79] See eg *Omoyuri v Secretary of State for the Home Department* [2001] Imm AR 175 where Simon Brown LJ found the notion that a 'devil cult' practising pagan rituals was in any true sense a religion deeply offensive. He stated that the rites of the Ogboni were merely the trappings of what should be recognized as an intrinsically criminal organization. See also 2.57–2.62 above. Note *L (China) v Secretary of State for the Home Department* [2004] EWCA Civ 1441 (n 55 above).

for the Home Department,[80] Farquharson LJ considered that a total ban on practising a religion would amount to persecution as it would constitute a wholesale chilling of a fundamental human right. In that case the issue of whether prosecution for certain prohibited activities that are fundamental to the religion amounted to persecution was left open.[81]

Proselytization cases   In many parts of the world the freedom to change one's   **6.48**
religion or to express different religious views from the prevailing orthodoxy is unacceptable.[82] Many of these situations are readily recognized, as is apparent from judicial statements. The question is what level of ill-treatment will suffice and how the holding of particular beliefs will be viewed by the agents of harm. For example, in *R (Wani) v Secretary of State for the Home Department & AIT*,[83] Collins J summarized the position of Ahmadis living in Pakistan:

> Ahmadis are discriminated against in Pakistan and are frequently subjected to violent attacks by Muslim fundamentalists. They are regarded as non-Muslims and the Pakistan Code forbids them to refer to themselves as Muslims and, in particular, prohibits them from proselytising. This prohibition can lead to problems for devout Ahmadis since one of the tenets of their faith is that they should promote their beliefs and so should proselytise. Having said that, there are large numbers of Ahmadis in Pakistan and, although there is discrimination and some violence, they are able to live there and it has never been accepted that an Ahmadi should be granted the right to remain in the United Kingdom simply because of the problems faced by Ahmadis in general.[84]

The case did not expressly consider what level of discrimination could amount to   **6.49**
persecution for the purposes of asylum protection. This was relevant in an earlier case, *Moezzi v Secretary of State for the Home Department*,[85] where the issue was dealt with directly. Mr Moezzi was an Iranian who married an Indian Hindu. If his wife did not abandon her faith, the marriage would not be recognized as valid and the child would be treated as illegitimate. The Court of Appeal dismissed the appeal on the basis that there was a 'risk of discrimination as compared to a risk of persecution' in the case.[86]

---

[80] [1990] Imm AR 61.

[81] See, for some recent Asylum and Immigration Tribunal decisions, *SH (Iran CG) v Secretary of State for the Home Department* [2006] UKAIT 00041 (Baha'i country guidance case); *MG (Sudan CG) v Secretary of State for the Home Department* [2006] UKAIT 00047 (Coptic Christians country guidance case); *FS (Iran CG) v Secretary of State for the Home Department* [2004] UKAIT 00303 (Iran and Christian converts); *YT (Eritrea CG) v Secretary of State for the Home Department* [2004] UKAIT 00218 (minority members of church). See for a case involving an in-country conversion: *MG (Iran) v Secretary of State for the Home Department* [2006] All ER (D) 356.

[82] See recent decision in *SS (Malaysia) v ECO, Kuala Lumpur* [2004] UKAIT 00091.

[83] [2005] EWHC 2815.

[84] Ibid [2].

[85] CA, 6 October 1988.

[86] See also comparison of cases from New Zealand, UK, US and Canada in Musalo (n 50 above).

6.50   In *Ahmad v Secretary of State for the Home Department*,[87] involving a claim by Ahmadis in Pakistan, the Court of Appeal held that generally individuals could not qualify for protection if they intentionally violated laws restricting their religious practice. A distinction was drawn in this case between a priest and an ordinary member of the religious community, and between a law which imposed restrictions on the practice of religion as opposed to an outright ban. On the facts of the case, the appeal was refused.

6.51   In *Iftikar Ahmed v Secretary of State for the Home Department*,[88] Simon Brown LJ noted that where an individual credibly asserts that he will act in a particular way in the future, however unreasonable it may be, any adverse consequences which would be reasonably likely to befall the protagonist on this account are to be assessed as part of the well-foundedness of the fear of persecution. However, such assertions may not be credible where it would be reasonable for asylum seekers to moderate their behaviour if they returned in order to avoid persecution. The question of what is considered to be a reasonable compromise will depend on the facts. The Court of Appeal, finding in the appellant's favour, noted that he had been subjected to harassment on a daily basis including physical violence, that his family were subjected to appalling treatment, and that his house was attacked and burned down on at least one occasion.[89]

6.52   The UNHCR Handbook states that mere membership of a particular religious community will not normally be enough to substantiate a claim to asylum.[90] While a country may be unsafe in certain areas for followers of a particular religion, it does not follow that the internal flight alternative is not available. In domestic law, the test which has been applied is whether it would be 'unduly harsh' to require the applicant to relocate.[91] In *R v Secretary of State for the Home Department, ex p Rahman*,[92] an Ahmadi lived with his wife in Lahore where, on the grounds of his religion, his factory had been burned down, he had been detained by the police, his family home had been attacked causing his wife to miscarry, and he had received numerous death threats. The Court of Appeal upheld the finding of the Adjudicator and ruled that the applicant could relocate to Rabwah as 'millions of [Ahmadis]

---

[87] [1990] Imm AR 61.

[88] [2000] INLR 1.

[89] See also four further cases involving Ahmadis: *Yasmin v Secretary of State for the Home Department* [1999] EWCA Civ 1633; *R v Secretary of State for the Home Department, ex p Arshad* (CA, 14 July 2000); *Tahir v Secretary of State for the Home Department* (CA, 4 July 1995); *Atibo v Immigration Officer* [1978] Imm AR 93. See also *MG (Iran) v SSHD* [2006] All ER (D) 356.

[90] UNHCR Handbook, para 73.

[91] *R v Secretary of State for the Home Department, ex p Robinson* [1998] QB 929.

[92] CA, 18 February 2000.

live there . . . [i]t depends on how they behave; what they do; and, as far as concerns religion, on the state of their religious activities'.[93]

However, an important point was recognized relating to the 'White List' of so-called **6.53** safe countries in the decision of *Secretary of State for the Home Department v Javed*,[94] namely that countries that are considered to be generally safe may not be safe for claims based on religion. In this case Javed argued that the decision by the Secretary of State to include Pakistan on the list of safe countries was irrational. The Court of Appeal found in his favour, noting the situation for Ahmadis, although the decision focused mostly on the position of women in that country.

Gender cases Recognition is expressly given in the UK Immigration Appellate **6.54** Authorities Gender Guidelines[95] to the persecution that women may face due to adherence to a particular religion. They state:

> Where the religion assigns particular roles or behavioural codes to women, a woman who refuses or fails to fulfil her assigned role or abide by the codes may have a well-founded fear of persecution on the ground of religion. Failure to abide by the behavioural codes set out for women may be perceived as evidence that a woman holds unacceptable religious opinions regardless of what she actually believes about religion.[96]

The Refugee Women's Legal Group has also noted that a woman's religious iden- **6.55** tity may be aligned with that of members of her family or community. As a result imputed or attributed religious identity may be important.[97]

One difficult issue in gender cases is the blurred line between practices such as **6.56** honour killings and female genital mutilation about which there is considerable debate as to whether they are rooted in tradition and custom as opposed to religion.[98] There is a tendency to analyse such claims under the rubric of a social group or in terms of political opinion.[99]

---

[93] See also *Ghafoor Khan v Secretary of State for the Home Department* [1999] EWCA Civ 1638 where the Court of Appeal stated there 'can be no blanket recognition of [Ahamdis] as refugees'.

[94] CA, 17 May 2001.

[95] N Berkovitz & C Jarvis, *Immigration Appellate Authority: Asylum Gender Guidelines* (Crown copyright, 2000).

[96] Ibid, paras 3.13–3.14.

[97] RWLG, *Gender Guidelines for the Determination of Asylum Claims in the UK* (July 1998).

[98] See A Wood, 'A Cultural Rite of Passage or a Form of Torture: Female Genital Mutilation from an International Law Perspective' (2002) 12 Hastings. Women's LJ 347.

[99] See UNHCR, *Guidelines on International Protection No 1: Gender-Related Persecution within the context of Article 1A(2) of the 1951 Convention and/or its 1967 Protocol relating to the Status of Refugees*, UN doc HCR/GIP/02/01, 7 May 2002. See *K and Fornah v SSHD* [2006] UKHL 46 for recent consideration of a particular social group in the context of female genital mutilation.

Conscientious objection to military service

6.57 As the Guidelines note, a number of religions require their adherents to abstain from military service as a central tenet of the religion. In countries where military service is compulsory, failure to perform that duty is frequently punishable by law.[100]

6.58 There have been a number of cases both domestically and before the Strasbourg court relating to people who have claimed refugee protection on the basis of domestic laws that require them to perform military service contrary to their religious or philosophical views. There may be different degrees of compulsion by the state. For example, a state may require a contribution to public funds by tax payers for the purpose of supporting the military, it may require all individuals to perform active service, or men only, or may require all individuals to perform military service with an option for those objecting on grounds of conscience to perform some other civic service.

International law

6.59 For the purposes of a claim for refugee status, the Guidelines draw a distinction between prosecution for failure to perform military service and persecution.[101] In general prosecution and punishment pursuant to a law of general application will not constitute persecution. However, there are exceptions to this where, for example, the purported general law is applied in a discriminatory manner, or where the punishment is excessive or disproportionately severe. Where there are alternatives to military service, there would not usually be a basis for a claim unless the alternatives were so unreasonable or burdensome as to constitute some form of punishment.[102]

Domestic law

6.60 As a matter of law this type of persecution has in principle not been recognized by the United Kingdom as giving rise to a well-founded fear of persecution per se. The justification given in *Doonetas v Secretary of State for the Home Department*,[103] was that the immediate cause of persecution is a refusal to obey a generally applicable and neutral law, and the fact that such refusal may be due to religious or other beliefs is a secondary factor. In that case it was also held that the law was not discriminatory because it applied to all religions and those who had no religious beliefs at all.

---

[100] Guidelines (n 51 above) paras 25–26.
[101] Ibid, para 26.
[102] See also UNHCR Handbook (n 47 above) para 169.
[103] TH/12339/75(820). Approved and applied in *Atibo v Immigration Officer, London (Heathrow Airport)* [1978] Imm AR 93.

In *Sepet and Bulbul v Secretary of State for the Home Department*,[104] two Kurds   **6.61**
objected to military service in Turkey on the basis that they believed that they would
be compelled to fight against fellow Kurds. They were not, however, opposed to all
military service as a matter of principle. The Tribunal recognized the right of the
state in general to call upon its nationals to perform military service and the con-
comitant obligation on the individual to serve, even where such service may result
in unpleasant or even fatal consequences which that individual would prefer to
avoid. It stated that normally the state would be permitted to enforce the obligation
to serve by prosecution and punishment of those who have evaded service. The
majority of the Court of Appeal in upholding the decision of the Tribunal noted
that there was no internationally recognized right of conscientious objection.[105]

This view was reinforced in the judgment of the House of Lords.[106] The fear of death   **6.62**
in active service cannot therefore ordinarily found the basis of a claim for refugee status.[107] Lord Bingham noted that '[w]hile, therefore there are indications of changed
thinking . . . there is as yet no authority to support the applicants' contention' but
he dismissed the claim 'with a measure of reluctance since [their claim] may well
reflect the international consensus of tomorrow'. However, importantly as the
Court of Appeal noted in *Sepet and Bulbul*:

> [T]here are circumstances in which a conscientious objector may rightly claim that
> punishment for draft evasion would amount to persecution: where the military serv-
> ice to which he is called involves acts, with which he may be associated, which are
> contrary to basic rules of human conduct; where the conditions of military service
> are themselves so harsh as to amount to persecution on the facts; where the punish-
> ment in question is disproportionately harsh or severe.[108]

ECHR law

The ECHR does not recognize the right of conscientious objection to military   **6.63**
service. Nor does any other international human rights instrument despite the

---

104 [2000] Imm AR 445.
105 [2001] EWCA Civ 681 [118] (Jonathan Parker LJ). But note that Waller LJ stated: 'But it
seems to me that the stage has been reached whereby it is recognised generally internationally, and
in particular by those states who are members of the Council of Europe, that conscientious objection to military service is a core entitlement. It is a breach of Art 9(1) to force a person to take part
in military action contrary to his/her conscience, not justified in normal times by Art 9(2). This entitlement has been recognised in the United States and in the courts of Canada.'
106 [2003] UKHL 15.
107 See *R v Secretary of State for the Home Department, ex p Fadli* [2001] IMM AR 392; *Adam v
Secretary of State for the Home Department* [2003] EWCA Civ 26.
108 [2001] EWCA Civ 681 (Laws LJ). Note that Lord Bingham in the House of Lords noted that
there was compelling support for the view that refugee status should be accorded to someone who
refused to carry out military service on the grounds that it would or might require him to commit
atrocities or gross human rights abuses or participate in a conflict condemned by the international
community.

fact that the Human Rights Committee believes that such a right may be derived from the protection afforded by Article 18 UDHR.[109] It has been considered by academic writers that the right to conscientiously object may form part of the right to freedom of conscience, but that compulsory military service may be justified on the grounds of public safety.[110] In 1988 a Council of Europe report referred to the importance of 'compelling reasons of conscience' in this context.[111] There is a growing body of opinion militating towards recognition of conscientious objection and allowing an alternative period of civic service instead. This has yet to be formally recognized in any legal instrument.[112]

6.64 A state may, therefore, legitimately require performance of military service in principle. But where it does so it should be 'reasonably necessary in a democratic society'. There should also be reasonableness and proportionality between the end and the means used to achieve the end. The scope and manner of implementation of military laws should be examined with particular reference to discrimination between certain groups in society. Where there is no possible form of alternative service, the likelihood of prosecution and punishment or persecution should be examined.[113]

6.65 In *Ulke v Turkey*[114] the ECtHR considered a case involving a Turkish citizen who complained of violations of Articles 3, 5, 8 and 9 on the grounds that he had been prosecuted and convicted for holding pacifist views and because he was a conscientious objector. He burned his call-up papers in a public press conference and was subsequently sentenced to six months' imprisonment and fined. He further served 701 days of imprisonment for desertion and was wanted by security forces for the execution of the remainder of his service. The ECtHR held that there had

---

[109] The HRC considers that where such a right is granted in law or practice, there should be no differentiation among conscientious objectors on the basis of the nature of their beliefs: see UN Doc CCPR/C//21/Rev.1/Add.4, 27 September 1993. See also *Krotov v Secretary of State for the Home Department* [2004] EWCA Civ 69 (concerning a desertion from the Russian army and refusal to fight in the Chechen war). It was held that refugee status might be available where service would involve an individual participating in acts contrary to basic rules of human conduct as defined by international law.

[110] J Fawcett, *The Application of the European Convention on Human Rights* (Clarendon Press, 1987). Note that Art 4 ECHR which prohibits slavery, servitude, forced or compulsory labour expressly provides in Art 4(3)(b) that 'forced or compulsory labour' shall not include any service of a military character or, in case of conscientious objectors in countries where they are recognized, service exacted instead of military service.

[111] In 1987 it was formally adopted as a policy of the Committee of Ministers (the legislative component of the Council of Europe) in a Recommendation R(87)8 addressed to member states.

[112] In *Prior v Canada* [1988] FCJ No 107, the court considered a claim by a taxpayer who objected to contributing to military expenditure. The court struck out the claim holding that there was no offence to conscience and that he had not been forced to act contrary to his beliefs.

[113] See Goodwin-Gill (n 1 above) para 4.3.2.2.

[114] Application 39437/98 (24 January 2006).

been a violation of Article 3 and that it was unnecessary to give a separate ruling on the complaints under Articles 5, 8 and 9. It noted that he remained under an obligation to perform his military service despite his convictions and punishment. He faced living the rest of his life with the risk of being sent to prison if he refused to perform military service. There were no specific provisions in Turkish law governing penalties for those who refused to wear uniform on conscientious or religious grounds. The numerous criminal prosecutions against him, and the cumulative effects of the criminal convictions, together with the possibility that he would be liable to prosecution for the rest of his life, had been disproportionate to the aim of ensuring that he did his military service.[115]

Family and child law

Family law issues arise in many cases involving the entry clearance of spouses, **6.66** partners and children. This is an area where issues of freedom of religion may indirectly come into play as the system is designed to recognize family law based upon Judeo-Christian heritage, which may discriminate in its effects upon other religions. Furthermore, immigration legislation may discriminate indirectly on grounds of religion.[116]

The Court of Appeal in *Singh v Entry Clearance Officer, New Delhi*,[117] recognized **6.67** the importance of viewing a case in the context of its particular social, cultural and religious setting. The case concerned whether the relationship between an Indian boy and his adoptive parents constituted family life for the purposes of Article 8, given that the adoption in the case which was valid under Indian law was not recognized by the United Kingdom because it fell outside para 6 of the Immigration Rules. Munby J expressly noted that:

> [I]n our multi-cultural and pluralistic society the family takes many forms. Indeed, in contemporary Britain the family takes an almost infinite variety of forms. Many marry according to the rites of non-Christian faiths . . . Many of these changes have given rise to profound misgivings in some quarters. We live in a society which on many social, ethical and religious topics no longer either thinks or speaks with one voice. These are topics on which men and women of different faiths or no faith at all hold starkly differing views. All of those views are entitled to the greatest respect but it is not for a judge to choose between them.[118]

A detailed analysis of family law and the recognition of marriages, divorces and **6.68** adoptions effected in accordance with particular religious beliefs is beyond the

---

[115] See also *Sert v Turkey*, Application 47491/99 (8 July 2004); *Stefanov v Bulgaria*, Application 32438/96 (3 May 2001); *Tsirlis and Kouloumpas v Greece*, Application 19233/91 and 19234/91 (29 May 1997).

[116] See *R (Baiai) v Secretary of State for the Home Department (No 3)* [2006] EWHC 1454 (Admin).

[117] [2004] EWCA Civ 1075.

[118] At [63], [64].

scope of this text.[119] However, it is worth considering the Immigration Rules relating to three areas concerning entry requirements for marriage, namely the general rule, child marriage, and polygamous marriage. While the notorious virginity tests, under the 'primary purpose rule' that effectively discriminated against spouses of South Asian origin seeking entry clearance to the United Kingdom, have long since been abolished, de facto discrimination in other forms may exist.[120] While it is not easy to mount a challenge to the Immigration Rules based upon the high threshold which has been set in *R (Razgar) v Secretary of State for the Home Department*,[121] nevertheless there may be cases on the facts where a challenge may be successful.

Marriage generally

6.69 To obtain admission as a spouse, the applicant must satisfy the entry clearance officer that the marriage is lawful and complies with the requirements of the Immigration Rules.[122] The parties must have capacity to marry and it must be a valid marriage in accordance with the law of the place of celebration. The IDI on Recognition of Marriage and Divorce deals with several of the issues relating to validity of marriage such as polygamy, telephone marriages, talaq (Islamic divorce), and customary divorces.[123]

Polygamous marriages

6.70 The common law rule is that all marriages celebrated in the United Kingdom must be monogamous. Additionally, a person domiciled in England and Wales is not permitted to marry polygamously. This rule is now codified in s 11 of the Matrimonial Causes Act 1973. A number of countries do however permit polygamy. Polygamy is further restricted in the United Kingdom by the criminal offence of bigamy.[124]

6.71 As regards immigration, the Immigration Rules prohibit more than one spouse from joining a spouse settled in the United Kingdom.[125] Previously, the law would not recognize a marriage that was potentially polygamous, namely where the couple could have more than one spouse under the relevant domestic law. This inevitably caused considerable hardship and has now been altered by statute.[126]

---

[119] See further C Hamilton, *Family, Law and Religion* (Sweet & Maxwell, 1995); D Pearl & W Menski, *Muslim Family Law* (Sweet & Maxwell, 1998).

[120] See 6.24 above.

[121] [2004] UKHL 27 [20]. See 6.20 above.

[122] See HC 395, paras 277–289.

[123] IDI, Ch 8, Annex B.

[124] Offences Against the Person Act 1861, s 57. See also *A-M v A-M (Divorce: Jurisdiction: Validity of Marriage)* [2001] 2 FLR 6.

[125] IA 1988, s 2; HC 395, paras 278–279.

[126] See the Private International Law (Miscellaneous Provisions) Act 1995 amending s 11(d) of the Matrimonial Causes Act 1973. See also IDI, Ch 8, Family Members, Annex C: Polygamous and potentially polygamous marriages. See also P Shah, 'Attitudes to Polygamy in English Law' (2003) 52 ICLQ 369.

A child of a polygamous marriage who has the right of abode is not prevented from entry to the United Kingdom. However, if a parent would be refused entry on the ground of polygamy, the Immigration Rules are not to be construed as permitting the parent's child to be granted entry clearance.[127] In particular circumstances refusal of entry might be challenged on Article 8 grounds outside of the Immigration Rules.[128]

Child marriage

A marriage between spouses where one or both are under the age of 16 is not valid **6.72** in the United Kingdom. There are however a number of countries where child marriage is valid under domestic law. Previously spouses under the age of 16 qualified for entry under the Immigration Rules. This was changed in 1986 when both parties to the marriage were required to be 16 and over. However, a spouse who married below the age of 16 would be entitled to enter on reaching the age of 18. From 21 December 2004, the Immigration Rules were changed again to prevent the grant of entry clearance, leave to enter or remain if either party to the marriage is below the age of 18 at the date of arrival or grant of leave in the United Kingdom.[129]

Religious leaders and workers

The Immigration Rules expressly provide for leave to enter in respect of ministers of **6.73** religion, missionaries, members of religious orders and visiting religious workers. Ministers of religion, missionaries and members of religious orders may be admitted for up to two years in the first instance if they hold current entry clearance.[130] Visiting religious workers and religious workers in non-pastoral roles may be admitted for up to six months and twelve months respectively in the first instance if they hold current entry clearance.[131] The provisions relating to visiting religious workers were introduced in express recognition that religious communities in the United Kingdom face difficulties in recruiting sufficient numbers of religious workers from within the country.[132]

Interesting questions arise as to the application of these provisions to members of **6.74** minority religions as the IDI expressly excludes certain religions. The Church of Scientology and the Unification Church (Moonies) are not accepted as religions for the purposes of the Immigration Rules and their members are expressly

---

[127] HC 395, para 296.
[128] See also *Macdonald's* (n 2 above) para 11.34.
[129] HC 395, para 277 as amended by HC 164.
[130] Ibid, paras 170(v), 171.
[131] Ibid, para 177C.
[132] Inserted by HC 769 with effect from 9 January 2006. See Explanatory Memorandum to the Statement of Changes in Immigration Rules laid on 19 December 2005 (HC 769).

precluded from being treated as ministers or missionaries.[133] Members of the Unification Church may, however, be admitted as visitors for up to six months.[134] The restrictions placed on these particular religious groups may well be subject to future challenge. The Home Office provides a list annexed to the IDI of particular religious organizations and the basis on which members may enter.[135]

6.75 It seems that this is an area which may be the subject of future challenge. It should be noted that the EA 2006 creates an exception to this for the purposes of people entering the country to provide services in connection with a religion or belief, such as a minister or clergyman.[136] This may curtail claims based upon discrimination.

Minister of religion

6.76 A minister of religion is a defined as a religious functionary whose main regular duties comprise the leading of a congregation in performing the rites and rituals of the faith, and in preaching the essentials of the creed.[137] To qualify for leave a minister must either have worked at least for one year as a minister of religion in any of the five years immediately prior to the date the application is made, or, where ordination is prescribed by a religious faith as the sole means of entering the ministry, have been ordained as a minister following at least one year's full time or two years' part time training for the ministry.[138] Ministers of religion now have to produce a certificate to demonstrate that they have passed the required spoken English language test.[139]

Missionaries

6.77 Missionaries are defined for the purposes of the Immigration Rules as persons who are directly engaged in spreading a religious doctrine and whose work is in essence neither administrative nor clerical.[140] To qualify for entry as a missionary a person must have trained as a missionary or have worked as one and must be sent to the United Kingdom by an overseas organization.[141]

---

[133] IDI, Ch 5, s 6 para 1 (August 2004). Note too that the Church of Scientology is not considered a religion for the purposes of registration as a charity by the UK Charity Commissioners. See also *Reverend Sun Myung Moon (USA) v ECO, Seoul* [2005] UKAIT 00112.

[134] IDI, Annex U.

[135] Ibid.

[136] Ibid, s 52(4)(g).

[137] HC 395, para 169(i).

[138] Ibid, para 170(i)(a). See *Begum (Kalsoon) v Visa Officer, Islamabad* [1988] Imm AR 325.

[139] As of 23 August 2004. HC 395, para 170(iva).

[140] Ibid, para 169(ii).

[141] Ibid, para 170(i)(b).

Members of a religious order

Members of a religious order are persons who are coming to live in a community **6.78** run by that order.[142] To qualify for admission they must be coming to live in a community maintained by the religious order of which they are members, and if intending to teach, do not intend to do so save at an establishment maintained by their order.[143]

Visiting religious workers

A visiting religious worker is a person coming to the United Kingdom for a short **6.79** period to perform religious duties at one or more locations in the country.[144] To qualify for entry as a visiting worker, he must (1) be an established religious worker based overseas; (2) submit a letter from a senior member or senior representative of one or more local religious communities in the United Kingdom confirming that he is invited to perform religious duties as a visiting religious worker at one or more locations in the United Kingdom and confirming the expected duration of that employment; and (3) have not been granted leave as a visiting religious worker in the twelve months prior to the application, and not be seeking leave to enter which, when amalgamated with his previous periods of leave in this category in the twelve months prior to the application, would total more than six months.[145]

A religious worker in a non-pastoral role is a person employed by the faith he is **6.80** coming to work for, whose duties include performing religious rites within the religious community, but not preaching to a congregation.[146] To qualify as a religious worker in a non-pastoral role a person must have (1) at least one year of full time training or work experience, or a period of part time training or work experience equivalent to one year of full time training or work experience, accrued in the five years preceding the application in the faith with which he has employment in the United Kingdom; (2) be able to show that, at the time of his application, at least one full time member of staff of the local religious community which the applicant is applying to join in the United Kingdom has a sufficient knowledge of English; (3) submit a letter from a senior member or senior representative of the local religious community which has invited him to the United Kingdom, confirming that he has been offered employment as a religious worker in a non-pastoral role in that religious community, and confirming the duration of that employment.[147]

---

[142] Ibid, para 169(iii).
[143] Ibid, para 170(i)(c).
[144] Ibid, para 177A(i).
[145] Ibid, para 177B(i)(a).
[146] Ibid, para 177A(ii).
[147] Ibid, para 177B(i)(b).

6.81 Additionally both visiting workers of religion and religious workers in non-pastoral roles must also satisfy the following additional requirements: (1) that they do not intend to take employment except as per the basis of their application; (2) they do not intend to undertake employment as a minister of religion, missionary or member of a religious order; (3) they will be able to maintain and accommodate themselves and any dependants without recourse to public funds, or will, with any dependants, be maintained and accommodated adequately by the religious community employing them; (4) they intend to leave the United Kingdom at the end of their leave in this category.[148]

---

[148] Ibid, para 177B(ii)–(v).

7

PLANNING, PRISONS, AND HEALTH AND SAFETY

Introduction

This chapter looks at a number of other areas of law where issues have arisen in **7.01** relation to religious freedom, individuals and religious organizations. Many of these areas such as planning involve decision making by public authorities who will be directly affected by equality legislation and must act compatibly with the protections contained in the European Convention on Human Rights ('ECHR').[1] It is necessary to consider in any particular area how the application of the Human Rights Act 1998 ('HRA 1998'), the Equality Act 2006 ('EA 2006') and the Race Relations Act 1976 ('RRA 1976') may affect the legal framework.[2]

Some of these areas involve exemptions from other generally applicable and **7.02** religiously neutral laws, to allow certain religious groups to carry out religious practices that they would otherwise be prevented from doing. An example of this is the statutory concession in respect of meat slaughter regulations to allow Muslim and Jewish communities to be able to provide halal and kosher meat.

---

[1] See 2.33–2.37 above for consideration of public authorities and HRA 1998, s 6.
[2] See Chapter 2 above for detailed treatment of the relevant legal provisions in these statutes.

The use of exemptions is far from novel as a legal tool. Most areas of law contain exceptions to the general rule, although where religion and culture are concerned this has been the subject of academic criticism.[3] Exemptions generally raise the question of whether other religious groups may be able to secure exemptions from general laws should they require them, and whether the granting of exemptions to one religious group but not to others amounts to unlawful discrimination.[4] In other areas of law, such as prison law, the statutory framework has made express provision for religion. As the religious make up of the population has altered so there has been a need to adapt the legal rules to accommodate other religious groups. Other areas still, such as planning law, do not as such treat the right to freedom of religion as requiring a different approach than that which is already envisaged in the balancing exercise in decision making.

7.03   This chapter first considers health and safety regulations where these have created difficulties for particular religious groups; it then looks at the subject of meat slaughter regulations and the exemptions which have been created for Jewish and Muslim groups. Following that it looks briefly at the religious issues that may arise in planning law and prison law. This chapter self-evidently contains a number of areas of law which are unconnected and which it is not easy to discuss collectively. However, there is merit in looking at these issues together as it enables interesting comparisons to be made across the board as to the way in which religious diversity is dealt with under the law.

Health and Safety Regulations

General comments

7.04   There are a number of specific exceptions to otherwise generally applicable statutory provisions in the area of legislation relating to health and safety.[5] This is an area where there are strong public policy reasons for requiring the population as a whole to be subject to the same standards. The prohibition of highly addictive and potentially harmful narcotics is one such area.[6] However, when the situation is looked at in the round and the various anomalies, lacunas and inconsistencies in the law are considered, it is not so apparent that exemptions cannot be justified even in the area of health and safety.

---

[3] See B Barry, *Culture and Equality* (Harvard University Press, 2002) and 1.34–1.35 above.
[4] Ibid.
[5] See J Waldron, 'One Law for All? The Logic of Cultural Accommodation' (2002) 59 Washington and Lee Law Review 3–35 for a discussion of the underlying principles relating to exemptions on religious and cultural grounds.
[6] See 2.13 and 2.80–2.84 above.

Historically, a number of these exemptions apply specifically to Sikhs, who have a **7.05**
number of specific requirements relating to religious dress.[7] In *Mandla v Dowell
Lee*,[8] Lord Fraser expressly recognized that turbans and beards provided a sign of
Sikh communal identity. Inevitably, some of these religious requirements will
come into conflict with regulations that prescribe a mandatory uniform or form
of dress, for example at school or in the workplace. There have to date been a number of cases concerning Sikh employees who were not permitted to manifest their
religious beliefs at work on grounds of health and safety requirements, which are
further discussed in Chapter 5 of this book.[9]

Protective head gear

A number of religions prescribe some form of head covering as a manifestation of **7.06**
the religion that may make the wearing of required protective head gear, such as a
hard hat on a building site or a motor cycle helmet, difficult. In the wake of a
number of cases concerning Sikhs, Parliament legislated in both areas to provide
specific exemption for Sikhs wearing turbans.[10] The Employment Act 1989
recognizes the right of Sikh construction workers to wear turbans at work and
provides an exemption from safety helmet requirements.[11] The effect of the
exemption is to set aside any liability that might otherwise be imposed upon an
employer who fails to ensure that all his workers wear safety helmets. Although the
definition of construction site covers both works of engineering construction and
steel and reinforced concrete structures, the exemption was narrowly construed
by the Tribunal in at least one decision.[12]

The Road Traffic Act 1988 contains an exemption for Sikhs riding motor cycles **7.07**
while wearing a turban.[13] An earlier statutory exemption was contained in the
Motor-Cycle Crash-Helmets (Religious Exemption) Act 1976.[14] This came into
force after the Commission gave judgment in *X v United Kingdom*,[15] a case brought
by a Sikh who had been convicted 20 times for not wearing a crash helmet.
The claimant contended at Strasbourg that his Article 9 rights had been violated.

---

[7] It is generally agreed that there are five symbols that Guru Gobind Singh requested his followers to wear, namely the kesh (uncut long hair); kanga (a comb); kara (a steel bracelet); kachha (long
underpants); and the kirpan (a small ceremonial sword).
[8] [1983] 2 AC 548, 1064. See 2.21–2.22 above.
[9] See 5.71–5.75 above.
[10] See 2.14 above.
[11] Employment Act 1989, s 11.
[12] *Dhanjal v British Steel General Steels* (Case No 50740191, 16 December 1993, IT) cited in R Jones
& W Gnanapala, *Ethnic Minorities in English Law* (Trentham Books, 2000) 228. See also 5.74 above.
[13] S 16(2).
[14] S 1 amending the Road Traffic Act 1988, s 17. Repealed by Road Traffic Act (Consequential
Provisions) Act 1988.
[15] Application 7992/77 (1978) 14 DR 234.

The Commission held that the requirement to wear a motorcycle helmet was justifiable on the ground of public safety. Notwithstanding the government's victory in Strasbourg, Parliament shortly afterwards decided to legislate expressly to allow the very practice which they had fought over in the courts. However, the Strasbourg case represents an important matter of principle and one which applies generally, namely that there would be no violation of Article 9 in a situation where any restriction could be justified under Article 9(2) as being a proportionate legislative response to health and safety concerns.[16]

7.08   The reasons and motivations for passing such legislation (including the recognition of the service of Sikhs in the British army) may be problematic and expose the government to criticism on the grounds of discrimination by other religious groups. But these exemptions, since they were enacted, have caused little controversy. In many areas of health and safety law there will no doubt be strong public policy rationale for the legislation to apply to everyone. It is far from clear that Articles 9 and 14 will assist other groups obtaining similar exemptions from general provisions designed to protect the health and safety of the public.[17] However, the provisions of the EA 2006 may provide the possibility for challenges to be made.[18]

Prohibited substances and objects

7.09   There are almost no statutory exemptions from laws relating to controlled substances such as cannabis on the grounds of religion. This is an area where the government has taken a clear line on public policy grounds. For example, in *R v Taylor*,[19] the defendant was prosecuted for possession of cannabis under the Misuse of Drugs Act 1971. He stated that as a Rastafarian the smoking of cannabis was part of his religion and argued that the prosecution infringed his rights under Article 9, or alternatively that the Crown had to prove that a prosecution was a necessary and appropriate response in fulfilment of a legitimate aim. The Crown at the trial had conceded that the use of cannabis was part of the defendant's religion but argued that the prosecution was justified. The judge found no way around the clear provisions in statute, contrasting the general prohibition on cannabis with an exemption created by criminal statute to allow Sikhs to carry ceremonial swords.[20]

---

[16]   See 2.80–2.84 above.

[17]   See *Singh Binder v Canada* [208/1986, Human Rights Committee Report 1990, Vol II A/45/40 IX F]. S was dismissed by the Canadian Railway Company as a maintenance electrician as a result of his refusal to wear protective headgear at work instead of his turban. The UNHRC held that the interference with S's religious practice was justified in the interests of public safety in accordance with Art 18(3) of the International Convenant on Civil and Political Rights 1966.

[18]   See 2.42–2.44 above.

[19]   [2001] EWCA Crim 2263; *R v Andrews* [2004] EWCA Crim 947.

[20]   A similar result was reached by the US Supreme Court in *Employment Division v Smith* 494 US 872; 110 SCt 1595 (1990) (relating to the smoking of peyote as part of the religious service). See 2.13–2.14 above.

One exception to this general principle in criminal law is contained in s 139 of the **7.10** Criminal Justice Act 1988. It was aimed at providing an exemption specifically for the Sikh practice of carrying a kirpan or small ceremonial sword. Unlike the exemptions relating to hard hats and motorcycle helmets, the legislation provides a statutory defence to a charge of carrying in a public place 'any article which has a blade or is sharply pointed'. It is a defence for 'a person charged with an offence under this section to prove that he had the article with him (a) for use at work; (b) for religious reasons; or (c) as part of any national costume'.[21] In *Multani v Commission Scolaire Marguerite-Bourgeoys*,[22] the Supreme Court of Canada struck down an order of a Quebec school board that prohibited a Sikh child from wearing a kirpan to school as a violation of freedom of religion under the Charter of Rights and Freedoms.

It is, therefore, arguably a more principled piece of legislation in that it does not **7.11** on the face of it discriminate in its ambit by confining itself to one particular religious group and allows any person to raise the religious or cultural defence.[23] The ambit of the exemption was tested in the prosecution of the Honoured Pendragon of the Glastonbury Order of Druids for carrying a sword in public. Although the Parliamentary record made it clear that this particular exemption was designed for the benefit of the Sikh community, the wording of the statute was neutral and the judge had little choice to apply it to the defendant, once his sincerely held religious beliefs were established.[24]

Where there are solid public policy reasons for regulating the carrying of sharp **7.12** and potentially lethal objects by members of the public, it is clear that restrictions will be justified under Articles 9 and 14. On the other hand, it is not likely to be in the public interest to prosecute people who carry such objects with no intent to use that object to harm another person and where there is no danger as such to the public. That said, it is likely that any other religious group seeking to obtain exemptions, particularly in the present climate of increasingly restrictive measures purporting to deal with terrorism offences, would face an uphill battle. Beyond this, it is unlikely that Strasbourg would interfere in domestic law by declaring neutral criminal laws prohibiting dangerous substances and items as violating the ECHR.[25]

Rituals, burials, and ceremonies

Festivals, public ceremonies and communal rituals are integral to many religions. **7.13** In terms of timing, these may conflict with education and work timetables and so

---

[21] Criminal Justice Act 1988, s 139(5)(b).
[22] (2006) SCC 6.
[23] See also *People v Singh* 135 Misc 2d 701; 516 NYS2d 412 (Criminal Court of the City of New York, 1987) (where the judge acknowledged that there was no basis in the statute to dismiss the case, but that the continuance of the prosecution would not serve the interests of justice or any useful purpose).
[24] Referred to in Barry (n 3 above) 51–2.
[25] See 2.80–2.84.

are considered in the relevant chapters above. They may also conflict with planning laws. For example, the conflict between the Druid community in the United Kingdom and the government over access to the ancient ceremonial site at Stonehenge has been the subject of considerable controversy. This is dealt with further below. Aside from this, festivals may impact on public order and safety. In England alone a wide variety of religious, national and cultural communities are able to celebrate as long as they do so within the confines of legislation such as the Public Order Act 1986.[26]

7.14 One issue that relates specifically to public health is the control of the waters and the prohibition on introducing pollutants into water ways and the sea. The most important legislation is the Water Industry Act 1991 and the Water Resources Act of 1991 which instructs the Environment Agency to police the use of water in England and Wales.[27] These two Acts, together with three others enacted at the same time, consolidated the previous legislation covering water which was spread over about 20 statutes. A number of provisions are designed to prevent pollution of water ways.[28]

7.15 Any scattering of human ashes on rivers is regulated by the Environment Agency working with British Waterways. Until relatively recently, the Environment Agency routinely refused permission apart from in tidal waters, on the grounds that so much water is extracted for drinking from the rivers that there could be a pollution implication. There is currently a concession by the government, the effect of which is to allow the Hindu population to scatter the ashes of their dead in certain rivers such as the Soar, Thames and Wye.[29] This is effectively by way of a policy adopted by the Environment Agency which deems the scattering of ashes in certain designated areas not to be pollution which would otherwise be regulated in accordance with a number of statutory provisions. However, it looks as if there may be challenges brought by religious organizations or individuals.[30]

7.16 Burial law in England and Wales is currently the subject of considerable parliamentary debate. Historically burial was the responsibility of the Church of England. However, in the nineteenth century urban growth meant that burial places were increasingly provided by local authorities and private cemeteries. Much of the older piecemeal legislation was replaced by the Local Authorities'

---

[26] See 2.16 above.

[27] See generally *Encyclopaedia of Environmental Law* (Sweet & Maxwell, 1997).

[28] See eg Water Resources Act 1991, s 85.

[29] The final samskar in the Hindu religion prescribes cremation for an individual after death and if possible that the ashes should be scattered in running water. Similarly Sikhs should also scatter the ashes of deceased relatives in running water so that the spirit is set free as the ashes are swept to the sea.

[30] Note that between November 2004 and February 2005 the Environment Agency carried out a public consultation on *Funeral Practices and the Environment*.

Cemeteries Order 1977.[31] But the Order does not apply to (1) Church of England or Church of Wales churchyards; (2) other religious burial grounds; (3) private cemeteries. This is an area which is ripe for review, as the Home Office acknowledges in its *Consultation: Burial Law and Policy in the 21st Century*.[32] A detailed discussion is beyond the scope of this book, but this is plainly an area where the HRA 1998 is likely to be engaged.[33]

Animal Rights

General comments

Religious slaughter as practised in a number of religions and most notably in Islam and Judaism is incompatible with the generally applicable regulations in many countries relating to meat and poultry slaughter. For this reason a number of states including the United Kingdom have introduced exemptions to the legislation that would otherwise prohibit slaughter in accordance with the religious doctrine.[34]   **7.17**

This issue is of interest in that it introduces the question of animal rights as opposed to human rights into the balance. Legally the protections contained in the ECHR provide no assistance for animals, only human individuals and legal persons such as groups, companies, and associations, themselves made up of individuals. However, the debates on animal rights are shifting. One jurisdiction, New Zealand, has already passed legislation prohibiting research on non-human hominids (chimpanzees, bonobos, gorillas and orangutans).[35] This genesis of this protection was a lobby group which argued that non-human hominids should be afforded similar rights to humans, ie not to be deprived of life, not to be subjected to torture or cruel treatment, and not to be subjected to medical or scientific experimentation.[36]   **7.18**

---

[31] SI 1977/204.

[32] (DCA, January 2004).

[33] See *Re Crawley Green Road Cemetery, Luton* [2001] Fam 308 (to refuse petitioner's petition for a faculty to remove the cremated remains of her late husband from consecrated land to non-consecrated land given her humanist beliefs would violate Art 9). See also *Dodson v Sweden*, Application 61564/00 (31 August 2004) (complaint under Art 8 about refusal to allow applicant to remove urn containing late husband's ashes was declared admissible).

[34] See generally A Shorten, *Cultural Exemptions: The Case of Religious Slaughter Legislation* (Mancept Working Paper, 2005).

[35] The Animal Welfare Act 1999 (New Zealand), which commenced on 1 January 2000, provides that the use of non-human hominids in research, testing, or teaching is not permitted unless the Director-General of Agriculture approves the use, and then, only if the use is in the interests of the non-human hominid itself or its species.

[36] See R Taylor, 'A Step at a Time: New Zealand's Progress Toward Hominid Rights' [2001] 7 Animal Law 35–43.

Meat slaughter regulations

7.19   Under the Welfare of Animals (Slaughter or Killing) Regulations 1995, animals
kept for the production of meat, skin, fur or other products must either be stunned
to cause immediate loss of consciousness until death is caused by bleeding, or be
killed outright using specified methods set out in the legislation.[37] These generally
applicable regulations cause difficulty for some religious groups. For example
Orthodox Jews regard meat as fit for consumption (kosher) only where the animal
has been slaughtered by using a sharp knife to cut the animal's throat in rapid and
uninterrupted movements severing the wind pipe, arteries and veins (shechita).
This to ensure that the greatest quantity of blood will flow as it is forbidden for
Jews to eat any blood. Many Muslims also require the animals to be alive at the
time of slaughter (and not stunned) and the blood to be drained from the carcass
in order to be permitted for consumption (halal). Not all religious adherents will
regard the act of stunning as killing the animal, though some will accept stunning
as a means of killing.

7.20   A religious exemption was introduced when the first legislation was passed regulating the slaughter methods for animals and has remained in place ever since.[38]
It is now contained in the Welfare of Animals (Slaughter or Killing) Regulations
1995.[39] The legal requirement for stunning does not apply to the slaughter of
animals or poultry by the Jewish method for the food of Jews by a Jew licensed by
the relevant governmental department (currently DEFRA) and duly licensed by
the Rabbinical Commission, or by the Muslim method for the food of Muslims
by a Muslim licensed by the relevant governmental department. The exemption
states that the slaughter should be without the infliction of unnecessary suffering.[40]
Ritual slaughter is also authorized by the European Convention for the Protection
of Animals for Slaughter[41] and by an EC Directive.[42]

7.21   The general rule and exemption raise a number of interesting legal issues. First,
whether the exemption is compatible with Article 9 and 14 in that it only grants

---

[37] The Regulations are made under the terms of the Slaughterhouses Act 1974 (applying to
cattle, sheep, goats, swine and horses), and the Slaughter of Poultry Act 1967 (applying to domestic
fowl and turkeys kept in captivity).

[38] See Slaughter of Animals Act 1933, s 6.

[39] SI 1995/731, reg 33. Note that the Welfare of Animals (Slaughter or Killing) (Amendment)
Regulations 1999, SI 1999/400, amend regs 14 and 22 of and Sch 12 to the 1995 Regulations, so as
to confine religious slaughter, in the case of animals, to licensed slaughterhouses and in the case of
birds to slaughterhouses as defined in the 1995 Regulations.

[40] 1995 Regulations, Sch 12 para 2.

[41] 10 May 1979. Article 17 permits states to derogate from the provisions concerning prior
stunning for slaughtering in accordance with religious rituals.

[42] Council Directive (EC) 93/119 on the protection of animals at the time of slaughter or killing
[1993] OJ L340/21. See also Council Directive (EEC) 74/577 on stunning of animals before
slaughter [1974] OJ L316/10.

an exemption to two religions but not others. Secondly, the exemption is limited to the slaughter of animals for food, but not for general sacrificial purposes. Thirdly, whether the exemptions are compatible with animal rights generally. It should be noted that these issues all engage underlying moral, political and philosophical ideas about animal rights, the extent of animal suffering, and whether killing animals is morally wrong, that are not discussed in any detail here but that need to be considered. The issue of whether another minority religion would be able to secure an exemption for its own particular practice by claiming a breach of Article 14 together with Article 9 has not yet been tested in domestic law.

A slightly different issue arose in *Cha'are Shalom Ve Tsedek v France*,[43] in which a **7.22** Jewish liturgical association with 600 members and 40,000 adherents, which ran 20 butcher shops administered by its own rabbinical committee, was not licensed by the Joint Rabbinical Committee in France to perform ritual slaughter. Ve Tsedek purported to require stricter slaughter rules than the Joint Rabbinical Committee (which represented the majority of about 700,000 Jews in France) in order to produce 'glatt' (smooth) meat. The French government produced evidence that there were shops where Ve Tsedek adherents could buy such meat. The Ministry of the Interior had previously refused to license the association on grounds that it was not sufficiently representative within the Jewish community and that it was not a religious body within the scope of the relevant domestic provisions.

In finding no violation of Article 9 alone or of Articles 14 and 9 taken together, the **7.23** European Court of Human Rights ('ECtHR') noted that it was in the general interest to avoid unregulated slaughter carried out in conditions of doubtful hygiene and that it was preferable for religious slaughter to be performed in slaughterhouses supervised by public authorities. The ECtHR found that there was in fact no interference as the applicant association could obtain supplies of 'glatt' meat from Belgium or other controlled butchers. It found that the right to freedom of religion did not extend to the right to take part in person in the performance of ritual slaughter and the subsequent certification process. It further noted that the restriction pursued a legitimate aim namely protection of public health and public order, in so far as organization by the state of the exercise of worship is conducive to religious harmony and tolerance. As regards Article 14, the majority ECtHR considered that the difference of treatment was limited in scope, pursued a legitimate aim, and was proportionate.[44]

---

43 [2000] ECHR 351, 27 June 2000.

44 Note however that the powerful minority dissent is well reasoned and should be considered in that it points out many of the problems inherent in the majority reasons. While it was accepted that states enjoyed a margin of appreciation in this area, the minority referred to the need to secure true religious pluralism.

7.24   The second and third issues give rise to consideration of a common principle, namely to what extent the rights of others should be taken into account and whether there are other aspects of the limitation under Article 9(2) that are relevant. In this regard the rights of others are likely to include the rights of animal activists to respect for their views, and the extent to which it would be possible to regulate animal sacrifice and ensure that it did not lead to public health concerns given that the sacrifice would not be carried out in supervised slaughter houses but more likely in the particular religious environment. Inevitably the balance between the rights will involve some consideration of the relative numbers affected on either side, and the relative importance of the respective rights, and in particular the degree of intrusion into the freedom of religion of the group or individual concerned.[45]

Planning Law

General comments

7.25   Although the English skyline contains church spires, minarets, cupola and other religious edifices, the establishment of a new building, or changing the use of an existing building for the purposes of a particular religion, will involve consideration of a range of factors under existing planning legislation and regulations. This will involve considerations of the use of green belt land, the degree of interference in the environment by a particular use of the land, noise emanating from forms of worship, and the rights of residents to peaceful enjoyment of their property under Article 1 Protocol 1 or family and privacy rights under Article 8. These considerations may evidently raise the issue of discrimination, as minority religious groups may find it more difficult to secure planning permission in certain areas than other religious organizations.[46]

7.26   The determination of planning permission applications is governed by the Town and Country Planning Act 1990. Section 70 refers to the considerations that apply to the determination of an application. It is couched in very flexible terms that do not purport to attribute specific weight to any one particular factor and generally allow for all material considerations to be taken into account.[47]

---

[45] See *Church of Lukumi Babalu Aye, Inc v City of Hialeah, Florida* 508 US 520 (1993) where the US Supreme Court considered the Santeria religion's practice of animal sacrifice in the open and found that the prohibitions contained in the applicable law had the appearance of targeting Santeria worshippers. The provisions did not withstand strict scrutiny and were declared unconstitutional in violation of the free exercise clause. See also *R (Countryside Alliance) v Attorney General* [2006] EWCA Civ 1677.

[46] See generally T Corner, 'Planning, the Environment and the European Convention of Human Rights' [1998] JPL 301–14.

[47] Town and Country Planning Act 1990, s 70(2). See generally R Turrall-Clarke & S Tromans, *Planning Law Practice and Precedents* (Sweet & Maxwell); V Moore, *A Practical Approach to Planning Law* (OUP, 2005).

It allows the local authority to grant planning permission on such conditions as it thinks fit.[48]

Some religious cases have provoked enormous controversy. For example, an application for the construction of an eruv (an area where some of the normal Sabbath restrictions on Jews are relaxed) in the London Borough of Barnet in the 1990s attracted nationwide attention. The proposed eruv consisted of a system of 85 poles with wires attached spanning a total area of six square miles. The planning committee rejected the application on the basis of visual impact and perceived harm to the Hampstead Garden Suburb Conservation Area. In an article appearing in The Economist shortly before the committee meeting, Lord McGregor, chairman of the Press Complaints Commission and past-chairman of the Hampstead Garden Suburb Trust expressed his fear that by introducing religious considerations into planning decisions the eruv would set a dangerous precedent. Ultimately the Secretary of State, following the Inspector's recommendation, granted planning permission on 20 September 1994.[49]   **7.27**

The social context (including religious worship requirements) in considerations of planning applications has been acknowledged for some time. In *Great Portland Estates plc v Westminster City Council*,[50] Lord Scarman stated that: 'the human factor is always present, of course indirectly as the background to the consideration of the character of land use. It can, however, and sometimes should, be given direct effect as an exceptional or special circumstance'.   **7.28**

The approach of the higher courts in the context of planning law, however, has been to assume that ECHR rights themselves do not warrant special treatment (except in the case of travellers) on the basis that the considerations that are involved are already factored into the balancing exercise envisaged by the legislative framework. In *Lough v First Secretary of State*,[51] the Court of Appeal held that Article 8 and Article 1 Protocol 1 rights have to be seen in the context of competing rights and are integral to the normal planning decision making process. As a result it was unnecessary for the decision maker to articulate the proportionality balancing exercise. There have been a number of criminal prosecutions of religious organizations following alleged breaches of planning permission and environmental laws, for example relating to noise pollution. Here there may be room for argument about the proportionality of a prosecution depending on the circumstances.[52]   **7.29**

---

[48] Ibid, s 70(1).
[49] DOE Ref:A/93/224571 and 229477.
[50] (1985) AC 661.
[51] [2004] EWCA Civ 905.
[52] See 2.13 above.

Use of land

7.30 In a number of earlier cases concerning the use of land, the fact that the proposed use is a religious one is not given additional significance. For example, in *Barnet Meeting Room Trust v Secretary of State for the Environment (No 2)*,[53] the Council had refused planning permission to erect a meeting room for worship on the edge of a green belt area in Barnet. The Council did not dispute the Trust's claim that it needed more accommodation in the area for Christian worship, and it had not suggested any other site, but refused on the grounds of the special character of the area. Although the room in question was a religious meeting place, the case was decided upon classic judicial review principles without specific reference to religious considerations.[54] This case was of course decided before the HRA 1998 came into force.

7.31 Following the enactment of the HRA 1998, it does not appear that Article 9 has had a significant impact on the result reached in individual cases. Some cases will no doubt continue to be considered without specific reference to freedom of religion. Even where Article 9 is referred to, the balancing exercise may effectively be similar to that which would have been carried out prior to the entry into force of the HRA 1998. In one recent case, *Islamic Education Society v Blackburn and Darwin Borough Council*,[55] the broadcast of the call to prayer (adhan) from a mosque was considered. There was evidence from a number of people in the local community who supported the amplification of the adhan five times a day during prescribed hours. However, the inspector rejected those views in favour of the twelve year Council policy on a number of grounds. The decision reveals a highly subjective approach taken to the religious issue.

7.32 One area that may be developed following the enactment of the HRA 1998 and the EA 2006 is religious discrimination. It is clear from the large number of planning appeals involving mosques, madrasas, religious meeting houses for Jehovah's Witnesses, Church of the Latter Day Saints and others, that planning is a significant issue for minority religions. Some of the planning decisions make reference to the relative intrusion of different types of religious worship, for example the broadcast of the call to prayer from the minaret as compared to the sound of church bells. Many local authorities appear not to have specific policies relating to religious difference and accommodation in their areas. These sorts of issues are evidently going to be very fact specific and dependent upon a number of factors

---

[53] [1993] JPL 739.

[54] See also *Northavon District Council v Secretary of State for the Environment and the Trustees of the Congregation of Jehovah's Witnesses* [1993] JPL 761.

[55] Application 10/04/0629 (PAD, 31 August 2005).

including the character of the land concerned, and the religious diversity of the local population.[56]

Some protection against discrimination was afforded to religious groups previ- **7.33**
ously under the RRA 1976, but, as referred to above, this did not protect all
religious groups.[57] However, as a general principle the need to perform a delicate
balancing exercise between different ethnic, cultural and religious groups in
society has been recognized. In *Brent London Borough Council v Swaminarayan
Hindu Mission*,[58] the inspector said:

> A multi-cultural society must accept the aspirations of different ethnic groups to pursue
> their religious and cultural activities in appropriate forms of developments. However,
> the planning system was designed to safeguard the general public interest. The needs of
> a particular group must be subject to planning policies, otherwise any semblance of
> control of land use would be continuously sacrificed to minority interests.

A further area where freedom of religion and discrimination may be engaged **7.34**
relates to the use of criminal prosecutions arising out of breaches of statutory
regulations relating to planning and environmental controls. For example, religious
organizations may be subject to criminal law sanctions where they fail to comply
with statutory notice requiring an immediate reduction in noise levels. Some
criminal law penalties contain the defence of 'reasonable excuse', and it may be
argued that the performance of religious duties amounts to a reasonable excuse.
Additionally, it may be argued in the circumstances of a particular case that a
criminal prosecution amounts to a disproportionate interference. This will clearly
depend upon the specific factual circumstances of the case.[59]

At the European level, the Strasbourg court is likely to uphold the decisions of the **7.35**
lower courts concluding that restrictions on planning permission pursue a legitimate aim and are proportionate in the circumstances.[60] This has certainly been
borne out by the existing case law in this area. In *ISKCON v United Kingdom*,[61]
the International Society for Krishna Consciousness operated a manor house for

---

[56] See *Cherwell District Council v Vadivale* (1991) 6 PAD 433 (permission refused for Hindu
applicant to use Old Rectory for wide range of religious meetings, celebrations and festivals at week-
ends on grounds of inconvenience to neighbours); *South Bucks and Chiltern District Council v Gold
Hill Baptist Church* (1989) 4 PAD 290 (application to erect a new church with access and car parking on prominent green belt site with distinctive rural character refused).

[57] It is unlawful for a planning authority to discriminate against a person in the carrying out of
any of its planning functions: see RRA 1976, s 19A (as inserted by s 55 of the Housing and Planning
Act 1986). See 2.21–2.28 above.

[58] (1987) 2 PAD 327 (permission refused for a marble temple of national significance with over
600 on-site parking places).

[59] See 2.13 above.

[60] See also 3.15–3.16 above.

[61] Application 20490/92 (1994) 76-A DR 90.

the purposes of theological education. The local authority served an enforce-ment notice on ISKCON alleging that by using the land for 'the purposes of a residential educational college and a religious community and public worship and public entertainment in connection with religious festivals' ISKCON had materially changed the use of the land, and that this material change of use amounted to a breach of planning control. ISKCON alleged a violation of Article 9, arguing that the interference was not necessary in a democratic society.[62]

7.36 The Commission found that ISKCON could not derive from the ECHR a right to 'exemption from the ordinary planning controls (provided due attention was paid to their interests), and that the individual applicants must accept that the enforcement of those planning controls affects the modalities of their worship and, so far as relevant, the education of their children'.[63] As regards future cases at the European level, Strasbourg is likely to give domestic states a wide margin in this area although it will no doubt scrutinize any criminal penalties imposed more carefully.

Access to holy sites

7.37 In *Chappell v United Kingdom*,[64] the Commission held that the closing of Stonehenge during summer solstice interfered with the Article 9 rights of Druids but was justified under Article 9(2). Subsequently, in *Pendragon v United Kingdom*,[65] the Commission considered a case involving services held at Stonehenge by the Glastonbury Druidic Order during the spring and autumn equinoxes and summer and winter solstices. Because non-Druidic people also held festivals in the surrounding area at the summer solstice, which one year caused a serious disturbance, English Heritage closed Stonehenge for the summer solstice. A member of the Order complained of violations of Articles 9, 10, 11 and 14, in that he was prevented from being present or carrying out a Druid ceremony at Stonehenge at sunrise on 21 June 1995, was arrested and detained in police cus-tody. The Commission declared the claim inadmissible, noting that there was no evidence that Druids were treated in any way differently from any other groups of people wishing or attempting to observe the summer solstice in the vicinity of Stonehenge.

---

[62] See *ISKCON v Secretary of State and Hertsmere Borough Council* (1992) 64 P & CR 85 for decision of domestic courts. See also 3.15 above.

[63] See also *Vergos v Greece*, Application 65501/01 (24 June 2004) (decision to refuse planning permission to build public prayer house on his own land was held to be in pursuit of the legitimate aim of protecting public order and rights of others under Art 9 and did not amount to discrimination).

[64] (1988) 10 EHRR CD 510. See also 3.16 above.

[65] Application 31416/96 (19 October 1998).

Prison Law

General comments

The United Kingdom is incarcerating an increasingly diverse religious popula- **7.38**
tion. The Church of England has long played an integral role in prisons in the
United Kingdom with a system of prison chaplains, recognition of the right to
worship, to attend religious services, and to receive last rites. As the prison population of the United Kingdom has become more religiously diverse, so it has been
accepted that there is a need to allow access for the spiritual leaders of the other
major world religions and to accommodate other religious beliefs. The HRA
1998, the EA 2006 and the RRA 1976 will all impact directly on this area.

It should be noted that the Prison Service is currently the only agency of the **7.39**
criminal justice system that also monitors religious affiliation. When prisoners
arrive at a prison they are asked to self-classify their religion.[66] That religion is
considered an important aspect of prison life is evident from the Prison Service
Order 4550: *Religion Manual* stating that the Prison Service recognizes and
respects the right of prisoners to practise their religion.[67] According to the 2002
statistics, the largest religious group in the prison were Anglicans (36 per cent)
followed by Roman Catholics (17 per cent), Muslims (8 per cent), other Christians
(3 per cent), Free Church (2 per cent) and Buddhist (1 per cent).[68] Sikhs, Hindus
and Jews each accounted for less than 1 per cent of the prison population.

Detailed consideration of all the issues that may arise in a prison environment are **7.40**
beyond the scope of this text.[69] However, as there have been a number of cases
from the United Kingdom that have reached Strasbourg relating to the conflict
between the religious rights of prisoners and prison laws and regulations it is
worth considering these here. In addition the widespread detention of asylum
seekers and those without valid leave to remain in the United Kingdom also raises
concerns where a substantial proportion of those detained are unlikely to be of the
majority religion. Given the inherent restrictions upon liberty involved in detention, and the practical and economic constraints of running a prison service, imprisonment is certainly going to interfere with a number of aspects of manifestations of
religion, from clothing to dietary and worship requirements. Many of these issues
mirror the concerns for religious groups within education and employment.

---

[66] Prison Act 1952, s 10(5). In *X v United Kingdom* (1983) 5 EHRR 487 it was held that requiring
a prisoner to register his religion in prison records did not interfere with his Art 9 rights.

[67] PSO 4550 of 30 October 2000 as amended.

[68] See *The Prison Population in 2002: Statistical Findings*, Home Office Findings No 228.

[69] For a detailed treatment of the law relating to prisons see S Livingstone, T Owen & A Macdonald,
Prison Law (OUP, 2003).

7.41   Different justifications for the restrictions on rights will of course apply in prisons, but it should be noted at the outset that the Prison Act 1952 provides no express authority whatsoever for the curtailment of a prisoner's basic rights other than his right to liberty. The legislative framework is still governed by the 1952 Act. In addition the Prison Rules 1999 are made under s 47 of the Act.[70] The statutory requirements governing the observance of religion are laid down in the Prison Rules 1999, Prison (Amendment) Rules 2000,[71] Prison (Amendment No 2) Rules 2000[72] and in the Young Offender Institution Rules 2000.[73]

7.42   It should also be noted that most of the restrictions on individual prisoners stem from secondary legislation and non-statutory administrative orders and instructions which themselves derive from the Home Secretary's rule-making power in the Prison Act 1952. As a result, challenges made on the basis of the HRA 1998 will enable the courts to quash decisions which violate a prisoner's fundamental rights, except in the rare situation of a particular restriction being mandated by primary legislation.

7.43   Before the advent of the HRA 1998, the House of Lords in *Raymond v Honey*[74] held that 'a convicted prisoner retains all civil rights which are not taken away expressly or by necessary implication'. This in turn had led the Court of Appeal in *R v Home Secretary, ex p Leech (No 2)*[75] to strike down an individual prison rule as ultra vires on the basis that it interfered with a prisoner's fundamental or constitutional rights. The House of Lords in *R v Secretary of State for the Home Department ex p Daly*[76] considered the appropriate standard for the review of interferences with prisoners' rights. The court in that case endorsed the principles set out in a range of cases leading to *Leech (No 2)* and confirmed that the test of proportionality is to be applied where a prisoner's rights have been interfered with. Lord Bingham in his judgment stated:

> Any custodial order inevitably curtails the enjoyment, by the person confined, of rights enjoyed by other citizens. He cannot move freely and choose his associates as they are entitled to do. It is indeed an important objective of such an order to curtail such rights, whether to punish him or to protect other members of the public or both. But the order does not wholly deprive the person confined of all rights enjoyed by other citizens. Some rights, perhaps in an attenuated or qualified form, survive the making of the order.[77]

---

[70] Note that unlike the Immigration Rules, which are issued as a House of Commons paper rather than by statutory instrument, the Prison Rules, SI 1999/728 as amended, are delegated legislation.

[71] SI 2000/1794.

[72] SI 2000/2641.

[73] SI 2000/3371.

[74] [1983] 1 AC 1.

[75] [1994] QB 198 (concerning r 33(3) of the 1964 Rules that gave a prison governor a general power to read every letter from a prisoner and stop any letter which he considered to be objectionable or of inordinate length).

[76] [2001] UKHL 26.

[77] Ibid [5].

For the purposes of a claim under the HRA 1998, both state run and private **7.44** prisons are directly bound by s 6. The contractor of a private prison will fall within the definition of s 6(3) as his functions in detaining people will clearly be functions of a public nature.[78] Although the HRA 1998 might have been considered to provide a powerful tool for means of redress in relation to prisons, in practice most cases have been decided on principles of common law, and the ECHR is rarely stated to lead to a different outcome than the common law.[79]

Inevitably, prison regulations will impact on various aspects of an individual's **7.45** religious views. Many of these will be self evidently justified. So, for example, in *X v United Kingdom*,[80] the Commission considered that a prison regulation which is applied generally to all prisoners requiring them to clean their cells was justified. In that case a high-caste Sikh prisoner argued that it was contrary to his religion to clean the floor of his cell. This argument was readily rejected, although the Commission noted that there was evidence that this was a genuinely held belief.[81]

Worship requirements

The Prison Act 1952 requires that every prison shall have a governor, a chaplain **7.46** and a medical officer and such other officers as may be necessary.[82] The chaplain shall be a clergyman of the Church of England.[83] The Secretary of State may appoint ministers of other denominations where the numbers of adherents to a particular religion require it.[84] The Secretary of State may allow ministers of other denominations to visit prisoners of his denomination in a prison where no minister of that denomination has been appointed.[85]

Rules 13–19 of the Prison Rules 1999 provide for visits by the prison chaplain and **7.47** minister (where appointed), services, religious books, and arrangements so that prisoners should not do unnecessary work on a Sunday, Christmas Day or Good Friday, or other recognized days of religious observance.[86] Although accommodation is made for non-Church of England religions, other religions are plainly not nearly

---

[78] See *Aston Cantlow and Wilmcote with Billesley Parochial Church Council v Wallbank* [2003] UKHL 37.

[79] Livingstone, Owen & Macdonald (n 69 above) para 2.106.

[80] Application 8231/78 (1982) 28 DR 5.

[81] See also *ELH and PBH v United Kingdom*, Applications 32094/96 and 32568/96 (1997) 91-A DR 61 (no violation of Art 9 in a case where a Catholic prisoner sought exemption from rules prohibiting conjugal visits on the basis that the alternative on offer (artificial insemination) was unacceptable to him as a Catholic).

[82] s 7(1).

[83] s 7(4).

[84] s 10(1).

[85] s 10(3).

[86] See also Young Offender Institution Rules 2000, rr 30–36 which have broadly similar provisions.

as well protected. For example, r 16(1) provides that the chaplain shall conduct a Church of England service at least once every Sunday, Christmas Day and Good Friday, and such celebrations of Holy Communion and weekday services as may be arranged. As regards other religions, r 16(2) merely states that prison ministers shall conduct a service for prisoners of their denominations at such times as may be arranged. Whereas chapels are used for Christian denominations, an identified area should be set aside for worship by members of other world religions.[87]

7.48 As regards Sunday work, r 18 states that arrangements shall be made so as not to require Christian prisoners to do any unnecessary work on Sunday, Christmas Day or Good Friday or prisoners of other religions to do any such work on their recognized days of religious observance. The Prison Service Instruction, *Religious Festivals Dates for 2006* sets out the festivals for some of the major world religions.[88]

7.49 However, there will inevitably be circumstances in which prison rules and regulations will interfere with aspects of religious worship.[89] In *X v United Kingdom*,[90] the Commission considered a claim by a high-risk prisoner who was prevented from attending Sunday service on security grounds. In *Omkarananda and Divine Light Zentrum v Switzerland*,[91] a prisoner claimed to be a light worshipper and therefore could not be incarcerated in a dark cell. In that case, it was held that he failed to establish that he held such a belief. However, had it been found that he had a genuinely held belief, no doubt the incarceration would have been considered a justified interference.[92] In *X v United Kingdom*,[93] a religious book was confiscated from a prisoner on the grounds that it contained a chapter on martial arts.[94]

---

[87] *Religion Manual* (n 67 above) paras 1.14–1.17.

[88] PSI 49/2005. It provides information on festivals for Buddhist, Christian, Hindu, Jewish, Muslim, Sikh and Pagan religions. Note that a special agreement has been made with the Pagan Federation due to the variance in emphasis on different festivals. Pagan prisoners may choose two out of eight dates where they must be excused from work. See also PSI 33/2005: *Practice of Paganism in Prison*, Annex H to Ch 1 of the *Religion Manual* (n 67 above).

[89] In *X v United Kingdom*, Application 8231/78 (1982) 28 DR 5, a Sikh prisoner objected to cleaning the floor of his cell on grounds of religion and culture. The Commission held that he had shown evidence that his religion may require a practice of high caste Sikhs of not cleaning floors but it regarded the interference with Art 9(1) as lawful for the protection of his health and that of other prisoners. It declared that aspect of the claim as manifestly ill-founded.

[90] (1983) 5 EHRR 289.

[91] Application 8118/77 (1981) 25 DR 105.

[92] Note that in *McFeeley v United Kingdom* (1980) 3 EHRR 161 one of the applicants complained that when he was in the punishment block he was not allowed to attend mass. This complaint was rejected for failure to exhaust domestic remedies.

[93] Application 6886/75 (1976) 5 DR 100.

[94] See also *X v Austria*, Application 1753/63 (1965) 16 Coll 20; and *McFeeley v United Kingdom* (1980) 3 EHRR 161, 203 (religious literature withdrawn on the grounds of misuse by prisoners as part of their protest resulted in a claim on this basis being manifestly unfounded).

Dietary requirements

The provision of food in a prison will evidently lead to interferences with some **7.50** individuals' exercise of their religion. Until 1988 remand prisoners could receive food from friends or relatives. However, r 24(1) of the Prison Rules 1999 provides that no prisoner shall be allowed to have any food other than that ordinarily provided except as authorized by the medical officer or practitioner.[95]

The *Religion Manual* states that prisoners must have a diet which accords with the **7.51** requirements of their religion 'as agreed between a relevant religious body and Prison Service Headquarters'.[96] Some prisons may allow special food to be brought in for religious festivals, although this can normally be prepared in the approved manner in the prison.[97]

Clothing

Clothing requirements are set out in the Prison Rules 1999. Rule 23(5) states that **7.52** a prisoner shall wear the clothing provided by the prison.[98] However, prisoners must be allowed to wear dress and headgear which accords with the requirements of their religion as agreed between a relevant religious body and Prison Service Headquarters.[99]

In *McFeeley v United Kingdom*,[100] the Commission considered whether Article 9 **7.53** guaranteed the right of prisoners to wear their own clothes. The applicants were prisoners convicted of terrorist offences under the law of Northern Ireland and refused on grounds of conscience to wear prison underclothes and footwear and to engage in prison work. The Commission held, in declaring the claim manifestly unfounded, that the applicants were seeking to derive from Article 9 a 'special category status' not covered by that provision. It held further that Article 9 could not be interpreted to include a right for the applicants to wear their own

---

[95] Note that the rule change was held to be intra vires the Prison Act 1952 in *R v Home Secretary, ex p Simmons* [1989] COD 332.

[96] *Religion Manual* (n 67 above) para 1.43.

[97] See *X v United Kingdom*, Application 5947/72 (1976) 5 DR 8; note too in *DS and ES v United Kingdom*, Application 13669/88 (1990) 65 DR 245 the applicants complained that the refusal of the prison authorities to facilitate the supply of an adequate kosher diet in prison constituted a violation of Art 9. The Commission did not address Art 9 in its decision denying admissibility, instead holding that domestic remedies had not been exhausted as they could have commenced judicial review proceedings.

[98] Note that unconvicted prisoners may wear clothing of their own in so far as it is suitable, tidy and clean (r 23(1)). Prisoners appearing before court may also wear their own clothing (r 40(3)).

[99] *Religion Manual* (n 67 above) para 1.44.

[100] (1980) 3 EHRR 161.

clothes in prison. In *X v United Kingdom*,[101] a Sikh prisoner claimed that the imposition of prison clothing was degrading as he recognized no authority between himself and his god. The Commission considered his claim that it was based on religious grounds, but rejected this as manifestly ill-founded as he had failed to substantiate this during his imprisonment. In *X v Austria*,[102] the refusal to allow Buddhist prisoners to grow a beard or to obtain a prayer chain was upheld.

---

[101] Application 8231/78 (1982) 28 DR 5.
[102] Application 1753/63 (1965) 16 Coll 20.

INDEX

All references are to paragraph number. Footnote references are indicated by the letter 'n' following the reference.

non-discrimination principle (*cont.*)
exemptions
schools with religious character 4.12
scope of 4.13
see also **discrimination**
non-refoulement principle
religious persecution 6.42
Nonconformists
legal restrictions on 1.06

Operational Enforcement Manual
and policies 6.06
origin of the species
as controversial teaching area 4.78
other people, rights and freedoms of
ECHR (Art 9) 2.86–2.87
Ottoman empire
millet system 1.31

pacifism
non-religious belief 2.57
parental and child rights 3.36–3.50
cases 3.43, 3.44, 3.45
common law 3.43
Conventions, Covenants and Declarations 3.37
domestic law 3.42–3.46
ECHR law 3.38, 3.39, 3.47–3.50
education system 3.41
parental preferences
school admissions (religious grounds)
4.29, 4.57–4.61
faith schools 4.53
persecution, religious
definitions/scope of protection 6.28–6.42
discrimination 6.37
domestic law 6.45–6.56
fear of on religious grounds 6.26–6.56
well-founded 6.33–6.34
forced conversion/compliance to religion 6.38–6.39
gender 6.40
cases 6.54–6.56
historical examples 6.26, 6.27
non-refoulement principle 6.42
proselytization cases 6.48–6.53
Refugee Convention *see* **Refugee Convention 1951**
religious freedom, limitations on exercise of
6.35–6.36
see also **Human Rights Committee; immigration and asylum; refugees**
philosophical and political theory 1.22–1.24
and working terms 5.47
planning law 7.25–7.37
balancing of interests 3.15
cases 7.28

controversial nature of religious cases 7.27
criminal prosecutions, breaches of statutory
regulations 7.34
higher courts, approach of 7.29
holy sites, access to 7.37
land, use of 7.30–7.36
legislation 7.26
primary purpose rule
immigration and asylum issues 6.24
prison law 7.38–7.53
clothing 7.52–7.53
dietary requirements 7.50–7.51
and religion 7.39
worship requirements 7.46–7.51
proportionality concept
balancing of interests 3.11
ECHR (Art 9) 2.88–2.91
immigration and asylum 6.20
school uniforms 4.88
proselytization cases
ECHR 3.14
protection from religion 2.63
religious persecution 6.48–6.53
'protected shop worker'
and Sunday trading 5.65
Protestantism
and Church of England 1.42
dissenting Protestants, legal restrictions on 1.06
Lollards (early group), destruction of 1.05
Protestant myth, Anglo-Saxon 1.03
public authorities
Department for Education and Skills
(DfES) 4.18
discrimination on grounds of religion or belief
immigration laws 6.09
prohibition on 4.15
employers as 5.45
employment legislation 5.07
'hybrid' bodies distinguished 2.33, 2.34
public order restrictions
justification for interference 2.80–2.82
pupil referral units
and state maintained schools 4.04

Race Relations Act 1976
difference of treatment 2.29
direct discrimination 2.26
and Directives 2.19, 2.20
education 4.07–4.09
employment 5.06
harassment, prohibition 2.30
immigration and asylum 6.07–6.09
indirect discrimination 2.27, 2.28
legal framework 2.06, 2.18–2.30